D0601498

ᵗ reᶜ
ʳsᶜ

1000
QUESTIONS
& ANSWERS
FACTFILE

1000
QUESTIONS
& ANSWERS
FACTFILE

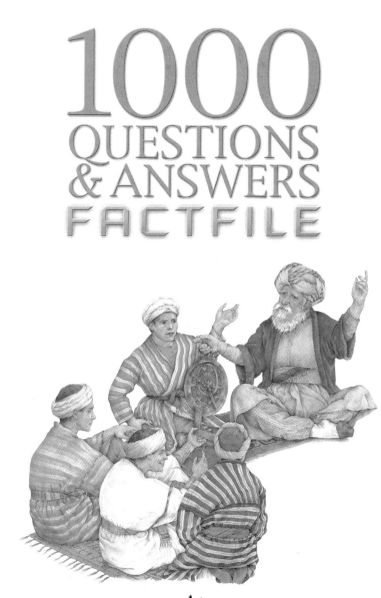

KINGFISHER

Kingfisher Publications Plc
New Penderel House
283–288 High Holborn
London WC1V 7HZ
www.kingfisherpub.com

First published by Kingfisher Publications Plc in 2002
First published in this format in 2006
10 9 8 7 6 5 4 3 2 1

1TR/0406/C&C/UNI/128MA/C

A CIP catalogue record for this book is available from the British Library.

ISBN-13: 978 0 7534 1313 5   ISBN-10: 0 7534 1313 2

Printed in China

Authors: **Robin Kerrod, Wendy Madgwick,
Sarah Reed, Fergus Collins, Philip Brooks**

Artwork archivists: Wendy Allison and Steve Robinson

Illustrations:

GD Achille, Jonathan Adams, Susanna Addario, Graham Allen, Marion Appleton, Norman Arlott, Julian Baker,
Sue Barclay, Andrew Beckett, Owain Bell, Gary Bines, Simone Boni, Richard Bonson, Peter Bull, J Burgess,
John Butler, Vanessa Card, Robin Carter, Jim Channel, Kuo Kang Chen, Dan Cole, Stephen Conlin, David Cook,
Peter Dennis, Francis D'Ohani, Francesca D'Ottavi, Sandra Doyle, R Draper, Lee Edwards, Angelika Elsebach,
James Field, Wayne Ford, Chris Forsey, Terry Gaby, Luigi Galante, Lee Gibbons, Peter Goodfellow, Jeremy Gower,
Ruby Green, Peter Gregory, Ray Grinaway, Alan Hardcastle, Martin Hargreaves, David Harley, Alan Harris, Nick
Harris, Nicholas Hewitson, Steve Homes, Tim Hayward, Adam Hook, Christian Hook, Biz Hull, David Hurrel,
Mark Iley, Ian Jackson, John James, Roger Kent, Martin Knowlden, Eddy Krähenbühl, Stuart Lafford, Terence
Lambert, Ruth Lindsay, Bernard Long, Mike Loates, Steiner Lund, Chris Lyons, David McAllister, Angus McBride,
Doreen McGuinness, Brian Mcintyre, Kevin Maddison, Shirley Mallinson, Janos Marffy, John Marshall, Josephine
Martin, Robert Morton, William Oliver, Nicki Palin, Alex Pang, Roger Payne, Bruce Pearson, Mark Pepe,
Melvyn Pickering, Sebastian Quigley, John Rignall, Andrew Robinson, Bernard Robinson, Eric Robson, Michael
Roffe, Mike Saunders, Chris Shields, Nick Shrewring, Tim Slade, Guy Smith, Tom Smith, Mark Stacey, Roger
Stewart, Mike Taylor, George Thompson, Ian Thompson, Shirley Tourret, Kevin Toy, Rose Walton, Wendy Webb,
Andrea Wheatcroft, Sohraya Willis, Ann Winterbotham, Dan Wright, David Wright

Picture credits

p.94 tl courtesy of the Department Library Services, American Museum of Natural History, Neg. no.410 764,
Shackelford 1925; p.204 tr Nokia; p.207 br Science Photo Library; p.209 c Science Photo Library/Mehau Kulyk;
p.227 cl Nokia; p.229 bl Mary Evans Picture Library; p.249 br Science Picture Library; p.263 b Princess Cruises

Contents

1000
QUESTIONS
& ANSWERS
FACTFILE
STARS AND
PLANETS

Contents

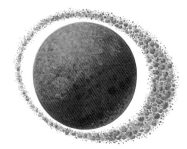

Looking at the Sky

The night sky is one of the most beautiful sights in nature. Stars beyond number shine out of a velvety blackness, bright planets wander among the stars and long-tailed comets come and go. Astronomy, the study of the night sky, is one of the most ancient sciences.

What can we see?

Although we can see a lot in the night sky with just our eyes, we can see much more through binoculars or telescopes. To the naked eye the Moon looks small, and we see few features. With binoculars and telescopes it looks larger, and we can see craters on its surface.

When did people first start studying the stars?

People must have been star-gazing for millions of years. But they probably began studying the night sky seriously only about 5,000 years ago. Early civilizations in the Middle East left records of their observations. The Babylonians were skilled observers, and we know the Egyptians were too, because they lined up their pyramids with certain constellations, or star patterns. In Britain, around 2800BCE, Stonehenge was built, possibly as a kind of observatory. Stones were lined up to show the positions of the Sun and Moon at different seasons. Ancient Chinese and Mayan astronomers left accurate records of their observations.

Stonehenge

Mayan astronomer

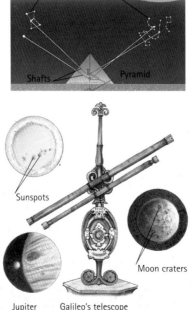

Constellations

Shafts

Pyramid

Ancient Egyptian astronomer-priests

Ancient Chinese star map

Aerial telescope

Who invented telescopes?

A Dutchman named Hans Lippershey built the first telescope in 1608. But it was Galileo, an Italian, who first used one to study the night sky. He made his first observations in the winter of 1609–10. He spied the moons of Jupiter, craters on Earth's Moon and spots on the Sun. Galileo's telescope was quite small. Later devices, known as 'aerial' telescopes, were around 50 metres long.

Sunspots

Jupiter

Moon craters

Galileo's telescope

How do radio telescopes work?

Stars give off radio waves as well as light waves. Astronomers have built telescopes to pick up these radio waves. Radio telescopes are not like light telescopes. Most are huge metal dishes, which can be tilted and turned to any part of the sky. The dishes pick up radio waves, or signals, and focus them onto an aerial. The signals are sent to a receiver and then to a computer, which changes them into images.

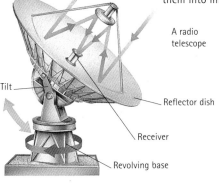

Radio waves from space

A radio telescope

Tilt

Reflector dish

Receiver

Revolving base

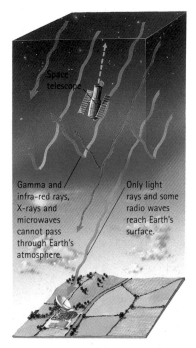

Space telescope

Gamma and infra-red rays, X-rays and microwaves cannot pass through Earth's atmosphere.

Only light rays and some radio waves reach Earth's surface.

Where do astronomers work?

Astronomers look at, or observe, the stars from observatories. The great domes on these observatories house big telescopes which use curved mirrors to collect the light from the stars. Some mirrors are as big as 10 metres across. Modern-day astronomers do not often look through these telescopes. Instead they use them as giant cameras and take pictures with them. Most observatories today are built on mountains, above the thickest part of the atmosphere, where the air is cleaner and clearer.

What is special about space telescopes?

Some of the outstanding discoveries of recent years have been made by space telescopes. Out in space, telescopes can get a much clearer view of the night sky than they can from Earth. Also, space telescopes can pick up invisible rays, such as X-rays, which cannot pass through the atmosphere.

11

Seeing Stars

Using just your eyes, you can see thousands of stars in the night sky. If you look closely, you will see that some are brighter than others. The bright stars make patterns that you can recognize every time you go star-gazing. We call them constellations.

1

2

3

4

5

6

Northern hemisphere
Plough
Celestial sphere
Earth's axis

Plane of equator

Equator

Plane of eclipse (path of the Sun)

Southern hemisphere

Southern Cross

The signs of the Zodiac

Can we all see the same stars?

Because Earth is round and just rotates on its north-south axis, we only see the stars above the hemisphere in which we live. Earth seems to be in the middle of a great dark ball, which we call the celestial sphere. People in the far north can always see the Plough but never the Southern Cross, which is seen in the far south. In the far south, no-one ever sees the Plough. People near the Equator can see almost all the stars at some time of the year.

What are star signs?

During the year, the Sun appears to move through the stars of the celestial sphere. It seems to pass through 12 main constellations, called the constellations of the Zodiac. They are also called star signs, and are important in astrology. Astrologers believe that human lives are affected by the stars.

Leo the Lion   Scorpio the Scorpion

The night sky in the
Southern hemisphere

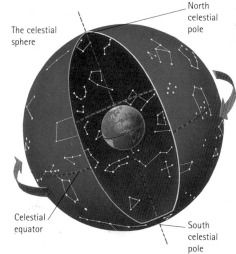

Some of the major constellations

Northern hemisphere	Southern hemisphere
1. Pegasus	1. Aquarius (The Water-bearer)
2. Perseus	2. Orion (The Hunter)
3. Pole Star	3. Scorpio (The Scorpion)
4. Plough (or Little Bear)	4. Southern Cross
5. Great Bear	5. Hydra (Water Snake)
6. Leo (The Lion)	6. Libra (Scales)

Why do the stars move across the sky?

If you go out star-gazing at night, you
will notice that the constellations gradually
move across the sky from east to west, as
the Sun does during the day. Ancient
astronomers thought that the stars were
fixed on the inside of the celestial sphere,
and that this sphere was spinning round
Earth, which stood still. We now know that
the opposite is true. It is Earth that is
moving and the stars that are standing still.
Earth spins round in space, moving from
west to east. This makes the stars appear
to travel in the opposite direction.

The celestial
sphere

North
celestial
pole

Celestial
equator

South
celestial
pole

13

Great Balls of Gas

Stars look like tiny bright specks in the night sky. But they are not tiny at all. They are in fact huge balls of searing hot gas. Stars look small only because they lie many million, million kilometres away. If you could get close to a star, you would find that it looked like our Sun, because the Sun is a star too.

Do stars last forever?

Just like living things, stars are born, grow older and, in time, die. The pictures below show two different ways in which stars die. After shining steadily for some time the stars swell up into a red giant. Some red giants shrink into a white, then a black dwarf. This will happen to the Sun one day. Other stars swell up from a red giant to a supergiant before exploding as a supernova.

Outer layers break away

Star

Red giant

Supergiant

Quick-fire Quiz

1. What is an exploding star called?
a) Supergiant
b) Supernova
c) Superstar

2. What will our Sun be one day?
a) A supernova
b) A black dwarf
c) A black hole

3. Which is the hottest?
a) Sun
b) Red giant
c) Blue-white star

4. Which is the smallest?
a) Sun
b) Supergiant
c) Pulsar

How big are stars?

We can measure the size of one star directly because it is so close. This is our own star, the Sun. The Sun measures nearly 1,400,000 kilometres across. Astronomers can work out the size of other stars too. They have discovered that there are many stars smaller than the Sun, and also many much larger. Astronomers call the Sun a dwarf star. They know of red giant stars tens of times bigger, and supergiant stars tens of times bigger still. Some supergiants measure 400 million kilometres across.

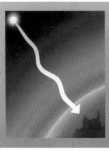

Why do stars twinkle?

When we look up at the heavens, we can see thousands of stars shining down, but they do not give out a steady light. They seem to twinkle, or change brightness all the time. In fact they do shine steadily but air currents in the Earth's atmosphere make the starlight bend this way and that. Some of the light gets into our eyes and some is bent away. So, to us on Earth, the stars seem to twinkle.

How hot are stars?

Stars are great globes of very hot gas, but their temperature varies quite a lot. Astronomers can tell the temperature of a star by the colour and brightness of the light it gives out. Yellowish stars like the Sun have a temperature of about 5,500°C. This compares with about 3,000°C for a dim red star to 30,000°C for a bright blue-white star.

White dwarf

Dead black dwarf

Why do some stars explode?

Massive stars explode when they come to the end of their lives. They swell up into huge supergiants. Supergiants are unstable, so they collapse and blast themselves to pieces in an explosion called a supernova. Supernovae are the biggest explosions in the Universe, as bright as billions of Suns put together.

Black hole

Star

Black hole

Supernova

What makes black holes black?

After a star explodes as a supernova, what is left of it shrinks rapidly. If it is really big, it shrinks almost to nothing. All that is left is a tiny region of space that has enormous gravity. The gravity is so great that the tiny region will suck in all nearby matter, including other stars. The name 'black hole' comes from the fact that the pull it exerts is so powerful that even light cannot escape from it.

What is a pulsar?

A smaller star that explodes as a supernova ends its life as a tiny star we call a pulsar. It gets this name because it 'pulsates', or sends out pulses of energy. Astronomers think that pulsars spin round fast and send out narrow beams of energy. On Earth we see a pulse of energy when this beam sweeps past us.

A pulsar passing Earth

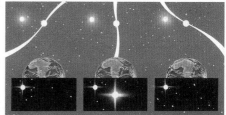

Pulsar

Galaxies

From Earth, space seems to be full of stars. But if you travelled a long way from Earth, you would in time leave the stars behind. Looking back, you would see that the stars form a kind of island in space. In other directions, you would see other star islands, which we call galaxies. The galaxies and the space they occupy make up the Universe.

Do all galaxies look the same?

Astronomers can see galaxies of all shapes and sizes through their telescopes. Some are known as barred spiral galaxies. They have curved arms coming from a bar through their centre (1). Ordinary spirals do not have the bar. Elliptical galaxies (2) have an oval shape. Galaxies with no particular shape are called irregulars (3).

The Local Group

Milky Way

Andromeda

What is the Local Group of galaxies?

There are thousands of galaxies in space. Many are in groups called clusters. The galaxy where we live is called the Milky Way, which is in a cluster we call the Local Group. The Milky Way is the second-largest galaxy in the Local Group. The largest is the Andromeda galaxy.

How do galaxies form?

Galaxies begin to form in clouds of dark gas so huge that even light would take hundreds of thousands of years to cross them. Over time, gravity begins to pull the particles of gas together. Gradually, the gas cloud shrinks and it becomes more and more dense. Here and there it becomes dense enough for stars to form. At the same time the gas cloud starts to rotate and flatten out.

1 A huge cloud of gas shrinks and becomes denser. Stars form in the centre.

2 The starry cloud spins, and flattens into a disc shape.

3 Matter in the disc collects on arms, where more stars form.

How did the Universe begin?

Astronomers believe that the Universe began with a huge explosion known as the Big Bang. They reckon it happened more than 15,000 million years ago. The Big Bang created a hot bubble of space that has been getting bigger and bigger ever since. Astronomers believe the Universe is constantly expanding.

Big Bang

The Universe expands after the Big Bang

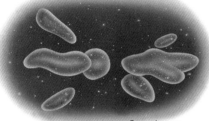

Superclusters

What makes up the Universe?

Simply speaking, the Universe is made up of matter and space. The matter is found as planets, moons and stars. The stars gather together into great galaxies, and the galaxies gather into groups, or clusters. Even the clusters gather together to form gigantic superclusters of galaxies. The Universe is made up of millions of these superclusters.

The Milky Way – a spiral galaxy

Quick-fire Quiz

1. What is the galaxy our Sun and its planets are in called?
a) The Heavens
b) The Milky Bar
c) The Milky Way

2. Which of these is brightest?
a) Star
b) Quasar
c) Galaxy

3. What began the Universe?
a) Gravity
b) Black holes
c) The Big Bang

4. Which of these is the Universe doing?
a) Expanding
b) Exploding
c) Shrinking

What are quasars?

Quasars look like stars. But they are so far away that, for us to detect them, they must be brighter than thousands of galaxies together. Astronomers think quasars get their great power from black holes. As matter is sucked into a black hole, enormous energy is given out as light and other radiation.

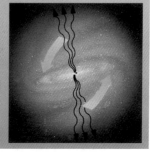

The Solar System

Every day, the Sun travels across the sky from east to west. It looks as if it circles Earth, but the opposite is true – Earth circles the Sun. Earth is part of the Sun's family, or Solar System. It is one of nine bodies called planets that circle the Sun.

How big is the Solar System?

Earth is nearly 150 million kilometres from the Sun. This seems a huge distance, but it is only a small step in space. The furthest planets lie thousands of millions of kilometres away from the Sun. The diagram on the right shows the orbits, or paths, of the nine planets round the Sun. The distance from one side of Pluto's orbit to the other is nearly 15,000 million kilometres.

Who first realized that Earth travels round the Sun?

Early astronomers thought the Sun and other planets circled the Earth. Nicolaus Copernicus (1473–1543) was a Polish priest and astronomer. He came up with the theory that the Sun was the centre of the Universe, and that Earth and the planets moved round it. This was the first real challenge to the idea that Earth was the centre of the Universe, which ancient astronomers believed. Copernicus published his theory while he lay dying in 1543, but religious leaders opposed his ideas for many years.

What happened at the birth of the Solar System?

1 The Solar System was born in a great cloud of gas and dust about 5,000 million years ago. There are many clouds like this, called nebulae, in the space between the stars.

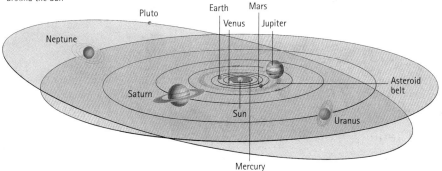

The orbits of the planets around the Sun

Pluto

Neptune

Earth Mars

Venus Jupiter

Saturn

Sun

Mercury

Asteroid belt

Uranus

5

6

7

2 Some parts of the cloud became much denser. Gas and dust in these areas started to stick together under the pull of their gravity. In time they formed into a ball-shaped mass.

3 The ball shrank and warmed up. Slowly, it started to glow, forming a 'baby' Sun by the time it was about 100,000 years old.

4 The baby Sun was spinning rapidly, flinging off masses of material into space. All the while it was shrinking and getting hotter and hotter.

5 In time, the baby Sun became hot enough to set off nuclear reactions. These produced the fantastic energy it needed to shine as a 'grown-up' star.

6 The ring of material thrown out earlier by the Sun began to clump together. It gradually formed larger and larger lumps at different distances from the Sun.

7 The large lumps grew into the planets we find today. Smaller lumps formed the moons of the planets, and even smaller lumps formed the asteroids.

Our Star, the Sun

The Sun is our local star. Like the other stars, it is a ball of very hot gas. It lies about 150 million kilometres from Earth, and is about 1.4 million kilometres across. The Sun pours huge amounts of energy into space. The light and heat that reach Earth make life possible.

Hydrogen atoms

Helium atom

Energy

Where does the Sun get its energy?

The energy that keeps the Sun shining is produced in its centre, or core. The pressure in the core is enormous, and the temperature reaches 15 million °C. Under these conditions, atoms of hydrogen gas fuse (join together) to form another gas, helium. This process is called nuclear fusion. It produces enormous amounts of energy.

What is the Sun's surface like?

The Sun's surface is a bubbling, boiling mass of very hot gas, constantly in motion, like a stormy sea. Here and there, fountains of flaming gas thousands of kilometres high shoot out. These are called prominences. Eventually, they curve over and fall back. Violent explosions called flares also often take place, blasting particles into space that can cause magnetic storms on Earth.

Rays of energy from the Sun

Earth's surface

What happens when the Sun warms Earth?

The Sun pours energy on to Earth, warming the land and the water in the oceans. Gases in the air trap the heat and warm the atmosphere. They act like a greenhouse, so the warming process is called the 'greenhouse effect'. One of the main gases that traps heat is carbon dioxide, produced when fuels burn.

Quick-fire Quiz

1. What is an explosion on the Sun called?
a) Prominence
b) Flare
c) Sunspot

2. What produces the Sun's energy?
a) Burning coal
b) Burning hydrogen
c) Nuclear fusion

3. Which gas in air traps heat?
a) Nitrogen
b) Carbon dioxide
c) Oxygen

4. How many more years will the Sun last?
a) 50 million
b) 500 million
c) 5,000 million

Is it safe to look at the Sun?

Never look directly at the Sun. Its light is so bright that it will damage your eyes and can even blind you. Instead, use binoculars or a telescope to throw an image onto paper, and look at that.

What is the Sun like inside?

The Sun is made up of a number of layers. In the centre is the very hot core, where energy is produced. This energy travels outwards by radiation, reaching the outer layer, called the convection region. There, currents of hot gas carry the energy to the surface (photosphere), where it escapes as light and heat. The temperature of the surface is about 5,500°C. Sunspots are dark patches on the surface. They are about 1,000°C cooler. Some sunspots grow to be bigger than Earth.

Earth, compared with a sunspot

Prominence

Cross-section of the Sun

Convection currents

Core

Radiation zone

Sunspots

Photosphere

Corona (the Sun's outer atmosphere)

How do eclipses happen?

Occasionally, the Moon moves across the face of the Sun during the day, blotting out its light and casting a dark shadow on Earth. Day turns suddenly into night. We call this a total eclipse of the Sun. Eclipses occur because, from Earth, the Moon seems to be almost the same size as the Sun and can cover it up. Total eclipses can only be seen over a small part of Earth because the Moon casts only a small shadow.

Moon's shadow

Moon

Sun

Earth

Total eclipse seen here

Partial eclipse seen here

Eclipse of the Sun

Will the Sun always shine?

1 The Sun was born, along with the rest of the Solar System, about 5,000 million years ago. It has been shining steadily ever since.

2 In another 5,000 million years' time, the Sun will swell up and get hotter. Earth's oceans will boil away and all life will die.

3 As the Sun gets bigger and hotter and redder, Earth will be scorched to a cinder. In time it may be swallowed by the Sun's outer layers.

4 Gradually, the red giant Sun will begin to shrink again. Eventually it will become a white dwarf star about the size of Earth.

The Planets

The nine planets are the most important members of the Sun's family. In order of distance from the Sun, they are Mercury, Venus, Earth, Mars, Jupiter, Saturn, Uranus, Neptune and Pluto. The first four are small rocky bodies. The next four are giants, made up mainly of gas. Pluto is a tiny ball of rock and ice.

Jupiter

Mercury

Venus

Earth

Mars

Which is the biggest planet?

Jupiter is by far the largest of the planets. It has more mass than all the other planets put together. It measures nearly 143,000 kilometres across, which is 11 times bigger than Earth. Even though it is so big, it takes less than 10 hours for it to spin round once. This means that its surface is spinning round at a speed of 45,000 kilometres an hour. This is 30 times faster than Earth spins.

How big are the planets?

The pictures on these two pages show the relative sizes of the planets. You might think that Earth is a big place. But look how much bigger some of the other planets are! Even the biggest planets, however, are dwarfed by the Sun. The Sun is nearly ten times bigger across than Jupiter, and it could swallow more than a million Earths. However, Earth is bigger than four of the planets – nearby Venus, Mars and Mercury, and tiny, distant Pluto.

Sun

Which planets have rings?

Once it was thought that Saturn was the only planet that had rings around it because they were the only ones that can be seen through a telescope. But close-up photographs taken by the *Voyager* space probes have shown us that the other three gas giants – Jupiter, Uranus and Neptune – have rings too. The rings around these other planets are much thinner, narrower and darker than Saturn's.

Why is Uranus sometimes called 'new'?

Astronomers have been studying the planets for thousands of years. They have watched the way they move, or 'wander', across the night sky, unlike the stars. But the ancient astronomers could only see five planets in the night sky. It was not until 1781 that someone built a telescope powerful enough to spot another planet, which came to be called Uranus. Uranus was the first of three 'new' planets to be discovered. Neptune was discovered in 1846, and Pluto in 1930.

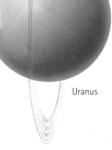

Uranus

Quick-fire Quiz

1. Which of these has rings?
a) Pluto
b) Saturn
c) Venus

2. How many planets are bigger than Earth?
a) Two
b) Three
c) Four

3. How fast does Jupiter spin?
a) 4,500km/h
b) 45,000km/h
c) 450,000km/h

4. When was the last planet discovered?
a) 1781
b) 1930
c) 1979

What is special about Saturn?

Two things are outstanding about Saturn. One is obvious when you look at the planet through a telescope. The planet is surrounded by a set of bright, shining rings. Many people think that these make Saturn the most beautiful object in the Solar System. The other special thing about Saturn is that it is the lightest (least dense) of all the planets. It is lighter even than water. This means that if you could place it in a huge bowl of water, it would float.

Rings

Saturn

Which planet is furthest from the Sun?

As far as we know, the most distant planet from the Sun is Pluto, the last 'new' planet to be discovered after Neptune. But Pluto is not always the furthest away. For 20 years between 1979 and 1999, Neptune was further still because during this time Pluto was travelling inside Neptune's orbit. Neptune will become the furthest planet again in a little over 200 years' time. Pluto travels more than 7,000 million kilometres away from the Sun. It takes nearly 248 Earth-years to circle the Sun once.

Pluto

Neptune

Mercury

Mercury is the planet closest to the Sun. It is also the fastest-moving planet, whizzing round the Sun in just 88 days. Being close to the Sun, Mercury gets extremely hot. Its surface is covered in thousands of craters, making it look rather like the Moon.

Mercury

Earth

How big is Mercury?
Mercury is the smallest of the rocky, Earth-like planets. With a diameter of only 4,880 kilometres, it is less than half the size of the Earth. The planet Pluto, a deep-frozen ball of rock and ice, is even smaller.

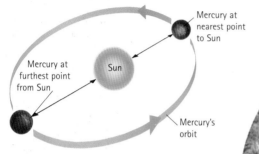

Mercury at nearest point to Sun

Mercury at furthest point from Sun

Sun

Mercury's orbit

What is strange about Mercury's orbit?
Most planets have a nearly circular orbit, or path, around the Sun. Mercury, however, has an oval orbit. At times it travels as far as 70 million kilometres away from the Sun. At others, it gets as close as 46 million kilometres.

Why does Mercury get so hot?
As it travels around the Sun, Mercury spins so slowly on its axis that a point on its surface stays in the Sun for nearly six Earth-months at a time. With the Sun so close and shining for so long, surface temperatures on Mercury soar to 430°C – hot enough to melt metals such as tin and lead.

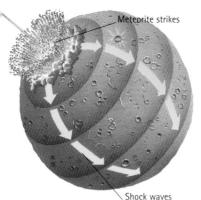

Meteorite strikes

Shock waves

Caloris basin

Craters

What has shaped Mercury's surface?

Billions of years ago, all the planets were bombarded by huge meteorites. On Earth, most craters made by the meteorites have been worn away by the action of the weather. Mercury has no weather because it has almost no atmosphere. So all the craters that formed ages ago remain, and the whole planet is covered with them. A huge one, called the Caloris Basin, was made by a giant meteorite that sent shock waves throughout the planet.

What is Mercury made of?

Like the Earth and the other rocky planets, Mercury is made up of different layers. Underneath a rocky crust there is a rocky mantle, and, at the centre, a huge metal core. The shrinking of the core has caused great ridges, up to 3 kilometres high, to appear on the surface.

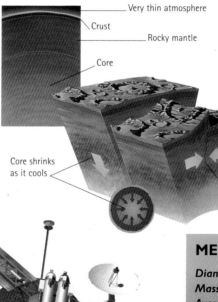

Very thin atmosphere

Crust

Rocky mantle

Core

Core shrinks as it cools

Mantle and crust are squeezed

Have any space probes visited Mercury?

Only one space probe has studied Mercury. Named *Mariner 10*, it flew to the planet in 1974, after visiting Venus. Its pictures revealed for the first time that Mercury looked rather like some parts of the Moon. *Mariner 10* flew past Mercury twice more. The US *Messenger* craft will fly by Mercury in 2008 and 2009, and will begin a year-long orbit of the planet in 2011.

Mariner 10

MERCURY DATA

Diameter at equator: *4,880km*
Mass: *0.06 times Earth's mass*
Average distance from Sun:
58 million km
Minimum distance from Earth:
91 million km
Length of day: *59 Earth-days*
Length of year: *88 Earth-days*
Temperature: *-185°C to 430°C*
Satellites: *0*

Venus

Venus is the planet whose orbit comes closest to Earth. We often see it shining in the western sky after sunset, which is why it is known as the Evening Star. Venus is a near twin of Earth in size, but it is a waterless world with a scorching climate.

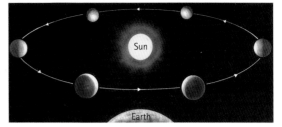

Venus in orbit

Why does Venus change shape?

From Earth, Venus seems to change its shape and size as time goes by. This is because it orbits closer to the Sun than Earth. When it is on the far side of the Sun, we see it as a small circle. As it moves closer to Earth, it gets bigger, but we only see it as a part-circle. Finally, it is just a thin crescent.

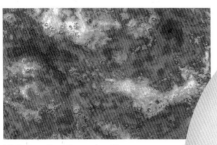

What is the surface of Venus like?

Space probes have shown that great plains cover much of Venus' surface. There are two big highland regions, which we can think of as continents. One is found in the north, and is called Ishtar Terra. The other lies near the equator, and is called Aphrodite Terra.

Venus landscape

Clouds cover the surface of Venus

Why is Venus so cloudy?

We cannot see Venus' surface from Earth because of thick clouds in its atmosphere. These clouds are not like the clouds we find on Earth, which are made up of tiny water droplets. Venus' clouds are made up of tiny droplets of sulphuric acid, one of the strongest acids we know. The sulphur has found its way into the atmosphere from the many volcanoes that have erupted on Venus over the years.

How can we see through Venus' clouds?

Space probes can see through Venus' clouds and show us what the planet's surface is like. But they do not 'see' in ordinary light. They 'see' with radar beams, because radar beams can go straight through clouds. The most successful radar probe, named *Magellan*, mapped the whole planet between 1990 and 1992.

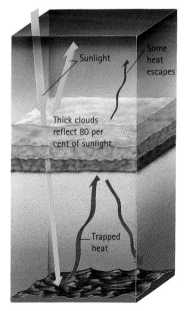

Magellan

What is Venus made of?

Venus is nearly the same size as Earth, and is probably similar in make-up. It has a hard rocky crust, but no great oceans as Earth has. Venus is far too hot for water to remain in liquid form. Beneath the crust is a mantle of heavier rock, and at the centre is a metal core, which may be partly liquid.

Why is Venus so hot?

The average temperature on Venus is more than twice as hot as an oven set on 'high'. This is because its atmosphere contains mainly carbon dioxide – a heavy gas that traps heat. Over the years it has caused the atmosphere to trap more and more heat, as a greenhouse does. The cloud layers trap the heat too, making the temperature reach a scorching 480°C.

Venus' atmosphere

Atmosphere

Crust

Mantle

Partly molten metallic core

Venus' structure

Sunlight

Some heat escapes

Thick clouds reflect 80 per cent of sunlight

Trapped heat

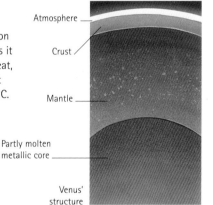

VENUS DATA

Diameter at equator: 12,100km
Average distance from Sun: 108 million km
Minimum distance from Earth: 42 million km
Turns on axis: 243 Earth-days
Circles Sun: 225 Earth-days
Surface temperature: 480°C
Satellites: 0

27

Earth

From space our home planet, Earth, appears to be mainly blue in colour. This is because of the colour of the oceans which cover over two-thirds of its surface. The land areas, or continents, cover less than a third. The layer of air above the surface is thin, but makes life on Earth possible.

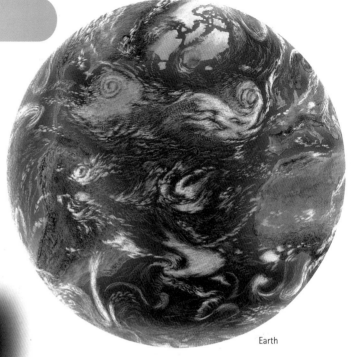

Earth

What causes day and night?

Almost every place on Earth has a time when it is light (day), followed by a time when it is dark (night). Day and night come about because Earth spins round in space, and different parts of its surface face the Sun. It is daytime when a place is on the side of Earth facing the Sun. It becomes night when the place is on the side of Earth facing away from the Sun.

Earth land and seascape

What makes Earth different?

A number of things make Earth different from the other planets. It is covered with great oceans of water, and its atmosphere contains lots of oxygen. The atmosphere also acts like a blanket, holding in enough of the Sun's heat to keep Earth at a comfortable temperature. The water, the oxygen and the temperature make Earth a suitable place for living things – at least one-and-a-half million different kinds of plants and animals.

How has Earth changed?

Earth formed about 4,600 million years ago when bits of matter in space came together (1). At first Earth was a great molten ball (2). It gradually cooled and the atmosphere and oceans eventually formed (3). In time, it changed into the world we know today (4 and 5), made up of layers of rock with a metal core. Our world is still changing. Currents in the rocks beneath the crust are widening the oceans, and driving the continents further apart (see below).

Atmosphere
Crust
Layers of mantle
Molten metal outer core
Solid metal inner core

Earth's structure

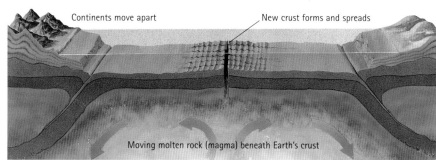

Continents move apart

New crust forms and spreads

Moving molten rock (magma) beneath Earth's crust

(see below)

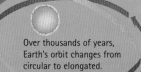

Over thousands of years, Earth's orbit changes from circular to elongated.

EARTH DATA

Diameter at equator: *12,756km*
Average distance from Sun: *149.6 million km*
Turns on axis: *23 hours 56 minutes*
Year length: *365.25 days*
Surface temperature: *-89°C to 58°C*
Satellites: *1 (the Moon)*

What causes the seasons?

The changes in weather that we call the seasons happen because of the way Earth's axis is tilted in space. Because of this tilt, a place leans more towards the Sun and is warmer at some times of the year than at others. It is this that causes the changing seasons. The place tilted towards the Sun has summer, while the place leaning away has winter.

Spring
Northern summer
Northern winter
Autumn
21 March
21 December
Sun
21 June longest day in the north
23 September
Southern summer
Spring
Autumn
Southern winter

Quick-fire Quiz

1. How many years old is Earth?
a) 4 million
b) 4,600 million
c) 6,000 million

2. How long does it take Earth to circle the Sun?
a) 265.25 days
b) 365.25 days
c) 465.25 days

3. What is Earth?
a) A star
b) A meteorite
c) A planet

4. What causes the seasons?
a) Tilting Earth
b) Tilting Sun
c) Tilting Moon

The Moon

Any object, or satellite, which orbits a planet is called a moon. Our Moon circles Earth once a month and is Earth's nearest neighbour in space. We can see it clearly through telescopes, and astronauts have explored it on foot. It is a small body – about a quarter the diameter of Earth. It has no atmosphere, no weather and no life.

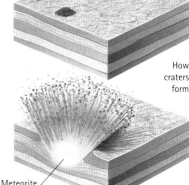

Meteorite

How craters form

Meteorite strikes the Moon

How did the Moon form?

Most astronomers think that the Moon formed after another large body smashed into Earth thousand of millions of years ago (1). Material from Earth and the other body were flung into space. In time, this material came together to form the Moon (2). This explains why Moon rocks are different from rocks on Earth.

1

2

Terraced crater

Concentric crater

Ray crater

Ghost crater

When did astronauts land on the Moon?

The first astronauts landed on the Moon on July 20, 1969. They were Edwin Aldrin and Neil Armstrong, the crew of the lunar landing module of the *Apollo 11* spacecraft. Armstrong was the first person to stand on the Moon. There were five more lunar landings – one more in 1969, two in 1971, and two in 1972.

Moon rock

What made the Moon's craters?

The surface of the Moon is covered with many thousands of pits, or craters. They have been made by meteorites raining down from outer space. Most large craters have stepped, or terraced, walls and mountain peaks in the middle. The largest craters are more than 200 kilometres across. Some young craters have bright streaks, or rays, coming from them, while only the tips of some old 'ghost' craters can be seen.

Where are the Moon's seas?

Early astronomers thought that the dark areas we see on the Moon might be seas. They called them 'maria', the Latin word for 'seas'. We know now that they are vast dusty plains, but we still call them seas. Most seas are found on the side of the Moon that always faces us, the near side. There are only one or two small seas on the opposite side, the far side.

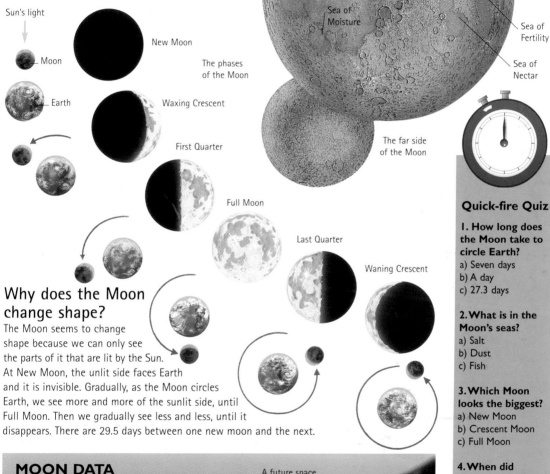

The near side of the Moon

Sea of Showers

Sea of Serenity

Sea of Crises

Ocean of Storms

Sea of Tranquillity

Copernicus

Sea of Moisture

Sea of Fertility

Sea of Nectar

Sun's light

Moon

Earth

New Moon

The phases of the Moon

Waxing Crescent

First Quarter

Full Moon

Last Quarter

Waning Crescent

The far side of the Moon

Why does the Moon change shape?

The Moon seems to change shape because we can only see the parts of it that are lit by the Sun. At New Moon, the unlit side faces Earth and it is invisible. Gradually, as the Moon circles Earth, we see more and more of the sunlit side, until Full Moon. Then we gradually see less and less, until it disappears. There are 29.5 days between one new moon and the next.

MOON DATA

Diameter at equator: 3,476km
Minimum distance from Earth: 356,000km
Time to circle Earth: 27.3 Earth-days
Surface temperature: -170°C to 110°C

A future space station on the Moon might look like this.

Quick-fire Quiz

1. How long does the Moon take to circle Earth?
a) Seven days
b) A day
c) 27.3 days

2. What is in the Moon's seas?
a) Salt
b) Dust
c) Fish

3. Which Moon looks the biggest?
a) New Moon
b) Crescent Moon
c) Full Moon

4. When did astronauts first land on the Moon?
a) 1965
b) 1969
c) 1972

31

Mars

Small and red in colour, Mars is more like Earth than any other planet. People once believed that intelligent beings lived on Mars – but space probes have shown that there are no Martians, and no other life on the planet. It is too cold, and the atmosphere is too thin for life to exist.

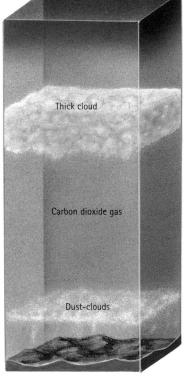

Mars' atmosphere

Thick cloud

Carbon dioxide gas

Dust-clouds

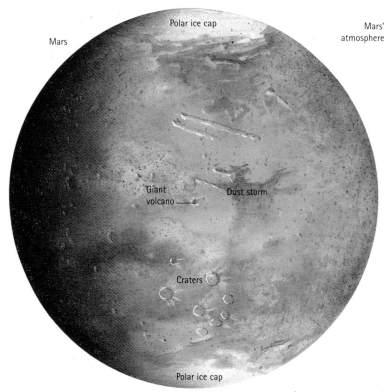

Mars

Polar ice cap

Giant volcano

Dust storm

Craters

Polar ice cap

How is Mars made up?

Mars is a rocky planet and it has a similar make-up to Earth. It has a hard crust, a rocky mantle and an iron core. Its atmosphere, however, is very much thinner than Earth's. The atmospheric pressure on Mars is only about a hundredth of what it is on Earth. The main gas in the Martian atmosphere is carbon dioxide, instead of nitrogen and oxygen, as on Earth. There is very little moisture in the atmosphere, and no oceans, lakes or rivers. Around the cold poles, the moisture freezes to form the planet's ice caps. Although Mars is similar to Earth in some ways, it is a lot smaller.

Why is Mars called the 'Red Planet'?

Astronomers call Mars the 'Red Planet' because of its colour. Its surface is reddish-orange. This colour comes from the rust-like iron minerals in the surface rocks and soil.

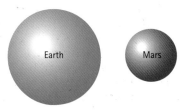

Earth

Mars

MARS DATA

Diameter at equator: 6,787km
Average distance from Sun:
228 million km
Minimum distance from Earth:
56 million km
Turns on axis:
24 hours 37 minutes
Circles Sun: 687 Earth-days
Surface temperature:
-110°C to 0°C
Satellites: 2

Viking lander

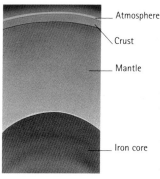

Deimos

Phobos

The *Sojourner* rover

Does Mars have moons?

Mars has two small moons, Phobos and Deimos. Phobos is the larger, but it is less than 30 kilometres across. Astronomers believe they were once asteroids, captured by Mars' gravity.

Which space probes explored Mars?

In 1965, *Mariner 4* flew past Mars and sent back pictures. *Mariner 6* and *7* also flew past, and *Mariner 9* went into orbit round it. Two *Viking* craft dropped landers onto the surface. In 1997, the *Pathfinder* probe landed, carrying a small vehicle called *Sojourner*, which investigated the surrounding rocks. Two larger Mars rovers landed in 2004.

Dust storm

Olympus Mons and the surface of Mars

Mars' structure

Atmosphere

Crust

Mantle

Iron core

What is Mars' surface like?

Mars' surface is dotted with vast deserts, craters and volcanoes. The highest volcano, Olympus Mons, is nearly 30 kilometres high. There is also a gash in the surface over 4,000 kilometres long and 7 kilometres deep in places. It has been called Mars' Grand Canyon, but its proper name is Mariner Valley. Smaller valleys look as if they have been made by flowing water, so astronomers think that Mars may once have had rivers and seas.

Quick-fire Quiz

1. What colour is Mars?
a) Yellow
b) Blue
c) Red

2. What is Mars' atmosphere made up of?
a) Oxygen
b) Carbon dioxide
c) Sulphur dioxide

3. What was the name of the first Mars rover?
a) Sojourner
b) Surveyor
c) Mariner

4. What were Mars' moons originally?
a) Planets
b) Comets
c) Asteroids

Jupiter

Jupiter is the giant among the planets. All the others could fit into it with room to spare, and it could swallow more than 1,300 bodies the size of Earth. Jupiter is a gassy planet, made up mainly of hydrogen. Its stormy atmosphere is full of clouds. Jupiter travels through space with a large family of moons, some as big as planets.

What makes Jupiter so colourful?

The coloured 'stripes' we see on Jupiter are different kinds of clouds in the thick atmosphere. Because Jupiter spins round quickly, these clouds are drawn out into bands parallel with the equator. The paler bands are called zones and the darker ones are called belts.

Jupiter's ring

What is Jupiter made of?

Jupiter is a great ball of gas and liquid gas. Its atmosphere is more than 1,000 kilometres deep and is made up mainly of hydrogen gas, with some helium. It is full of clouds of ice, ammonia and ammonium compounds. At the bottom of the atmosphere the great pressure turns the hydrogen into a liquid. Deeper down, rapidly increasing pressure turns the hydrogen into a kind of liquid metal. Right at the centre, there is a small core of rock.

The Great Red Spot

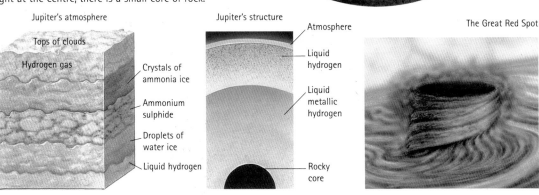

Jupiter's atmosphere

Tops of clouds

Hydrogen gas

Crystals of ammonia ice

Ammonium sulphide

Droplets of water ice

Liquid hydrogen

Jupiter's structure

Atmosphere

Liquid hydrogen

Liquid metallic hydrogen

Rocky core

The Great Red Spot

Europa

Callisto

Io

Ganymede

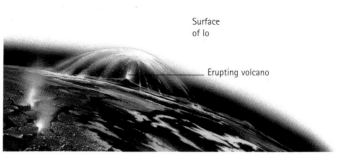

Surface of Io

Erupting volcano

What's special about Io?

Io has been nicknamed the 'pizza moon' because it is so colourful. It is a very unusual moon because it has active volcanoes on it. These pour out liquid sulphur, which is a rich yellow-orange, giving Io its brilliant and varied colours. The *Voyager 1* probe discovered Io's volcanoes when it flew past Jupiter in 1979.

How many moons does Jupiter have?

Jupiter has at least 63 moons. We can see the four biggest with binoculars. The Italian astronomer Galileo discovered them in 1610, so they are known as the Galilean moons. In order of distance from Jupiter, they are Io, Europa, Ganymede and Callisto. With a diameter of 5,262 kilometres, Ganymede is the largest of Jupiter's moons and, at roughly the same size as planet Mercury, is the biggest moon in the Solar System. The smallest of Jupiter's moons, recently discovered, measure about one kilometre across.

What is the Great Red Spot?

The most prominent feature on Jupiter's surface is a large red oval region called the Great Red Spot. Astronomers did not know what it was until space probes looked at it closely. We now know it is a gigantic swirling storm, rather like a huge hurricane on Earth. It measures about 40,000 kilometres across – three times the size of Earth.

JUPITER DATA

Diameter at equator: 142,800km
Average distance from Sun: 778 million km
Minimum distance from Earth: 590 million km
Turns on axis: 9 hours 50 minutes
Circles Sun: 11.9 Earth-years
Temperature at cloud tops: -150°C
Satellites: 63 known

Which probes have visited Jupiter?

Pioneer 10 flew past Jupiter in 1973 and took the first close-up photographs of its colourful atmosphere. *Pioneer 11* followed the next year, and travelled on to Saturn. *Voyagers 1* and *2* flew past in 1979, sending back astounding pictures and information. In 1995, the *Galileo* probe went into orbit round Jupiter after dropping a probe into its atmosphere.

Galileo probe

Quick-fire Quiz

1. Which of these is Jupiter mainly made up of?
a) Rock
b) Carbon dioxide
c) Hydrogen

2. What is the Great Red Spot?
a) A storm
b) A sea
c) A sunspot

3. Which is Jupiter's biggest moon?
a) Io
b) Callisto
c) Ganymede

4. What makes Io colourful?
a) Its clouds
b) Its volcanoes
c) Its oceans

Saturn

Saturn is the second biggest planet, after Jupiter. Like Jupiter, it is a giant ball of gas. Saturn is a favourite planet among astronomers because of its shining rings. The rings appear to change shape year by year as the planet makes its way round the Sun.

SATURN DATA

Diameter at equator: 120,000km
Diameter of visible rings: 270,000km
Average distance from Sun:
  1,427 million km
Minimum distance from Earth:
  1,200 million km
Turns on axis: 10 hours 40 minutes
Circles Sun: 29.5 Earth-years
Temperature at cloud tops:
  -170°C
Satellites: 46 known

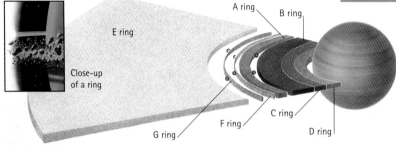

E ring

Close-up of a ring

A ring

B ring

C ring

D ring

F ring

G ring

What are Saturn's rings made of?

Saturn is surrounded by many rings, but only three can be seen from Earth – the A, B and C rings. The other rings were discovered by space probes. The rings look like solid sheets, but they are not. They are made up of millions upon millions of bits of ice, whizzing round the planet at high speed. The bits vary in size from specks of dust to large chunks. In places, the rings are less than 50 metres thick.

Saturn's atmosphere

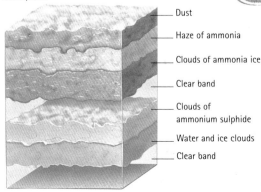

Dust

Haze of ammonia

Clouds of ammonia ice

Clear band

Clouds of ammonium sulphide

Water and ice clouds

Clear band

Why is Saturn so cloudy?

Saturn is a very cloudy planet. The clouds form into bands parallel to the equator because the planet is spinning round so fast. These bands are not as easy to see as they are on Jupiter because of the haze that tops the atmosphere. There seem to be three main cloud layers on Saturn, located at different levels, with clear areas in between. The upper layers of clouds are made up of ammonia and ammonium compounds. At the lowest level, the clouds seem to be made up of water and ice particles, like the clouds we have on Earth.

What's Saturn like inside?

Saturn is a gas giant, which means that it is composed mainly of gas and liquid gas. Its cloudy atmosphere is made up almost entirely of hydrogen and helium. Below that lies a vast, deep ocean of liquid hydrogen. Deeper down is a layer of hydrogen in the form of a liquid metal. At the centre of the planet, there is a small core of rock.

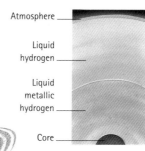

Atmosphere

Liquid hydrogen

Liquid metallic hydrogen

Core

Saturn's structure

Quick-fire Quiz

1. How far is Saturn from the Sun?
a) 14 million km
b) 142 million km
c) 1,427 million km

2. Which is Saturn's biggest moon?
a) Pan
b) Titan
c) Rhea

3. What are Saturn's rings made up of?
a) Rock
b) Ice
c) Metal

4. What colour is Titan's atmosphere?
a) Orange
b) Red
c) Blue

Titan

What are Saturn's moons like?

Saturn has at least 46 moons – 36 of which have been officially named. Only five have a diameter greater than 1,000 kilometres – Tethys, Dione, Rhea, Titan and Iapetus. The biggest is Titan. With a diameter of 5,140 kilometres, it is the second largest moon in the entire Solar System, and the only one that has a thick atmosphere.

Saturn

What is Titan's surface like?

Titan's thick atmosphere is made up mainly of nitrogen gas. It is orange in colour and full of hazy clouds that stop us seeing what its surface is like. Astronomers reckon that it may be covered with great lakes or seas of liquid methane, and there may be land areas covered with methane ice and snow. In January 2005, the *Cassini* spacecraft dropped the *Huygens* landing probe on to the surface, to see what the conditions are like there.

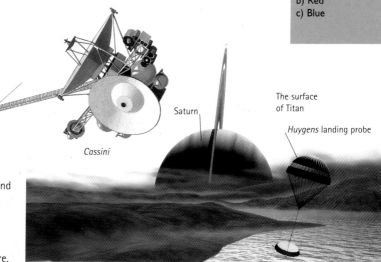

Cassini

Saturn

The surface of Titan

Huygens landing probe

Uranus

Uranus is the third biggest planet, and is four times bigger across than Earth. It is so far from the Earth that it is barely visible with the naked eye. Because of this it was not discovered until the 1700s, with the help of a telescope.

Who discovered Uranus?

In March 1781, an English astronomer named William Herschel was looking at the sky through a telescope. He spied what he thought must be a new comet, but it was actually a new planet. Until then, astronomers knew of only six planets. The new planet, which was later called Uranus, turned out to be twice as far away from the Sun as Saturn.

Why is Uranus sometimes called the topsy–turvy planet?

All planets spin as they orbit the Sun. We say they spin round their axis (an imaginary line that goes through their north and south poles). In most planets the axis is nearly upright as the planet spins. But Uranus spins on an axis at right-angles to normal, so it is as if Uranus is lying on its side. This means that, at times in its orbit, Uranus' poles point straight at the Sun. As a result, they become hotter than the rest of the planet, instead of always being colder, as on Earth.

How many rings does Uranus have?

Astronomers used to think that Saturn was the only planet that had rings circling it. But, in 1977, they discovered that Uranus had rings too. There are about 11 main rings, made up of bits of rock up to a metre across, which whizz round the planet at high speed. The particles in some of the rings are kept in place by tiny 'shepherd' moons.

Uranus in orbit

Sun

Axis

Orbit

Direction of Uranus' rotation

Which probe has visited Uranus?

We can find out very little about Uranus through Earth-based telescopes because it is so far away. Most of what we know came from the *Voyager 2* spacecraft, which visited Uranus in 1986. *Voyager 2* had earlier visited Jupiter (1979) and Saturn (1981). It has now gone far beyond the planets, and will soon leave the Solar System and begin a journey to the stars.

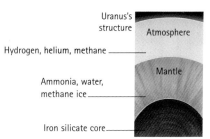

Uranus's structure

Atmosphere

Hydrogen, helium, methane

Mantle

Ammonia, water, methane ice

Iron silicate core

What is Uranus made of?

Uranus has a thick atmosphere of hydrogen, helium and methane, and a mantle of water, ammonia and methane ice. At the centre there is an iron silicate core.

Voyager 2

What are Uranus' moons like?

We can only see the five largest of Uranus' moons from Earth – Miranda, Ariel, Umbriel, Titania and Oberon. Ten smaller moons were discovered by *Voyager 2*. The Hubble Space Telescope discovered 12 more, bringing the total to 27 moons. Titania is the biggest moon. It is about 1,600 kilometres across.

Miranda

Ariel

Titania

URANUS DATA

Diameter at equator: 51,000km

Average distance from Sun: 2,870 million km

Minimum distance from Earth: 2,600 million km

Turns on axis: 17 hours 14 minutes

Circles Sun: 84 Earth-years

Temperature at cloud tops: -200°C

Satellites: 27

Quick-fire Quiz

1. What makes Uranus unique?
a) It has many moons
b) Its large size
c) A highly tilted axis

2. What do shepherd moons keep in place?
a) Space sheep
b) Meteorites
c) Ring particles

3. When was Uranus discovered?
a) In 1681
b) In 1781
c) In 1881

4. Which is Uranus' biggest moon?
a) Miranda
b) Ariel
c) Titania

What is special about Miranda?

Miranda is the smallest moon that can be seen from Earth, with a diameter of only about 500 kilometres. Close-up photographs show it to be the most interesting moon of all. Its surface is a patchwork of different kinds of landscape - craters, grooves, cliffs and valleys. Astronomers think that, ages ago, Miranda shattered into pieces when it collided with another body. Then the pieces came together to create the landscape we see today.

The surface of Miranda

Neptune and Pluto

Neptune and Pluto were the last planets to be discovered. They lie thousands of millions of kilometres away from Earth, at the edge of the Solar System. Neptune is a gas giant, very like Uranus. Pluto is a tiny ice ball, smaller than our own Moon.

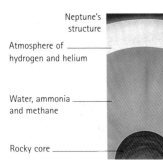

Why is Neptune blue?

Neptune is a lovely blue colour, rather like Earth. This colour comes about because the atmosphere contains a gas called methane. Methane absorbs the red colours in sunlight, and makes the light coming from Neptune's atmosphere appear blue. Dark spots that sometimes appear in Neptune's atmosphere are violent storms.

Neptune's structure

Atmosphere of hydrogen and helium

Water, ammonia and methane

Rocky core

Does Neptune have moons?

Through a telescope, we can see two moons circling around Neptune – Triton and Nereid. When *Voyager 2* visited the planet, it found six more. Using improved ground-based telescopes, astronomers found five more satellites in 2002 and 2003, bringing the total to 13. Triton is by far the biggest moon, measuring some 2,700 kilometres across. It circles the planet in the opposite direction from most moons.

Nereid

Proteus

Triton

What is Neptune like?

Neptune has a similar make-up to its twin planet, Uranus. It has an atmosphere made up mainly of hydrogen, together with some helium. Beneath this there is a huge, deep, hot ocean of water and liquid gases, including methane. In the centre, there is a core of rock, which may be about the same size as Earth.

Voyager 2 over Neptune

When did Voyager 2 visit Neptune?

Neptune was the last planet *Voyager 2* visited on its 12-year journey. Launched in 1977, *Voyager 2* passed about 5,000 kilometres above Neptune's cloud tops on August 24, 1989 – closer than to any other planet. By then, it was more than 4,000 million kilometres from Earth, and its radio signals took more than four hours to get back.

NEPTUNE DATA

Diameter at equator:
49,500km

Average distance from Sun:
4,500 million km

Minimum distance from Earth:
4,300 million km

Turns on axis: 17 hours 6 minutes

Circles Sun: 165 Earth-years

Temperature at cloud tops:
-210°C

Satellites: 13

PLUTO DATA

Diameter at equator: 2,250km

Average distance from Sun:
5,900 million km

Minimum distance from Earth:
4,300 million km

Turns on axis: 6 Earth-days 9 hours

Circles Sun: 248 Earth-years

Surface temperature: -230°C

Satellites: 1

Who found Pluto?

Percival Lowell

United States astronomer Percival Lowell built his own observatory, and led a search for a ninth planet. An astronomer who worked there, Clyde Tombaugh, finally discovered it in 1930.

What is special about Charon?

Pluto's only moon, Charon, is unique in the Solar System, as it is half as big across as Pluto itself. No other moon is as big compared with its planet. Also, it circles Pluto in the same time it takes Pluto to spin round once. This makes Charon appear fixed in Pluto's sky.

Charon

Pluto

What do we know about Pluto?

We do not know much about Pluto because it is so far away. At its furthest, it travels more than 7,000 million kilometres from the Sun. Even in powerful telescopes, it looks only like a faint star. So far, no space probes have visited the planet. All we know is that Pluto is a deep-frozen ball of rock and ice. It probably has a covering of 'snow', made up of frozen methane gas.

Pluto's structure

Thin atmosphere of methane and nitrogen

Mantle of ice

Rocky core

What would Charon look like from Pluto?

Because it appears fixed in Pluto's sky, Charon can only be seen from one side of the planet. From that side, Charon would appear huge, much bigger than the Moon does on Earth. This is because Charon circles very close to Pluto, only about 20,000 kilometres away. Our Moon circles 20 times further from us.

Quick-fire Quiz

1. Which is largest?
a) Charon
b) Neptune
c) Pluto

2. Which is Neptune's biggest moon?
a) Charon
b) Nereid
c) Triton

3. Who discovered Pluto?
a) Percival Lowell
b) Clyde Tombaugh
c) William Herschel

4. *Voyager 2* reached Neptune from Earth after how long?
a) 5 years
b) 9 years
c) 12 years

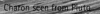

Charon seen from Pluto

Web Addresses

www.bbc.co.uk/science/space
This site provides lots of information on many aspects of space. You will find space news, chat rooms, space games and links to other space-related sites.

www.NASA.gov
This is the official NASA site, which provides news and information on space research and travel at all levels.

Kids.msfc.nasa.gov
This is devoted to introducing kids to the wonders of space and space travel. Log on and find out all sorts of fascinating facts, play games, do projects, join a Kids Club, write space stories and even get your own Nasa Kids email address.

www.enchantedlearning.com/subjects/astronomy
This is an interesting site for all ages. A comprehensive online site about space and astronomy, with fun activities, quizzes and puzzles, as well as hard information on all aspects of the Solar System. It also has lots of links to other space-related sites.

www.bbc.co.uk/history/discovery/revolutions/
launch_ani_cosmology.shtml
This is a lively animation showing how the theories of cosmology have changed over the centuries, from Aristotle to Galileo.

homeschooling.gomilpitas.com/explore/astronomy.htm
This site offers lots of lessons, interactive activities and experiments on all aspects of space. Follow the links to different websites offering a huge range of information.

www.seti.org/game/index.html
Play space science adventure games, complete with glossary, at this site put together by SETI – the organization dedicated to the Search for Extra-Terrestrial Intelligence.

KidsAstronomy.com
This site offers in-depth information on astronomy, current space topics, and includes interactive games.

www.spacekids.com
This is a fun site for kids with videos, games, photos, jokes, news and homework help.

starchild.gsfc.nasa.gov/docs/StarChild/StarChild.html
This learning centre for young astronomers is graded at different levels. It offers good graphics, articles with an attached glossary, as well as activities and plenty of fun facts.

www.thinkquest.org/library/index.html
The ThinkQuest Library is a collection of more than 5,500 educational websites designed by participants in the ThinkQuest competitions. To see what they have produced on stars and planets, check out subjects such as stars, planets, Solar System and Universe.

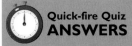

Quick-fire Quiz ANSWERS

Page 11 Looking at the Sky
1. b   2. c   3. b   4. b

Page 13 Seeing Stars
1. b   2. c   3. b   4. b

Page 15 Great Balls of Gas
1. b   2. b   3. c   4. c

Page 17 Galaxies
1. c   2. b   3. c   4. a

Page 19 The Solar System
1. b   2. c   3. b   4. c

Page 21 Our Star, the Sun
1. b   2. c   3. b   4. c

Page 23 The Planets
1. b   2. c   3. b   4. b

Page 25 Mercury
1. b   2. c   3. b   4. a

Page 27 Venus
1. c   2. b   3. c   4. a

Page 29 Earth
1. b   2. b   3. c   4. a

Page 31 The Moon
1. c   2. b   3. c   4. b

Page 33 Mars
1. c   2. b   3. a   4. c

Page 35 Jupiter
1. c   2. a   3. c   4. b

Page 37 Saturn
1. c   2. b   3. b   4. a

Page 39 Uranus
1. c   2. c   3. b   4. c

Page 41 Neptune and Pluto
1. b   2. c   3. b   4. c

1000
QUESTIONS
& ANSWERS
FACTFILE

PLANET
EARTH

Contents

Earth's Formation

In the vastness of outer space lies a star system, or galaxy, known as the Milky Way. Inside this galaxy is our Solar System – a bright star orbited by nine planets. The planet that is third closest to this star, which we call the Sun, is a unique, life-supporting planet called Earth.

Why is Earth unique?

Earth is a rocky planet and is more than a million times smaller than the Sun. Unlike the other eight planets in the Solar System, Earth has water and an atmosphere that contains oxygen. This means that life can exist on Earth.

How did Earth form?

1 The Sun was formed when a nebula – a vast cloud of gas and dust – shrank under the pull of gravity. Hot clouds of dust and gases spun around the newly formed Sun.

2 When the specks of dust collided, lumps formed, and gravity pulled these lumps together, creating a large, spinning fiery ball. Heavy elements such as iron sank to the centre of the molten ball.

3 Lighter metals and rocks rose to the surface of the ball, which cooled enough for a solid, hard shell to form.

4 Gases escaped from the planet and formed an atmosphere with clouds. As rain fell, oceans were formed and these contained oxygen-producing plants.

5 Over time, the planet became the one we live on today – planet Earth, but it continues to change.

Who proved that Earth is round?

For thousands of years, it was a common belief that Earth was flat. After all, it appears flat to the naked eye. But in 1522, Portuguese explorer Ferdinand Magellan's ship *Victoria* completed a historic journey – it sailed all the way around the world. This proved once and for all that Earth was round.

Who was Copernicus?

Copernicus

Before 1500, most people believed that the Sun and planets revolved around Earth. In 1530, Polish astronomer Nicolaus Copernicus (left) wrote a book showing that Earth spins on an axis and, along with the other planets, journeys around the Sun. His ideas outraged many people at the time, and the book was banned until 1830.

How long does it take Earth to orbit the Sun?

It takes 365.25 days (one year) for Earth to complete its orbit around the Sun. Earth spins on an axis that runs from the North Pole to the South Pole. It takes 24 hours (one day) for Earth to spin right round on its axis.

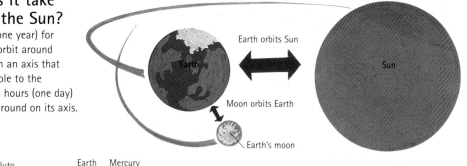

Earth orbits Sun

Earth

Sun

Moon orbits Earth

Earth's moon

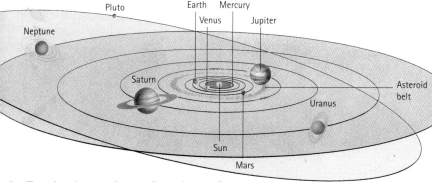

Pluto

Neptune

Earth   Mercury

Venus

Jupiter

Saturn

Asteroid belt

Uranus

Sun

Mars

Is Earth the only rocky planet?

No, the nine planets of our solar system are divided into two groups – rocky planets and gaseous or icy planets. The four planets closest to the Sun – Mercury, Venus, Earth and Mars – are rocky. Jupiter, Saturn, Uranus, Neptune and Pluto are gaseous or icy planets.

How old is Earth?

Earth formed at the same time as the Sun and the other eight planets of our Solar System. By studying rocks and fossils, scientists have estimated that this was about 4.6 billion years ago.

5

Crust to Core

Explorers have charted the continents and seas of Earth's surface, and satellites have beamed back pictures of our planet from space. Geologists (scientists who study Earth), however, have sought an understanding of what Earth is made of, and what lies beneath the surface crust.

Crust

Mantle

Outer core

Inner core

What is Earth made of?

It is about 6,400 kilometres from the surface of Earth to its centre. Earth is made up of different layers of rock and metal. There are three main zones – an outer crust, the mantle below and the core at the centre. The outer crust is made of rock, and is divided into two parts – continental crust and oceanic crust. The mantle, which lies beneath the crust, is made up of molten rock and is about 2,800 kilometres thick. The core of Earth consists mainly of the metals nickel and iron. It is hot and dense and is divided into two areas – a liquid outer core and a solid inner core.

Ocean

Crust

Mantle

How do we know what's inside Earth?

Geologists cannot be absolutely certain what the inside of Earth is like, but they can discover a lot from examining the rocks spewed out from volcanoes. They can also use seismic waves from both earthquakes and nuclear bomb tests to build up a three-dimensional picture of the planet. Seismic waves move quickly through hard, dense rock, and more slowly through soft rock. In the 1960s, scientists tried to drill through the ocean crust to the mantle (left), but failed as the project was too expensive.

Earth data

Age: 4.6 billion years
Mass: 5.9 billion, billion tonnes
Circumference (distance around Earth at equator): 40,091km
Distance from surface to centre: 6,400km
Temperature at centre: 5,000°C

How does Earth aid navigation?

As Earth spins in space, electric currents below its surface cause it to act like a magnet. Like a bar magnet, Earth has two magnetic poles and a magnetic field. If a magnetized needle is floated in a bowl of water, it will align itself with Earth's magnetic poles, creating a simple compass. Some animals such as pigeons and dolphins also use the Earth's magnetic field to navigate.

Is Earth round?

From space, Earth looks spherical. However, it is not perfectly round. In fact, it is slightly flatter at the top and bottom – the Poles – and it bulges slightly at the middle around the equator.

How high is the sky?

The sky, or atmosphere, surrounds Earth and contains a mixture of gases that makes life on the planet possible. The atmosphere is made up of several layers and reaches about 1,600 kilometres into space.

The troposphere is the lowest layer and contains enough air for plants and animals to breathe. The air in the stratosphere is much thinner and contains a thin layer of 'ozone' – a type of oxygen gas that warms the atmosphere and absorbs harmful rays from the Sun. The other layers in the atmosphere are the mesophere, the ionosphere and the exosphere.

Exosphere

Ionosphere

Mesosphere

Stratosphere
Troposphere

Ozone layer

Quick-fire Quiz

1. What are scientists who study Earth called?
a) Geographers
b) Geologists
c) Genealogists

2. How thick is the mantle?
a) 2,800km
b) 280km
c) 28,000km

3. What is Earth's core made of?
a) Oxygen and nitrogen
b) Granite and marble
c) Nickel and iron

4. What is the layer of atmosphere that we live in called?
a) Troposphere
b) Ozone
c) Stratosphere

Water

From space, Earth looks blue. This is because 71 per cent of the surface of the planet is covered by water. About 97 per cent of the planet's water is in the sea and is salty. The remaining water is in the rivers, lakes and glaciers.

Pacific Ocean

In which sea is it easy to float?

Sea water contains common salt and other minerals. On average, the sea is 3.5 per cent salt. However, the Dead Sea, an inland sea, is 25 per cent salt. High salt content gives water great buoyancy, and so it is very easy for swimmers to float in the Dead Sea.

Which is the biggest ocean?

Oceans are huge areas of sea water. There are four oceans – the Pacific, the Atlantic, the Indian and the Arctic. The Pacific is the largest and the deepest. It is more than twice as big as the second largest ocean, the Atlantic. The Pacific is wide enough to fit all the continents, and deep enough to swallow Mount Everest, the world's highest mountain.

Water falls as snow in mountainous areas

Water is transferred inland as clouds move with winds

Plants give off water in a process called 'transpiration'

Water evaporates from lakes and rivers as it flows back into oceans

What is the 'water cycle'?

The world's water is constantly being recycled (above). Rain falls onto the land and into the oceans. The Sun's rays heat Earth, and water evaporates back into the atmosphere. As the water in the atmosphere cools, it condenses to form rain clouds.

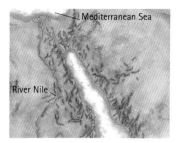
Mediterranean Sea

River Nile

Which is the world's longest river?

The longest river in the world is the Nile in Africa (left). It runs 6,695 kilometres from its source in Lake Victoria, Burundi, to the Mediterranean Sea. Rivers not only play an important role in shaping the landscape, they are also a vital resource for humans, providing food and water for drinking and irrigation. The Nile is such a long river that it is even visible from space!

Quick-fire Quiz

1. How much of Earth's surface is covered by water?
a) 21%
b) 51%
c) 71%

2. Which is the second largest ocean?
a) Arctic
b) Atlantic
c) Indian

3. Which is the largest sea?
a) South China Sea
b) Red Sea
c) Dead Sea

4. How long is the Nile?
a) 5,595km
b) 6,695km
c) 7,795km

How do lakes form?

Lakes can form in a variety of ways. Oxbow lakes are formed when a loop of a winding, or 'meandering', river gets cut off from the river. Volcanic lakes form in the natural hollows of old volcanoes. Lakes can also form in rift valleys, which occur when the land in between two faults – fractures in Earth's crust – slips away.

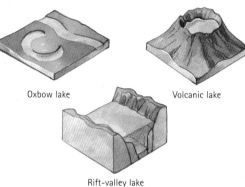
Oxbow lake

Volcanic lake

Rift-valley lake

What causes waves and tides?

As wind blows over the ocean's surface, friction between the air and water causes wavelets on the surface. These grow bigger, creating waves with crests that are separated by 'troughs'. Tides are caused by Earth's spin and the gravitational pulls of the Moon and Sun.

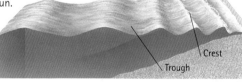

Crest

Trough

Water falls as rain on oceans

Water evaporates from oceans

What's the difference between seas and oceans?

Seas are sections of oceans, but are partly cut off from them by land. The largest sea, the South China Sea, is part of the Pacific Ocean. Most seas and oceans are rich in marine life and mineral resources.

Land

Earth's crust is divided into sections called 'plates' that are moved about by the mantle over millions of years. Continental crust – crust that makes up Earth's land – is 30 to 40 kilometres thick.

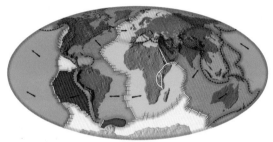

The different colours represent the tectonic plates of Earth's crust. The arrows indicate the direction each plate is moving in.

What are tectonic plates?

The surface of the Earth is made up of about 20 tectonic plates (above) that move slowly over Earth's surface, causing continents to collide and split apart. Areas where plates pull apart from each other are called 'divergence zones', and areas where plates push against each other are called 'convergence zones'.

How has Earth changed?

1 About 200 million years ago, all the continents were joined together in one giant land mass called Pangaea.

Pangaea

2 By about 130 million years ago, Pangaea had split into a northern continent called Laurasia, and a southern continent called Gondwanaland.

Laurasia

Gondwanaland

3 By about 65 million years ago, Gondwanaland had split into Africa and South America, and Laurasia was splitting into North America and Eurasia.

North America

Eurasia

South America

Africa

4 In 65 million years from now, it is likely that North America will split from South America to join Asia. It is also likely that Africa will group closely together with Europe.

North and South America

Africa

What evidence of plate movement is there?

The shapes of the east coast of North and South America and the west coast of Europe and Africa indicate that they were once joined. Also, scientists have found matches between rocks, fossils, plants and animals from different continents – ostriches from Africa and rheas from South America probably share an ancestor.

Quick-fire Quiz

1. Which is the smallest continent?
a) Antarctica
b) Europe
c) Asia

2. What are areas where tectonic plates pull apart called?
a) Convergence zones
b) Divergence zones
c) Continental zones

3. How thick are continental land masses?
a) 20 to 30km
b) 30 to 40km
c) 40 to 50km

4. Which ocean is getting smaller?
a) Atlantic
b) Indian
c) Pacific

How many continents are there?

There are seven continents – North America, South America, Africa, Asia, Europe, Antarctica and Australasia. Europe, attached to Asia, is the smallest continent and it is argued that it is really part of Asia. Australasia is made up of Australia, New Zealand and other Pacific Islands. India is a 'subcontinent' of Asia as it is so large and distinct.

How else have tectonic plates shaped the world?

Plate movement has not only mapped out our continents, but it has also created many geographical features. Mountains are formed when plates crumple land as they collide, and volcanoes erupt when plates dive under the mantle and melt or split apart (below). Earthquakes occur where tectonic plates move past each other.

Are the continents still moving?

Yes! North America and Europe are estimated to be moving seven centimetres further apart every year. This means that the Atlantic Ocean is getting wider and the Pacific Ocean is getting smaller.

53

Earthquakes

Earthquakes can be devastating natural disasters. More than a million earthquakes are detected each year, but only a fraction of these are strong enough to cause damage.

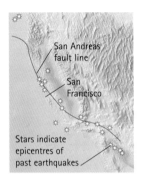

Epicentre

Focus

Shock waves

What is a 'fault' line?

As plates of continental and oceanic crust slide and push against each other, they cause rocks to snap, forming a line of weakness called a 'fault'. Earthquakes occur along these fault lines. The San Andreas Fault (right) runs down the west coast of North America and is one of the biggest fault lines in the world. In 1906, a catastrophic earthquake along the fault caused 500 deaths in San Francisco.

San Andreas fault line

San Francisco

Stars indicate epicentres of past earthquakes

What are shock waves?

Shock waves are waves of energy caused by earthquakes. The source of the waves is called the 'focus' of the quake, and the point on the surface above the focus is referred to as the 'epicentre'. There are two kinds of shock waves. 'Body' waves travel through the rock beneath the surface, causing it to compress, expand and move up and down. 'Surface' waves reach Earth's surface and have a rolling motion, just like ocean waves. Usually, an earthquake causes most damage at the epicentre, and less further away.

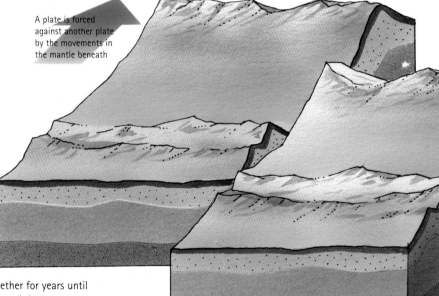

A plate is forced against another plate by the movements in the mantle beneath

How are earthquakes caused?

As Earth's plates push and shove against each other, they place enormous stress on rocks near the top of the crust. Instead of rubbing smoothly past each other, they may lock together for years until the strain gets too much and the pent-up energy is released. This causes an earthquake, sending shock waves through the rocks.

What is a 'tsunami'?

When an earthquake happens beneath the sea, it can create enormous tidal waves called 'tsunamis'. Tsunamis can reach heights of 30 metres or more by the time they reach coastlines, and can cause vast amounts of damage.

What should you do in an earthquake?

Perhaps the greatest danger in an earthquake is that a building will collapse on top of you. Standing in a doorway or taking shelter under a table may save your life. Architects and engineers try to construct buildings that resist collapse (left). These buildings have deep foundations in solid rock and must be able to bend slightly.

Trans-America Pyramid, San Francisco, USA

How are earthquakes measured?

Earthquakes are recorded by 'seismographs' and measured on two scales. The Mercalli Scale is based on the effects of earthquakes. The Richter Scale is based on the size of shock waves.

Mercalli Scale	Richter Scale
1 Very slight: detected by instruments	less than 3
2 Feeble: felt by people resting	3–3.4
3 Slight: like heavy trucks passing	3.5–4
4 Moderate: windows rattle	4.1–4.4
5 Rather strong: wakes sleeping people	4.5–4.8
6 Strong: trees sway, walls crack	4.9–5.4
7 Very strong: buildings crack	5.5–6
8 Destructive: buildings move	6.1–6.5
9 Ruinous: ground cracks	6.6–7
10 Disastrous: landslides	7.1–7.3
11 Very disastrous: railways break	7.4–8.1
12 Catastrophic: total devastation	8.1 and over

What damage can earthquakes cause?

Depending on the strength of the earthquake, areas can be completely devastated. The ground shakes and ripples, and huge cracks open up. Buildings collapse, and electricity lines, water mains and gas pipes are destroyed. Fires often start, causing further chaos. Some earthquakes have caused the deaths of thousands of people. Approximately 90,000 people were killed by an earthquake in northern Pakistan in October 2005.

As the plates attempt to move past each other, tension builds up and will be released in the form of an earthquake

Quick-fire Quiz

1. Which fault line is on the west coast of North America?
a) San Andreas Fault
b) San Francisco Fault
c) Great American Fault

2. Where does most of an earthquake's damage usually occur?
a) Under the ground
b) In space
c) At the epicentre

3. What is probably the greatest danger to human life in an earthquake?
a) Buildings collapsing
b) Electric shocks
c) Molten lava

4. Which type of damage would an earthquake measuring 7.1 on the Richter scale cause?
a) Feeble
b) Disastrous
c) Catastrophic

Mountains

Formed over millions of years, mountains create some of the world's most dramatic landscapes. Most occur in ranges that stretch for hundreds of kilometres, and many of these ranges will continue to grow upwards before erosion eventually reduces them to the size of hills.

Pressure applied by crust buckles rock

Fold mountains

How are mountains formed?

Volcanic mountains are formed by molten rock that has escaped through cracks in the crust and built up on the surface. Block mountains occur when a chunk of land is thrust above neighbouring rock along fault lines in Earth's crust. The mountains in the great ranges are fold mountains. They are formed when two slabs of continental crust collide, buckling the rock and sediment between them (above). The Himalayas were formed in this way (right).

India hits Asia, crumpling both continental crusts and forming the Himalayan mountain range

Where are mountains found?

Mountains can be found all over the world (above). The greatest mountain ranges are the 'Rockies' of North America, the Alps of Europe, the Andes of South America and the highest of them all – the Himalayas in Asia.

How do mountains stay upright?

It is thought that Earth's crust 'floats' on the mantle beneath. Mountains have 'roots' that reach deep below ground level and support them.

What life can be found on mountains?

Animals and plants that live on mountains have to be able to survive extreme temperatures and high winds. Trees are unable to survive above a certain altitude known as the 'tree line'. However, hardy alpine plants can grow higher up. Mountain animals such as llamas, yaks, goats and hares have thick, woolly coats to keep out the cold.

Why are some mountains rugged and others smooth?

Young mountains, such as the Himalayas, have steep, rugged peaks and sides. Over time, the peaks and sides will be eroded by water, rain, ice and wind. This means that older mountains are smoother and less high.

Which is the highest mountain?

The world's highest peak is Mount Everest (below). It is part of the Himalayas in Asia and is 8,848 metres high. On May 29, 1953, New Zealand mountaineer Edmund Hillary and his Sherpa guide, Tenzing Norgay (right), made history by reaching the summit of Everest. Mauna Kea in Hawaii is 10,000 metres high. However, 6,000 metres of the mountain lies beneath the ocean.

Edmund Hillary and Tenzing Norgay

Quick-fire Quiz

1. Which mountain range is found in South America?
a) Alps
b) Rockies
c) Andes

2. Which type of mountain are the great ranges?
a) Volcanic mountains
b) Fold mountains
c) Block mountains

3. What is the line above which trees are unable to grow called?
a) Tree line
b) Growth line
c) Altitude line

4. How high is Mauna Kea?
a) 8,000m
b) 9,000m
c) 10,000m

Volcanoes

An erupting volcano spewing hot molten rock is one of the most dramatic sights on Earth. Volcanic eruptions are caused by disturbances in Earth's crust. There are about 500 active volcanoes in the world.

What are volcanoes?

Volcanoes are openings in Earth's crust from which hot molten rock (magma), ash and gas spurt. The magma, which is called lava after eruption, cools around the openings to form cone shapes. Volcanoes often occur in mountain ranges on land, but they can also form on ocean floors, rising above sea level (above).

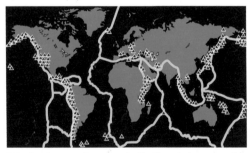

Pink triangles are active volcanoes. Plate boundaries are in yellow

Magma chamber

Where are volcanoes found?

Most of Earth's volcanoes are located along plate boundaries (above), where tectonic plates meet, because this is where crust is weakest. There are so many volcanoes surrounding the Pacific Ocean that it is known as the 'ring of fire'. A few volcanoes occur away from plate edges above 'hot spots' – areas where Earth's crust is thin and magma can burn through. Some islands are the tops of volcanoes that have emerged from the ocean floor. The Hawaiian Islands are examples of this.

Cinder-cone volcano

Composite volcano

Shield volcano

Are there different types of volcano?

A volcano's shape depends on how thick the magma is and the force with which it is spewed out. A cinder cone is formed after a huge explosion, which occurs if there is a lot of gas in the magma. The cone of the volcano is made mostly of volcanic ash. A composite volcano erupts regularly, and is usually very tall and made of alternating layers of lava and ash. The lava is thick and sticky, and does not flow far before it solidifies. A shield volcano has several craters and is formed when magma is thin and runny. It spreads across a wide area to form a low dome shape.

What are 'geysers'?

'Geysers' are found in volcanic areas where hot rocks lie near Earth's surface. Underground water is heated to boiling point by the rocks and then shoots a fountain of hot water into the air. In New Zealand and Iceland, the power from geysers and hot springs is used to make electricity. One of the world's most famous geysers is *Old Faithful* in Yellowstone National Park, USA, which shoots up a jet of water and steam every 70 minutes.

What is a dormant volcano?

A dormant volcano is a volcano that has been quiet for hundreds of years. However, there is always a danger that a dormant volcano may suddenly erupt. A volcano that has permanently stopped erupting is said to be 'extinct'.

What happens when a volcano erupts?

Deep beneath a volcano lies a magma chamber (left). Pressure builds up inside the chamber and the magma escapes through a chimney-like vent. During an eruption, rock and ash are spewed out with the magma.

Rocks, Fossils and Minerals

Earth's many and varied landscapes are all shaped out of rock. There are three main types of rock – igneous, metamorphic and sedimentary – and they are all formed in different ways.

Amethyst

What are minerals?

All rocks are made up of building blocks called minerals. Minerals are natural chemical compounds, and nearly all consist of just eight chemical elements – oxygen, silicon, calcium, magnesium, potassium, aluminium, iron and sodium. When minerals are cut and polished and considered to be beautiful and durable enough to wear as jewellery, they are known as gemstones, or gems (left). Gems are valued according to their hardness, density, colour and how they reflect light.

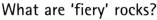

Opal   Diamond   Ruby   Emerald

What are 'fiery' rocks?

After molten magma forces its way through cracks in Earth's crust, it gradually cools, forms crystals and becomes a hard mass of igneous rock. The word 'igneous' comes from the Latin word for fire. Granite (left) and basalt are examples of igneous rock.

Granite

Igneous rock

What is metamorphic rock?

Metamorphic rock is igneous or sedimentary rock that has been changed by great heat or pressure. For example, magma under the ground can bake surrounding limestone and change it into marble. The forces that build new mountains also create metamorphic rock, changing soft mudstone into hard slate (left).

Metamorphic rock formed by heat from magma underground

Slate

Metamorphic rock formed by pressure from folding crust

Slate

Magma chamber   Marble

How do fossils form?

Fossils are the remains of animals and plants that lived more than 10,000 years ago. Most fossils are formed in sedimentary rock.

1 When a sea animal such as an ammonite dies, its body sinks to the sea bed. The soft parts rot away, leaving hard shell.

2 The shell is buried under more and more sediment and, over time, this sediment hardens into rock.

3 Over millions of years, the rock in which the fossil lies may shift, and the fossil could find itself thrust up to become part of a new mountain range.

4 Eventually, the effects of weathering and erosion wear away the rock and expose the fossil.

How is limestone formed?

Limestone is a sedimentary rock. All sedimentary rock is made from sediments such as shells, sand and mud that settle on the bottom of seas, lakes and rivers. Sediments pile up in layers, and pressure from the higher layers squeezes out water from the lower layers. The squashed sediments cement together to form solid rock. Limestone is formed from the shells and skeletons of tiny sea creatures. Sandstone and chalk (right) are also sedimentary rocks.

Chalk

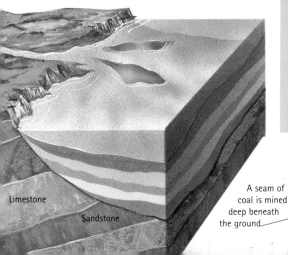

Limestone

Sandstone

A seam of coal is mined deep beneath the ground

What use are rocks, fossils and minerals?

Rocks are used as building materials, and some minerals are useful in industry – silicon is used to make glass, and diamonds make good cutting tools (some drills are tipped with diamonds). Coal, a 'fossil fuel', is mined from deep underground (below). It is the remains of prehistoric plants that built up in thick layers. The layers were flooded by the sea and covered with sand, which, over millions of years, compressed the layers into coal.

Quick-fire Quiz

1. Which type of rock is granite?
a) Igneous
b) Sedimentary
c) Metamorphic

2. Which is a sedimentary rock?
a) Chalk
b) Basalt
c) Marble

3. Which metamorphic rock can limestone be changed into?
a) Slate
b) Granite
c) Marble

4. In which type of rock are fossils usually found?
a) Igneous
b) Sedimentary
c) Metamorphic

Climate

Climate is the average weather conditions of a region, season by season. Many factors affect climate – global position, ocean currents and the 'greenhouse effect'. As these factors continue to change, so, too, will Earth's climate.

Why does Earth have seasons?

Earth has seasons because its axis tilts and, as it orbits the Sun, one hemisphere is always tipped closer to the Sun than the other hemisphere. When the northern hemisphere is closer to the Sun – from March 21 to September 21 – it will experience spring and summer, while the southern hemisphere will be in autumn and winter. When the southern hemisphere is closer to the Sun – from September 21 to March 21 – it will have spring and summer, while the northern hemisphere will experience its autumn and winter.

Spring in NH

Autumn in SH

Summer in NH

Sun

Winter in NH

Winter in SH

Summer in SH

Autumn in NH

Spring in SH

Key –
NH   northern hemisphere
SH   southern hemisphere

Why are some places hotter than others?

Different parts of the world have different temperatures. As Earth is round, the Sun does not heat it evenly (below). Areas near the equator always have a hot climate because the Sun is directly overhead. Further away from the equator, the Sun's rays are spread over a much larger area so it is not as hot. Although equatorial regions do not experience much change in temperature, they do have rainy and dry seasons.

Sun's rays spread over very large area – cold at North Pole

Sun's rays spread over large area – warm

Sun's rays directed at small area – hot at equator

Equator

Warm

Cold at South Pole

Pacific Ocean

South America

Australia   Warm water

Cold water

How do ocean currents affect climates?

Ocean currents bring warm or cold water to continental coasts. Then air masses are heated or cooled by the water, and this affects the climate in the local area. Warm currents move westward across the Pacific (above), providing south-east Asia and northern Australia with a warm, humid climate.

Climate zones of the world

Polar   Cold   Temperate   Arid   Tropical

How does global position affect climate?

Climate depends on many geographical factors – mountainous areas are cold, and places close to the ocean are wetter than inland regions. Global position also affects climate (left). Polar regions are snowy and icy, and even areas that have 'cold' climates may be frozen for months on end. Temperate climates have warm summers, cool winters and rain. Arid, desert areas are hot and dry, and tropical areas are hot and wet.

What is an 'ice age'?

An 'ice age' is a period when part of Earth is permanently covered by ice. As the Poles are frozen, we are in an ice age now. Some ice ages are more severe than others – millions of years ago, ice sheets covered most of Earth during ice ages. The last severe ice age took place between about 20,000 and 80,000 years ago (right).

Average July temperatures
15°C
10°C
5°C
0°C

Severe ice age

200,000   160,000   140,000   80,000   40,000   20,000   present

Years before present

What is the 'greenhouse effect'?

Some of the Sun's heat is not absorbed by Earth and is reflected back into space. Gases in Earth's atmosphere such as carbon dioxides, nitrogen oxides and chlorofluorocarbons (CFCs) trap some of this heat and radiate it back to Earth. This is the 'greenhouse effect'. Without the greenhouse effect, it would be too cold on Earth for life to exist. However, too many CFCs, which are released by industry, have entered the atmosphere, and this is causing an excess of heat to be trapped. This causes 'global warming', which is harmful and alters Earth's climate over time.

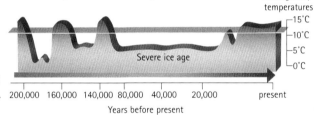

Sun's heat enters atmosphere

Some radiated heat escapes

Sun's heat reflected back to space

Radiated heat trapped in atmosphere causes global warming

Quick-fire Quiz

1. Why does Earth have seasons?
a) The Sun's axis tilts
b) The equator tilts
c) Earth's axis tilts

2. When does the southern hemisphere have spring and summer?
a) March 21 to September 21
b) September 21 to March 21
c) January 21 to July 21

3. Which climate has warm summers and cool winters?
a) Cold
b) Temperate
c) Arid

4. What do places near to oceans experience?
a) Cold weather
b) Dry weather
c) Wet weather

63

Weather

Weather is the day-to-day changes in atmospheric conditions – sunshine, rainfall and wind speeds. Some areas have similar weather every day, while others have very changeable weather.

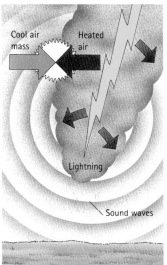

Lightning

Cool air mass

Heated air

Sound waves

Why does it snow?

Tiny water droplets in clouds freeze to form ice crystals. These six-sided crystals can bind together and create beautiful snowflakes (left). The ice crystals are quite heavy so they will fall from the clouds. If the temperature of the air below the clouds is less than 0°C, the ice crystals will remain frozen and fall as snow. If the air is above 0°C, the ice crystals will melt and fall as rain.

How are clouds made?

Water vapour in the air condenses into tiny droplets. The droplets are not heavy enough to fall as rain, and instead they group together to form clouds. Different conditions form clouds of different types and shapes (below). Cirrocumulus clouds look like ripples. Altocumulus clouds are white and puffy. Cumulus clouds are big, cauliflower-shaped clouds. Stratus clouds are flat and low-lying.

What are thunder and lightning?

In a storm cloud, air currents force water droplets to crash into each other until they become electrically charged. Lightning is the huge spark of electricity produced as the charge is released. Lightning heats the air near to it so quickly that it produces a loud, booming noise – thunder (above). To work out how far away a storm is, count the seconds between the lightning and thunder – five seconds indicates 1.6 kilometres.

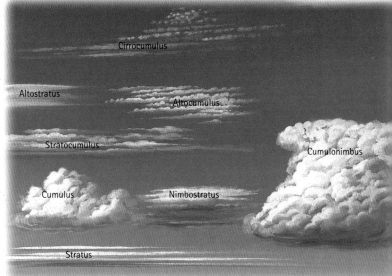

Cirrocumulus

Altostratus

Altocumulus

Stratocumulus

Cumulonimbus

Cumulus

Nimbostratus

Stratus

How are rainbows caused?

Rainbows appear in the sky after rain and are the reflection of the Sun in raindrops. The raindrops split the sunlight into a 'spectrum' of colours – red, orange, yellow, green, blue, indigo and violet (right). To see a rainbow, your back must be to the Sun.

How is weather forecast?

The science of studying weather systems is called meteorology. Information on temperature, cloud type, wind speed, air pressure, rain and snow is collected regularly from places all over the world. As well as information from the ground, meteorologists can get an accurate picture of the weather from satellites in space (left). The information is sent to forecasting stations and plotted onto charts. Meteorologists can make fairly accurate forecasts up to a week ahead.

Weather satellite

What are tornadoes, hurricanes, typhoons and cyclones?

A tornado is a twisting storm funnel about 100 metres wide. The winds inside the tornado can reach speeds of 350 km/h. Tornadoes move in straight lines across land and are most common on the Great Plains of North America (right). At the centre, or 'eye', of a tornado is an area of pressure so low that it can cause buildings to explode. Hurricanes are much bigger storms that form over tropical waters in the Atlantic. They are so powerful that when they strike land, they can devastate crops, forests and buildings. Storms that form over the Pacific are called typhoons, and ones that occur over the Indian Ocean are called cyclones.

Quick-fire Quiz

1. Which clouds are flat and low-lying?
a) Cirrus
b) Stratus
c) Cumulus

2. What are tropical storms that form in the Pacific called?
a) Hurricanes
b) Typhoons
c) Cyclones

3. What is the study of weather systems called?
a) Meteorology
b) Microbiology
c) Weatherology

4. What is lightning?
a) Spark of electricity
b) Crashing air currents
c) Loud booming noises

Polar Regions

The North and South Poles are at the north and south points of Earth's axis. The polar regions of the Arctic (north) and Antarctica (south) are the coldest areas on Earth (below). Ice and snow stretch as far as the eye can see.

Arctic

Antarctica

Do any people live in Antarctica?

Only scientists live in Antarctica, and they normally stay only in the summer months. The land is not owned by any country and an Antarctic Treaty, signed by 32 countries, ensures the land is only used for research. Tourism is increasing in the area which means that waste disposal is a problem – the freezing temperatures preserve waste rather than rot it away.

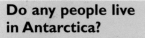

Is there any land in the Arctic Circle?

There is no land at the North Pole itself – just a mass of pack ice. However, most of Greenland and parts of Canada, Alaska and Scandinavia lie within the Arctic Circle. Antarctica is a continental land mass covered by an ice sheet.

How cold is Antarctica?

Antarctica is the world's coldest continent. Temperatures inland range from -25°C to -89°C. The lowest temperature ever recorded on Earth was -89.2°C at Vostok in Antarctica. Ice sheets are up to three kilometres thick, and the ice and snow reflect the Sun's heat back into space. Icy winds can blow at speeds of up to 145 km/h. It has not rained in Antarctica for two million years.

What are icebergs?

Icebergs are parts of the Arctic and Antarctic ice sheets that have broken off into the ocean. Icebergs vary in size and shape, and some can be the size of a small country. As much as 90 per cent of an iceberg is underwater, and this is why they are hazardous to ships, which are often unable to detect them.

What are glaciers?

A glacier is a large body of ice that moves slowly through mountain valleys and polar regions. Glaciers move less than two metres a day, but are so big that they can dramatically shape and carve the land that they pass through. During the past ice ages, much of Europe, North America, South Africa and Asia were covered by glaciers. When glaciers meet the ocean, chunks can break off into the sea and form icebergs (below).

Quick-fire Quiz

1. Where is the South Pole?
   a) Arctic
   b) Antarctica
   c) Greenland

2. Where are polar bears found?
   a) Arctic
   b) Antarctica
   c) Australia

3. How far do glaciers move each day?
   a) Less than 2m
   b) 10 to 20m
   c) 50 to 100m

4. Which country lies within the Arctic Circle?
   a) Ireland
   b) Iceland
   c) Greenland

What is tundra?

Tundra (above) is the land around the Arctic Circle in between the northern conifer forests and the permanent ice sheets around the North Pole. The surface soil in the tundra only thaws for a few weeks in the summer, but below the surface, the ground is permanently frozen. This means that vegetation cannot extend its roots very deep, and only small shrubs, mosses and trees can grow there.

How do animals survive polar climates?

Polar animals have thick coats or layers of fat (blubber) to keep warm. Polar mammals usually have small ears and snouts to avoid losing too much heat. Penguins, whales, seals and seabirds fish in the icy seas, and musk oxen graze on plants in the tundra, where they live all year round. Polar bears live in the Arctic only, and penguins live in Antarctica only.

Arctic tern

Penguins   Seal   Musk ox   Polar bear

Deserts

Deserts are regions where the annual rainfall is less than 250 millimetres, but some deserts have no rain for several years. Deserts are the driest places on Earth and are often very windy. Few plants can survive in these conditions.

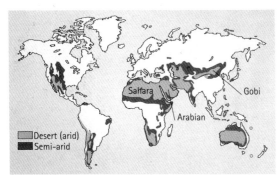

Which are the largest deserts?

The three largest deserts in the world are the Sahara, the Arabian and the Gobi (above). The Sahara covers about one third of Africa, measuring about 8.6 million square kilometres. The Arabian Desert and the Gobi in Asia measure 2.3 and 1.2 million square kilometres respectively. Australia has several deserts that cover a huge area of land.

Wind direction

Dunes 'migrate' in direction of wind

How are dunes formed?

Many deserts have sandy mounds called dunes. Dunes are formed when the wind blows steadily from one direction. Sand grains lodge against stones or bushes and, over time, the sand piles up, forming dunes. Whole dunes are moved along by the wind as sand on the gently inclined, wind-facing side of the dune is swept over the top of the dune (above). Dunes shaped like crescent moons are called 'barchan dunes'.

Are deserts always hot?

Daytime temperatures can rise to a scorching 50°C in some deserts. Once the sun sets, however, temperatures can drop dramatically because there are few clouds over deserts to keep the day's heat in. The difference between day and night temperatures in the western Sahara can be more than 45°C, whereas the Gobi has a more temperate climate. Many people consider the polar regions to be cold deserts as they have no rain.

Are all deserts sandy?

Most deserts are rocky, not sandy. Only about 11 per cent of the Sahara is sandy. Many deserts contain huge, strange-shaped rocks that have been formed by wind erosion.

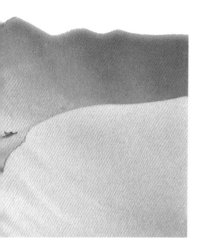

What is an oasis?

Deserts are very dry places. An oasis (above) is a small fertile area in a desert where water from beneath the ground reaches the surface. Many oases occur naturally, although they can be created artificially by digging wells in places where water lies close to the surface. Plants can grow near oases, but elsewhere some plants lie dormant and wait patiently for rain.

Can people live in deserts?

Many people who live in deserts are nomads, who wander from place to place in search of food and water. Permanent settlements are formed around oases and, as it is now possible to make artificial oases, more and more people are now living in desert lands.

What life is found in deserts?

Many desert animals, such as foxes, jack rabbits and coyotes, are nocturnal, sleeping during the scorching hot day and coming out to find food at night when it is cooler. Some desert animals are able to survive with little or no water – camels can go for many days without drinking. Desert plants store water in their fleshy stems and leaves. Cacti swell after rain and gradually get thinner as they use the water.

Quick-fire Quiz

1. Which is the largest desert?
a) Arabian
b) Gobi
c) Sahara

2. What is a sandy mound in a desert called?
a) A castle
b) A dune
c) An oasis

3. Which people wander from place to place seeking food?
a) Nomads
b) Normans
c) Nocturnals

4. What are many desert animals?
a) Nocturnal
b) Amphibious
c) Heavy sleepers

Grasslands

Lying just beyond the edges of deserts and in the dry interiors of continents are grasslands. In these regions, rain falls during only one season of the year. The land is too dry for many trees to grow, but drought-resistant grasses flourish.

Why are grasslands good for grazing?

Large areas of the grasslands of North America, South America, Australia and New Zealand are used to graze sheep or cattle (left). As grass leaves grow from the base of a plant, they can survive and grow even if the tops of the plant are eaten by cattle or sheep. This makes grassland areas ideal for ranches, which rear livestock. Grasslands are also used to grow food crops such as wheat and corn.

Where are grasslands found?

There are more than 8,000 different species of grasses around the world. Grasslands are found all over the world in the dry central areas of continents, and on the edges of deserts (below). The grassland of Europe and Asia is called 'steppe'. In South America, it is called 'pampas', and in North America, it is 'prairie'. The grasslands of Africa, India and Australia are called 'savannah'.

When were the prairies a 'Dust Bowl'?

The grassland climate is very dry, and long droughts are common. In the 1930s, there was a severe drought in the prairies of central North America. Overgrazing and poor farming reduced the ground to dust, and strong winds brought dust storms to the region. The area became known as the 'Dust Bowl'.

Grasslands of the world

Prairie
Steppe
Savannah
Pampas
Savannah

Which animals live in grasslands?

The animal species that live in grasslands vary from continent to continent. The prairies of North America (left) used to be home to buffalo, and are still the habitat of falcons, coyotes and prairie dogs. The Australian savannah is home to kangaroos, koalas, emus and kookaburras. The savannah of Africa (below) shelters a rich array of wildlife – from elephants and giraffes to lions and antelopes.

Quick-fire Quiz

1. What is Asia's grassland called?
a) Steppe
b) Pampas
c) Savannah

2. How many species of grasses are there?
a) More than 2,000
b) More than 5,000
c) More than 8,000

3. Where was the 'Dust Bowl'?
a) European steppes
b) African savannah
c) North American prairies

4. Where do kookaburras live?
a) South American pampas
b) African savannah
c) Australian savannah

What is 'slash-and-burn'?

Because grassland is useful for growing crops and grazing livestock, humans have looked for ways to extend it. By setting fire to vegetation during the dry season, woody plants are destroyed and this encourages new growth. The process is called 'slash-and-burn'.

71

Forests

Forests are huge areas of land covered with trees. There are many types of forest – coniferous, deciduous and the spectacular tropical rainforests. A huge variety of wildlife and vegetation can be found deep within forests.

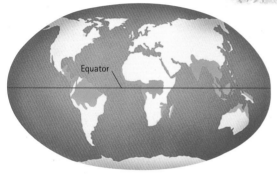

Equator

Rainforests of the world

What is the rainforest's 'canopy'?

There are several different levels in a rainforest. The forest floor is home to shrubs, climbing plants, moss and fungi. It is very dark, and the floor is covered in decaying leaves and plants. The 'canopy' (above) is the top of thousands of mature trees. It forms a kind of roof over the rainforest. Many forest animals such as brightly coloured birds and monkeys live in it. Above the canopy, a few taller trees break through, providing homes for big birds of prey.

How often does it rain in a rainforest?

Rainforests, or jungles, grow near the equator (above) where temperatures are high and the air is moist – it rains nearly every day. The conditions are ideal for wildlife. In fact, about half the world's plant and animal species are found in rainforests.

How do rainforests help us breathe?

Rainforests play a vital role in Earth's oxygen cycle. The mass of vegetation in the vast rainforests takes in enormous amounts of carbon dioxide. The carbon dioxide is converted by the plants into oxygen, which is returned to Earth's atmosphere. This is one of the reasons why environmentalists are determined to halt the destruction of rainforests.

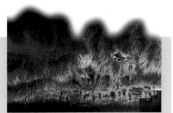

How do forest fires start?

Forest fires may be started by lightning, arson or even from the Sun's rays magnified through an empty glass bottle. Fires often spread very quickly in forests – at speeds of up to two kilometres a minute. Firefighters battle against the huge fires, often helped by aeroplanes that dump huge loads of water onto the flames. Fires can rage for months, and the damage they cause is enormous – homes are destroyed, and air for thousands of kilometres around is polluted.

How do humans use forests?

Forests are rich resources for humans. They provide timber, food and medicines. Timber, which can be burnt for heating and cooking, is used for building and for making products such as paper. The sap from rubber trees can be made into rubber tyres and gloves. Rainforests provide foods such as coffee, cocoa, nutmeg and pepper. Many rainforest plants are used to develop medicines – quinine, used to treat malaria, comes from cinchona trees. The rainforests are now under threat of destruction as more and more trees are cut down.

What's the difference between a deciduous and a coniferous forest?

Deciduous trees, such as the oak (left), shed their leaves in winter. An oak tree can house more than 300 animal species. Coniferous trees, such as the fir tree (left), have hard narrow leaves, or 'needles', that they keep all year round. For this reason, conifers are known as 'evergreens'. The biggest forest in the world is coniferous. It stretches across the top of Asia and Europe. Coniferous forests thrive in cold areas with long winters, whereas deciduous forests grow in more temperate regions.

Fir tree (coniferous)   Oak tree (deciduous)

Quick-fire Quiz

1. What proportion of the world's plants and animals is found in rainforests?
a) One fifth
b) One third
c) One half

2. Which type of forest grows in temperate regions?
a) Deciduous
b) Coniferous
c) Rainforest

3. Which tree does quinine come from?
a) Cinchona
b) Rubber
c) Palm

4. Which type of forest is the largest?
a) Deciduous
b) Coniferous
c) Rainforest

What do woodland animals eat?

Deciduous and coniferous forests are found in North America, Europe and northern Asia. Most animals that live in these woodlands eat leaves and seeds, but some birds eat insects, and some animals eat meat – the wild boar eats mice as well as fungi and acorns. The grey squirrel leaps among the trees in search of fruit and birds' eggs, while deer nibble leaves, shaping the lower branches of trees. Foxes emerge at night to hunt small mammals such as rabbits and mice.

Life on Earth

Earth is the only planet in the Universe that is known to support life. Millions of species of plants and animals currently live in the oceans and on the land, but 95 per cent of all species that have ever existed are now extinct.

Simple organisms
3,000 million years ago
(mya)

When did life on Earth begin?

Life on Earth began about 3,000 million years ago when chemicals dissolved in the oceans and simple bacteria grew. Then marine plants developed, producing oxygen that enabled marine animals to form. Over time, life developed on land.

What is evolution?

Seed-feeding   Berry-feeding

Insect-feeding   Cactus-feeding

Evolution is the way in which the characteristics of living things change over time. According to Darwin's theory of natural selection, only 'successful' animals will survive over time – animals with useless characteristics will either become extinct or will adapt. Darwin noted that evolution had adapted the beaks of finches on the Galapagos Islands (left) to suit different foods.

Charles Darwin

When did humans first appear?

Modern humans (*homo sapiens sapiens*) probably originated in Africa about 120,000 years ago. When European Neanderthal man became extinct about 35,000 years ago, *homo sapiens sapiens* became dominant.

Modern mammals
10,000 years ago (ya)

Dinosaurs
220–75 mya

Early mammals
70 mya

Homo sapiens
sapiens
120,000 ya

Neanderthal man
100,000–35,000 ya

Homo erectus
1.5–0.5 mya

Homo habilis
2–1.5 mya

Australopithecus
4–1 mya

Dryopithecus
15 mya

How do plants differ from animals?

Plants, unlike animals, are able to produce their own food. They do this by 'photosynthesis' – a process that enables them to convert water into energy with the aid of sunlight and natural solar cells, or chloroplasts (right).

Sunlight

Chloroplasts
in leaf cells

Which is the most common type of animal?

Explorers and scientists have discovered more than one million animal species, and 97 per cent of these are invertebrates. Invertebrates are animals without backbones, and they include insects, spiders, jellyfish, worms and molluscs. Vertebrate species – animals with backbones – include reptiles, birds, fish, amphibians and mammals.

Marine life
600–375 mya

Amphibians
375–275 mya

Reptiles
275 mya

Quick-fire Quiz

1. When did life on Earth begin?
a) 300 million years ago
b) 3,000 million years ago
c) 30,000 million years ago

2. How many animal species have been found?
a) 1 million
b) 5 million
c) 10 million

3. What percentage of animal species are invertebrates?
a) 50%
b) 79%
c) 97%

4. Where do ostriches live?
a) Africa
b) Australia
c) South America

Do animals always stay in the same habitat?

Many animals migrate to warmer climates to avoid the cold weather and food shortages of winter. The longest migration is of the Arctic tern, which travels 40,000 kilometres from the Arctic to Antarctica each year (above). Some migrations are related to reproduction – loggerhead turtles swim up to 2,000 kilometres to their birthplace, where they lay more eggs. Many animals do not migrate, and some are found naturally in only one particular part of the world – kangaroos are found only in Australia, ostriches live only in Africa and giant anteaters are found only in South America.

What is a 'food chain'?

Living things need energy. Plants, which convert light energy into food, are eaten by insects or herbivores, which are then eaten by other animals. When living things die, they rot and release nutrients into the ground. In this way, energy is passed along a 'food chain'. Animals and plants can belong to many different chains. The 'food web' is the interconnection of different chains.

1 Water plants produce energy from the Sun, soil and water.

2 Freshwater shrimps and snails eat the plants.

3 Trout feed on the shrimps and snails.

4 An otter preys on the trout.

5 The otter dies and its body decomposes.

6 Bacteria, flies and maggots feed on the otter, which returns nutrients to the soil.

Human Landscape

Humans have dramatically changed the face of Earth. Farming, industrialization and the growth of towns and cities have all had a huge impact on the way we live and on the environment.

What is a city?

A city is a large, important town. It has a big population and is usually a centre of commerce and industry. Most cities have grown over many centuries from small towns or villages. Today, nearly half of the world's population live in cities, which are often overcrowded. To create more working and living space, many cities have tall buildings called skyscrapers (right).

How many people are there in the world?

The world's population is over 6 billion. It has grown very quickly – in 1800 it was only about one billion. At the moment, on average three people are born every second, but it is still difficult for experts to predict how much the population will grow in the future. Depending on future birth rates, the population in 2100 (right) could be 7.5 billion, 11 billion or more than 13 billion. Poorer countries often have faster birth rates than richer ones. This can cause long-term problems for the poorer countries because they have limited food supplies and resources.

Population in billions

The world's population is over 6 billion

13
12
11
10
9
8
7
6
5
4
3
2
1

1600 1700 1800 1900 2000 2100

Which city has the largest population?

It is not easy to measure city populations. Statistics vary according to how and when populations are counted. Official population counts, or censuses, are carried out every few years and provide the most accurate estimates. Tokyo in Japan probably has the largest population (estimated at about 35 million), and Mexico City has the second largest (22 million). Bombay, India, and São Paulo, Brazil, follow with populations of about 20 million.

What is a developing country?

A developing country is a nation that has not experienced the development of new technologies and growth in wealth that many richer countries have. Developing countries are usually located in the southern hemisphere, where extreme climates and lack of resources make progress difficult. Many developing countries have high levels of debt after borrowing money from developed countries and world banking organizations. A nation's wealth is judged by examining its Gross National Product (GNP) – income generated per year. Japan, which is a developed country, has a higher GNP than India (right), a developing country.

India

How have changes in farming methods 'industrialized' countries?

The increased use of machinery and improvements in farming methods have resulted in farming being less 'labour intensive'. This means that only a few farm workers are needed to work the land. In the past, most people worked on farms, producing food for hundreds of people, but now many have left the countryside to take up jobs in the towns and cities. This enables countries to 'industrialize' by developing their industries, factories and economy. Many people in poorer countries still work in agriculture.

What is an 'ageing' population?

A country with an 'ageing population' has a low birth rate due to people choosing not to have large families, as well as high life expectancies because of good medical care. The average age of the population will be high. Ageing populations are usually found in developed countries. Developing countries, where people have more children and shorter life expectancies, have young populations. In Africa, nearly 50 per cent of the population is under the age of 15.

Quick-fire Quiz

1. What is today's estimated world population?
   a) 1.3 billion
   b) 3 billion
   c) 5.8 billion

2. How many people are born every second?
   a) One
   b) Three
   c) Ten

3. What does 'GNP' stand for?
   a) General National Population
   b) Great National Possibilities
   c) Gross National Product

4. Which countries have ageing populations?
   a) Developed countries
   b) Developing countries
   c) African countries

Earth's Resources

Earth is rich in natural resources that we can use to make energy, goods and materials. Many of these natural resources are extracted from deep within the ground, or from under the sea.

What is a renewable resource?

A renewable resource is a resource we can use without permanently reducing the amount available to us. Sun, wind and water are all renewable resources and there are many ways that we can produce energy from them (below). Coal, oil, gas and wood are non-renewable resources and one day they will run out. Scientists believe that gas and oil supplies could run out in a few decades.

Wind turbines drive generators

Mirrors direct sunlight to a liquid in a solar tower. The liquid is heated and creates steam to drive generators

Salt-water ponds trap Sun's heat

Solar panels provide energy for homes

What are 'fossil fuels'?

Coal, oil and natural gas are all 'fossil fuels'. They are called this because they are made from the remains of fossilized plants and tiny animals. Oil is made from the remains of tiny sea creatures that lived millions of years ago. Oil rigs (above) are used to extract oil from deep beneath the sea bed. An oil rig is a platform with powerful drills that cut down into the rock. Once the oil has been reached, it is pumped up and sent down pipelines to land, where it is made into petrol and other products.

How can we get energy from water?

Water is a very valuable source of energy. It can be used to produce electric and mechanical power. Hydroelectric plants use water from rivers, waterfalls and dams to spin enormous wheels called turbines, which generate an electric current. Ocean waves are also a good source of power (right). Waves rock floats that absorb the energy and use it to drive pumps. The pumps force a liquid to spin the turbines and generate electricity.

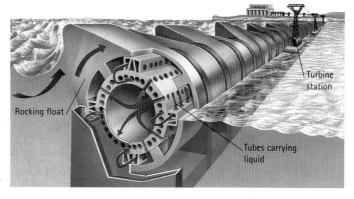

Turbine station

Rocking float

Tubes carrying liquid

What is nuclear energy?

Nuclear energy is created when tiny particles – neutrons – are fired at uranium atoms, causing the atoms to split (below). This process is called nuclear 'fission'. It releases more neutrons and heat, which is used to generate an electric current. 'Fusion' is a different nuclear reaction that constantly occurs on the Sun's surface.

Sun's surface

Neutrons released

Heat energy produced

Neutron fired at uranium atom

Atom splits

Uranium atom

Quarry

Surface ores removed with power shovels

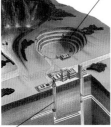

Shafts and tunnels access ores deep below surface

How are metals extracted from the ground?

Metal deposits near the ground's surface are the easiest to extract. Miners scoop them out, using explosives to break up any layers of rock in the way. If the metal ores are deep underground, miners have to tunnel through solid rock and cut them out. Stones used for building, such as marble and slate, are cut or blasted from the ground in a process called quarrying.

Is it possible to create new land?

Yes! Since medieval times, land has been reclaimed from the sea. In the 1920s, a large part of the Netherlands (right) was reclaimed by enclosing it with a massive dam. Today, roughly one quarter of the land area of the Netherlands is reclaimed land. Italy, Japan and England also have areas of reclaimed land.

Land reclaimed
- before 1900
- after 1900

Netherlands

Do all countries have the resources they need?

Raw materials and energy sources are not evenly spread throughout the world. Russia, the USA and Brazil are all rich in minerals, but some countries must import raw materials. Heavy materials are transported by sea – oil is shipped in huge tankers (right).

Caring for Earth

Humans have done a great deal of damage to Earth. Forests have disappeared, natural vegetation has been cleared to make way for farmland, towns and cities, and industrialization has polluted the seas, rivers and atmosphere. Governments and environmentalists have looked for ways to reduce the damage humans have caused.

What is 'recycling'?

Many of Earth's natural raw materials have been used up by humans. Instead of being thrown away, some materials can be 'recycled' (made into something new). For example, old glass bottles and jars can be crushed and melted to make new glass objects. Aluminium cans, plastic bags and bottles, newspapers, cardboard boxes and old clothes can also be recycled.

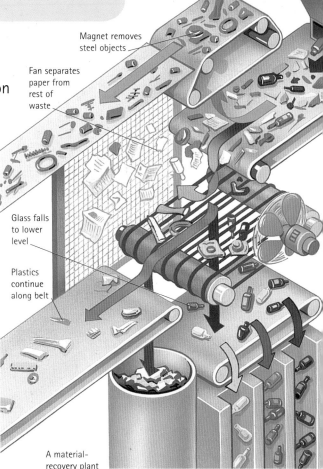

Mixed waste

Magnet removes steel objects

Fan separates paper from rest of waste

Glass falls to lower level

Plastics continue along belt

A material-recovery plant

Why is there a hole in the sky?

About 25 kilometres up in the atmosphere is a thin layer of ozone that protects Earth from the Sun's ultraviolet rays. An excess of the chemical CFC (chlorofluorocarbon) has destroyed part of the layer, creating a hole over Antarctica. CFCs were used in fridges, aerosol cans and fast-food packaging, but they are now banned.

What are animal reservations?

Destruction of natural environments and hunting have led to many animal species becoming endangered or even extinct. Animal reservations provide a protected, natural wilderness for endangered species to live in without being at risk from game hunters.

How is industrial land reclaimed?

1 Factories spew smoke and chemicals into the atmosphere, polluting land and rivers. Rubbish tips and mines destroy natural vegetation.

2 Rubbish tips and old industrial sites can be cleared and covered with a thick soil layer and turned into recreational land. Open-cast pits can be flooded to make new lakes.

Quick-fire Quiz

1. Which is the term for making old materials into something new?
   a) Rewinding
   b) Rebuilding
   c) Recycling

2. How high up is the ozone layer?
   a) 25km
   b) 250km
   c) 2,500km

3. What produces acid rain?
   a) Carbon dioxide and oxygen
   b) Ozone and carbon monoxide
   c) Sulphur dioxide and nitrogen dioxide

4. What does 'CFC' stand for?
   a) Cancer-forming chemical
   b) Chlorofluorocarbon
   c) Carbon fuel chemical

Acid rain

Waste gases produced by industry

What is 'acid rain'?

Burning fossil fuels release sulphur dioxide and nitrogen dioxide into the air where they mix with water to form a weak acid. This eventually falls as 'acid rain' (above). Acid rain can fall far away from where the pollution occurred. It kills many trees and acidifies rivers and lakes, harming wildlife. Reducing our use of fossil fuels will help reduce the problem of acid rain.

How can we combat deforestation?

To protect rainforests from deforestation – being destroyed – tropical timber is grown in plantations. Special fast-growing trees that can grow several metres each year are cultivated.

Web Addresses

www.enchantedlearning.com/subjects/rainforests

This is a charming site for teachers and pupils alike where you will find information, games and teaching materials on, among other topics, rainforests, geography, oceans and biomes.

www.funbrain.com/where/index.html

This is a great geography game, available at different levels and also available as a two-player version, which will get you up to speed with world geography. Choose your map and pick your level then find out where things are in the world.

kids.earth.nasa.gov

This is NASA's planet Earth site for kids and is full of interesting information and activities.

www.kidsplanet.org

A fun, imaginative site for kids on all aspects of planet Earth from the web of life, explained by a garden spider, to fact sheets, games and ecological and environmental issues.

www.eduweb.com/amazon.html
www.eduweb.com/adventure.html

Explore the geography of the Equadorian Amazon through online games and activities. Understand how eco-friendly projects work by playing interactive games such as Amazon Interactive, Tracking the Tiger Trade, Build-A-Prairie and The Watershed Game.

www.nationalgeographic.com/kids

This varied site offers lots of information on planet Earth, zoology and science, as well as games and activities.

mbgnet.mobot.org

Explore the different habitats of the world and learn about the people, animals and plants that live in each area.

www.howstuffworks.com/rainforest.htm

An educational site offering useful and interesting articles, with links, about rainforests, the animals that live there and what is happening to them in the world today.

www.animalsoftherainforest.com

An educational rainforest site with large images, covering a range of topics from wildlife to deforestation. There are lots of links to other sites.

www.rainforestheroes.com/kidscorner/action

A site that offers practical solutions on how to protect rainforests. Includes activities to do at home, which will help you to understand all about the rainforests.

www.thinkquest.org/library/index.html

The ThinkQuest Library is a collection of over 5,500 educational websites designed by participants in the ThinkQuest competitions. To see what they have produced on planet Earth, check out subjects such as Earth, volcano, rivers, mountains and ice age.

www.nwf.org/kids

This US National Wildlife site offers games, eco-tours, led by 'Ranger Rick', with lots of information given and questions asked, backed up by a glossary. The site also features lots of cool things to do to understand and help the planet.

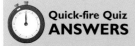

Quick-fire Quiz ANSWERS

Page 47 Earth's Formation
1. a 2. c 3. b 4. a

Page 49 Crust to Core
1. b 2. a 3. c 4. a

Page 51 Water
1. c 2. b 3. a 4. b

Page 53 Land
1. b 2. b 3. b 4. c

Page 55 Earthquakes
1. a 2. c 3. a 4. b

Page 57 Mountains
1. c 2. b 3. a 4. c

Page 59 Volcanoes
1. c 2. a 3. a 4. a

Page 61 Rocks, Fossils and Minerals
1. a 2. a 3. c 4. b

Page 63 Climate
1. c 2. b 3. b 4. c

Page 65 Weather
1. b 2. b 3. a 4. a

Page 67 Polar Regions
1. b 2. a 3. a 4. c

Page 69 Deserts
1. c 2. b 3. a 4. a

Page 71 Grasslands
1. a 2. c 3. c 4. c

Page 73 Forests
1. c 2. a 3. a 4. b

Page 75 Life on Earth
1. b 2. a 3. c 4. a

Page 77 Human Landscape
1. c 2. b 3. c 4. a

Page 79 Earth's Resources
1. a 2. a 3. b 4. b

Page 81 Caring for Earth
1. c 2. a 3. c 4. b

1000
QUESTIONS
& ANSWERS
FACTFILE
DINOSAURS

Contents

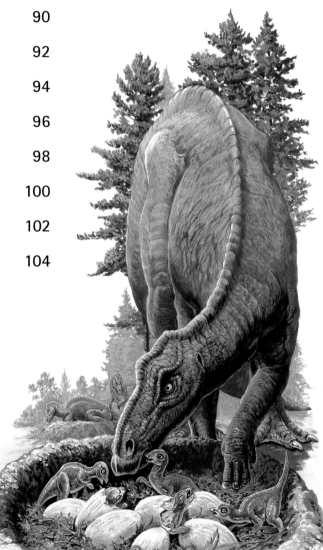

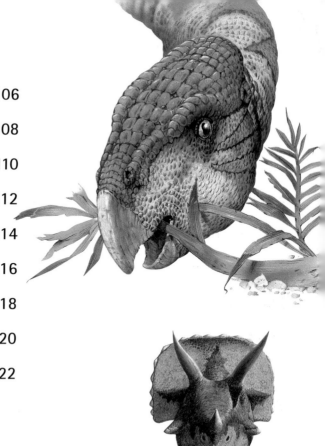

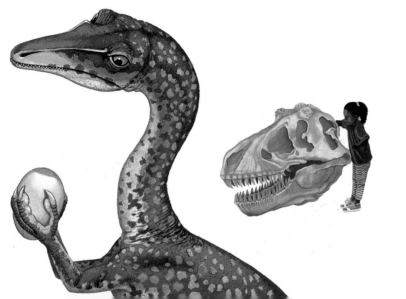

Digging up the Facts

Millions of years ago dinosaurs ruled the Earth, but they died out long before people existed. We only know about dinosaurs from their fossils – animal and plant remains that have been preserved in rocks, and which we can still see today.

How are fossils dug up?

When a dinosaur fossil is found, fossil experts, called palaeontologists, carefully clear away the overlying rocks. They photograph, measure and record the position of each bone. Then the bones are dug up, wrapped in layers of paper and plaster and left to dry. This plaster 'coat' protects the fossil on its journey to the museum, where the fossil is rebuilt. Sometimes a whole dinosaur skeleton is put together in this way.

How is a fossil formed?

When an animal or plant dies, it usually rots away. However, if it is buried quickly by mud or sand, parts of it may survive. Over millions of years it will turn into a fossil.

1 A dinosaur dies and its flesh is eaten or rots away.

2 Its skeleton is covered by layers of mud or sand.

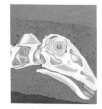

3 Slowly, mud turns to rock, and bones become fossils.

4 As the rock wears away, the fossil is revealed.

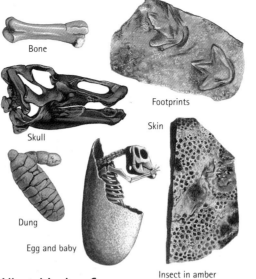

Bone

Footprints

Skin

Skull

Dung

Egg and baby

Insect in amber

What kinds of fossils are there?

Fossil bones and teeth are not the only dinosaur remains. Fossil imprints of their scaly skin, footprints and nests of eggs have all been found. Scientists can even tell what dinosaurs ate from their fossilized dung. Some fossils form in other ways. For example, an insect trapped in the sticky resin of a tree can be fossilized when the resin turns into hard amber.

Quick-fire Quiz

1. What are fossil experts called?
a) Fossiologists
b) Palaeontologists
c) Rock collectors

2. Where are most fossils found?
a) Soil
b) Wood
c) Rock

3. Who invented the word 'dinosaur'?
a) Mary Mantell
b) Edwin Cope
c) Richard Owen

4. What does *Megalosaurus* mean?
a) Fierce lizard
b) Big lizard
c) Toothed lizard

Georges Cuvier

Mary Mantell

Gideon Mantell

Richard Owen

Edwin Cope

Othniel Marsh

William Buckland

One name or two?

Dinosaur names are in Latin and have two parts – the genus name and the species name. They are written in italics and the genus name has a capital letter, e.g. *Tyrannosaurus rex*. Similar species of dinosaur are put in the same genus, which is the name usually used.

Who found the first dinosaur bones?

Dinosaur bones were first found hundreds of years ago, but people thought they were from giants or dragons. In 1822, Georges Cuvier suggested they belonged to giant reptiles. In 1824, William Buckland named the first dinosaur *Megalosaurus* (big lizard). A year later, fossil hunters Mary and Gideon Mantell named a second dinosaur, *Iguanodon*. Then, in 1842, Richard Owen called them 'dinosaurs', meaning 'terrible lizards'. In America over 130 new kinds of dinosaur were found by Edward Cope and Othniel Marsh.

Colour and Camouflage

No-one knows for sure what colour dinosaurs were. A few pieces of fossil dinosaur skin have been found, but the colour faded millions of years ago. Perhaps they had similar colours to reptiles today.

What use are colours?

Skin colour can help animals to hide, to attract a mate or to act as a warning. Many dinosaurs were probably camouflaged. Their skins may have been patterned to blend in with their surroundings. *Deinonychus* could have been sand-coloured, like lions today, to blend in with the sandy ground or dry, yellow plants. Or perhaps *Deinonychus* were striped like tigers so that they could hide among the vegetation until the pack was ready to attack.

Deinonychus

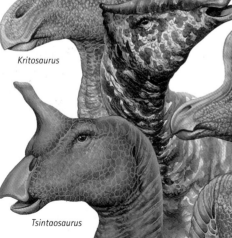

Saurolophus

Kritosaurus

Corythosaurus

Tsintaosaurus

Edmontosaurus

Could dinosaurs see in colour?

No-one knows for sure. We do know that some dinosaurs, called hadrosaurs, had crests, frills and inflatable air sacs on their heads. The hadrosaurs' heads and crests were probably brightly coloured so that they could be seen easily. Perhaps the dinosaurs also used their crests to send signals to each other. Several modern-day reptiles send signals in this way, so it is likely that some dinosaurs could see colours.

Were male and female dinosaurs different colours?

Mallard ducks

It is quite possible that they were. The male and female adults of many animals today, including some birds and lizards, are very differently coloured. The male may use his bright colours to attract a female or to warn off other males. Females may have dull, drab colours so they are less easy to spot when sitting on eggs or looking after babies. When artists first started drawing dinosaurs they tended to make them all brown or green, but now dinosaurs are often shown with very colourful markings.

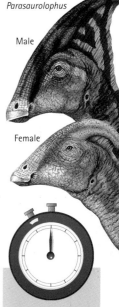

Parasaurolophus

Male

Female

Striped dinosaurs?

A zebra's stripes breaks up its outline, making it hard for a predator to pick one animal out from the herd. Dinosaurs which lived in herds may have had stripes for the same reason.

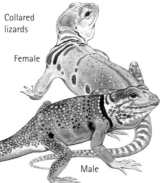

Collared lizards

Female

Male

Smooth or scaly?

Fossils and mummified skin show that many dinosaurs had skin covered with lumps and bumps for protection. Several colourful reptiles today have similar skins, so some experts think dinosaurs were also brightly coloured.

Quick-fire Quiz

1. Which of these had a large crest?
a) *Deinonychus*
b) *Corythosaurus*
c) *Kritosaurus*

2. Why was dinosaur skin bumpy?
a) For protection
b) For warmth
c) For camouflage

3. Why might dinosaurs have had stripes?
a) To show off
b) To confuse predators
c) To attract mates

4. What is camouflage?
a) Blending in with the surroundings
b) Changing colour
c) Having bright warning colours

Dinosaur Giants

Dinosaurs are the biggest land animals that have ever lived on Earth. The largest were the plant-eating sauropods. There were several kinds and they all had enormous bodies, long necks and small heads. Some were as tall as a four-storey building.

Which is the largest complete fossil dinosaur?

The biggest almost complete skeleton found so far is that of *Brachiosaurus*. This dinosaur was so tall it could raise its head 13 metres above the ground. One *Brachiosaurus* would have weighed as much as ten large elephants.

Which was the heaviest dinosaur?

Only a few bones of *Supersaurus* and *Ultrasaurus* have been found but they both outweigh *Brachiosaurus*. *Ultrasaurus* holds the record at almost 30 metres long, 12 metres high and up to 130 tonnes in weight. That is as heavy as 20 large elephants.

Brachiosaurus

Diplodocus

Apatosaurus

The huge sauropods were many times bigger than today's largest land animal, the elephant.

Which dinosaurs had the heaviest bones?

Sauropod dinosaurs had the biggest and heaviest bones. A thigh bone weighing 450 kilograms has been found. Early fossil-hunters struggled to get their finds home. Now helicopters are often used.

Some sauropod hip bones are bigger than an adult man.

Were dinosaurs brainy?

Dinosaurs may have been big, but they were not all very bright. Most of them, like this *Stegosaurus*, had a small brain. Weight for weight, *Brachiosaurus* had the smallest brain of almost any known dinosaur. Its brain weighed only one hundred thousandth of its body weight. You are much brainier: a human brain weighs a fortieth of an adult's body weight. But fossils show us that some dinosaurs had much bigger brains and were probably quite smart.

How big did dinosaurs grow?

It is hard to work out the size of the biggest dinosaurs because only a few bones have been found. Experts think that *Ultrasaurus* was the heaviest and that *Seismosaurus* was the longest (39–52 metres). That's longer than a blue whale – the biggest animal alive today.

Blue whale

Which was the biggest carnivore?

Tyrannosaurus rex was one of the biggest meat-eating dinosaurs. It grew up to 14 metres long and over 5 metres high. Its head alone was over a metre in length. It could have opened its mouth wide enough to swallow you whole!

Quick-fire Quiz

1. How long was *Tyrannosaurus'* head?
a) Over 10m
b) Over 2m
c) Over 1m

2. Which dinosaurs lived under water?
a) None of them
b) *Stegosaurus*
c) *Brachiosaurus*

3. Which is the most complete sauropod skeleton?
a) *Brachiosaurus*
b) *Tyrannosaurus*
c) *Ultrasaurus*

4. What is the biggest animal alive today?
a) Elephant
b) *Seismosaurus*
c) Blue whale

Which dinosaur had the biggest feet?

The front feet of sauropods such as *Brachiosaurus* were huge — up to a metre long. Some fossilized sauropod footprints are big enough to sit in. A sauropod's feet had to be big to support the dinosaur's great weight. Palaeontologists can work out an animal's size, weight and speed from its footprints.

No dinosaur could ever really have lived like this.

Did dinosaurs live under water?

No. People once thought that *Brachiosaurus* was too big to live on land. They thought it supported its weight by living in water and breathing through the nostrils on the top of its head. We now know this was not true. The pressure of the water would have crushed its ribs and stopped *Brachiosaurus* from breathing.

91

Small Dinosaurs

Not all dinosaurs were huge. Some were as small as modern-day lizards. Fewer fossils of small dinosaurs have been found because they were often eaten by other dinosaurs and their fragile bones were easily broken.

What did small dinosaurs eat?

1 Some small dinosaurs ate plants, while others fed on insects, worms or small reptiles. Tiny *Lesothosaurus* lived in herds and fed on plants. It relied on speed to outrun predators.

What is the smallest dinosaur skeleton?

A *Mussaurus* (mouse-lizard) skeleton found in Argentina in South America was tiny enough to fit into the palm of your hand. The skeleton was a baby dinosaur with a big head, eyes and feet. Small eggs, about 2.5 centimetres long, were found nearby. An adult *Mussaurus* would have been about 3 metres long.

Which were the smallest dinosaurs?

One of the earliest and smallest meat-eating dinosaurs was *Saltopus*. At just 60 centimetres long its body was the same size as that of a large chicken. *Saltopus* was a speedy hunter and could catch fast-moving lizards and flying insects. In 1984, a small plant-eating dinosaur, *Leaellynasaura*, was found in Australia. It was about the same size as *Saltopus*. However, some scientists think that the fossils were not fully grown and that adult *Leaellynasaura* may have been up to 2 metres long.

Leaellynasaura

Saltopus

2 *Compsognathus* was the size of a large pet cat. It moved quickly, using its speed to catch fast-moving prey like insects and lizards. One fossil *Compsognathus* skeleton has been found with the remains of its last meal, a lizard, inside it.

3 *Hypsilophodon* was a speedy little dinosaur that grew to about 2 metres long. It lived in forests and used its horny beak to nip off juicy shoots from plants.

4 Wolf-sized *Oviraptor* may have darted along at up to 50 kilometres an hour. It hunted lizards and small mammals and raided other dinosaurs' nests to snatch the eggs.

How big were dinosaur babies?

Newly hatched dinosaur babies were very small. You could have held this baby *Protoceratops* in your hand. One baby *Troodon* fossil has been found that is only 7 centimetres long — the size of a large hen's egg.

Did small dinosaurs defend themselves?

Scutellosaurus was only the size of a cat, but this little plant-eater was no easy meal for big dinosaurs. It was protected by rows of small bony knobs along its back and tail, and was the smallest armour-plated dinosaur.

Dinosaur Babies

Less than 100 years ago, scientists were not sure how dinosaur babies were born. In 1923, an expedition to the Gobi Desert in Mongolia found a nest of fossilized dinosaur eggs, laid over 100 million years earlier. This proved that dinosaurs laid eggs on land.

Who found the first eggs?

Roy Chapman Andrews discovered the first dinosaur eggs in 1923 in the Gobi Desert. He worked for the American Museum of Natural History and led many exciting dinosaur-hunting expeditions. He even used specially adapted cars to drive across the Gobi desert. Some people think he was the original 'Indiana Jones'.

How big were dinosaurs' eggs?

Dinosaur eggs were laid in clutches of ten to 40. Their size varied according to the size of the adult, but the eggs were small for such large animals. For example, a 30-metre long female probably laid eggs about 60 centimetres long. A really huge egg was not possible because it would need such a thick shell the baby could not break out of it.

Some dinosaur eggs had rough shells and others had smooth.

Did dinosaurs build nests?

1 Some dinosaurs, such as the *Maiasaura*, certainly built nests. *Maiasaura* lived in herds. Every year the females gathered at the same nesting site. We know this because a huge nesting area has been found in Montana, United States.

Did dinosaurs look after their babies?

Experts think that some kinds of baby dinosaurs, such as young *Maiasaura*, were not very well developed. The adults probably fed their newly hatched young on soft plant shoots until they were able to fend for themselves. The babies of other dinosaurs, such as *Orodromeus*, were well developed and could probably run soon after they hatched. So perhaps, like many reptiles today, these dinosaurs laid lots of eggs and left their hatchlings to look after themselves.

2 Female *Maiasaura* made a low mound of mud about 2 metres across. Each female dug out a nest and lined it with twigs and leaves.

Did dinosaurs egg sit?

In 1993, 70 years after Roy Chapman Andrews found the first dinosaur eggs, another expedition set out for the Gobi Desert. This time, the scientists discovered the fossilized remains of an *Oviraptor* sitting on a nest of eggs. The find proved that some kinds of dinosaurs sat on their eggs to hatch them, in the same way that birds do today.

Quick-fire Quiz

1. Where were the first eggs found?
a) Sahara Desert
b) Gobi Desert
c) Kalahari Desert

2. Which dinosaur stole eggs?
a) *Troodon*
b) *Triceratops*
c) *Maiasaura*

3. Who found the first eggs?
a) Indiana Jones
b) Richard Owen
c) Roy Chapman Andrews

4. What were *Maiasaura* nests made of?
a) Stones
b) Mud
c) Paper

Did dinosaurs defend their young?

Armoured dinosaurs like *Triceratops* may have defended their young by charging a would-be predator. Scientists think a herd of adult plant-eaters on the move defended their young by keeping them in the middle of the herd.

3 Each female laid about 20 to 25 eggs in the nest. She covered them with more plants to keep them warm.

4 The *Maiasaura* mother guarded her eggs carefully. Egg-thieves, such as *Troodon*, were always ready to snatch an easy meal.

5 The *Maiasaura* hatchlings broke out of their egg shells using a special sharp tooth on their snouts.

Communication

Animals cannot talk to each other, so they communicate in other ways. They use sounds, smells, touch and visual signals to tell each other what is going on. Dinosaurs may have used similar methods to send 'messages' to one another.

Why was making a noise useful?

Dinosaurs may have used sound to warn of danger or keep in touch with other members of a large herd. *Parasaurolophus* may have hooted a warning if danger threatened. The duck-billed dinosaur *Edmontosaurus* may have blown up a bag of skin over its nose and bellowed loudly at rival males. Young dinosaurs may have squeaked to get an adult's attention.

What sounds did dinosaurs make?

Dinosaurs had complex ears and could probably hear well, so they may have used many different sounds to send signals to each other. Like reptiles alive today, most dinosaurs could probably hiss or grunt and large ones may have roared. A few, like the hadrosaurs, probably made distinctive calls to each other through their horns, crests and inflatable nose flaps. Scientists believe this is possible because, when they blew through models of different hadrosaur skulls, they found that each skull gave a different sound.

Tsintaosaurus

Edmontosaurus

Corythosaurus

Male peacock displaying

Lambeosaurus

Did dinosaurs display like birds?

Experts think that some male dinosaurs displayed to the females during the mating season. Just as peacocks display their coloured feathers, male dinosaurs may have displayed bright head crests, spines or neck ruffs to attract females and warn off rival males.

Did dinosaurs use their noses?

Fossils of dinosaurs' brains suggest that many dinosaurs had a good sense of smell and most dinosaurs had well-developed nostrils. A strong sense of smell would have helped dinosaurs sniff out food. If, as some scientists think, dinosaurs gave off scent signals, they may also have used their sense of smell to find a mate. *Brachiosaurus* had huge nostrils on the top of its head. No-one knows why, but perhaps they allowed it to eat water plants and breathe at the same time.

Brachiosaurus

Parasaurolophus herd

Quick-fire Quiz

1. Which dinosaur group had head crests?
a) Hadrosaurs
b) Theropods
c) Lizards

2. Which dinosaur had an inflatable nose flap?
a) *Edmontosaurus*
b) *Brachiosaurus*
c) *Lambeosaurus*

3. Which dinosaur had a hollow crest?
a) *Tyrannosaurus*
b) *Brachiosaurus*
c) *Parasaurolophus*

4. Where were *Brachiosaurus'* nostrils?
a) On the end of its nose
b) It didn't have any
c) On top of its head

How did noisy noses work?

Hadrosaurs such as *Parasaurolophus* and *Lambeosaurus* had hollow crests. Air passages extended from the nose through the crest and down into the throat. The dinosaurs could hoot and honk as they breathed in and out. Different types of crest produced different notes.

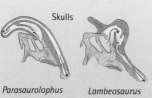
Skulls
Parasaurolophus   *Lambeosaurus*

Could dinosaurs taste their food?

Many dinosaurs had tongues and they could probably taste and smell their food, like most animals today. Reptiles such as snakes use their forked tongue to 'taste' the air for traces of prey. But there is no evidence to suggest that any dinosaurs had tongues that could do this.

Plant-Eaters

Most dinosaurs were herbivores. This means they ate plants not meat. Plant-eating dinosaurs came in all shapes and sizes from small two-legged dinosaurs to huge sauropods. Plants are hard to digest so, to get enough energy from their food, many spent most of the day eating.

Lizard or bird hips?

Experts divide dinosaurs into two groups by the shape of their hips. Sauropod plant-eaters

1

2

3

(1) had lizard hips. Their big stomachs unbalanced them so they had to walk on four legs. Two-legged theropod meat-eaters (2) also had lizard hips. Plant-eating bird-hipped dinosaurs (3) evolved later. Many walked on two legs with their big stomach slung between their back legs. Armoured bird-hipped plant-eaters were so heavy that they walked on four legs.

Psittacosaurus

Did dinosaurs eat leaves?

Leaves were the main diet of many plant-eaters. *Psittacosaurus* probably snipped leaves off with its bird-like beak, then sliced them into smaller bits with its scissor-like teeth. Like the giraffe, *Brachiosaurus* used its long neck to graze on leafy treetops.

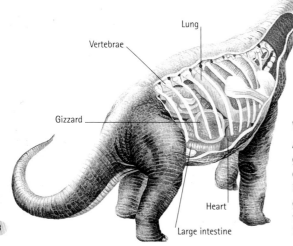

Lung

Vertebrae

Gizzard

Heart

Large intestine

Why were sauropods so big?

A sauropod's huge body was filled almost entirely with its guts. Sauropods like *Brachiosaurus* ate up to 200 kilograms of plants a day, so they needed a big stomach and long intestines to digest this tough food. Experts once had to guess what a dinosaur's insides looked like, but in 1998 two dinosaurs from China were found with their guts intact. These should tell us more about what dinosaurs ate.

Lufengosaurus

1 2 3 4 5

Did plant–eaters have teeth?

Most plant-eating dinosaurs had teeth, and experts can tell what food a dinosaur ate by looking at these. *Lufengosaurus*, an early sauropod, had many small peg-like teeth with jagged edges. These were great for nipping off soft leaves, but no use for chewing, so *Lufengosaurus* swallowed its food whole.

Why were teeth different shapes?

The size and shape of a dinosaur's teeth depended on what it ate. The ornithopod *Heterodontosaurus* had sharp, narrow front teeth (1) for cutting and slicing. *Plateosaurus* (2) and sauropods like *Diplodocus* (3) and *Apatosaurus* (4) had peg-like teeth to shred and crush food. *Stegosaurus* (5) had leaf-shaped teeth for slicing and munching soft plants.

Why did dinosaurs swallow stones?

Small stones have been found in the rib cages of many dinosaurs. Few dinosaurs could move their jaws from side to side, so they could not chew their food. They swallowed it whole and probably swallowed small stones (gastroliths) to help them grind food as it churned about in their stomachs. Chickens swallow grit to do the same thing.

Shunosaurus

Quick-fire Quiz

1. What are gastroliths?
a) Grinding teeth
b) Stomach stones
c) Plants

2. Which dinosaur had leaf-shaped teeth?
a) *Diplodocus*
b) *Apatosaurus*
c) *Stegosaurus*

3. Which dinosaur had a bird-like beak?
a) *Shunosaurus*
b) *Brachiosaurus*
c) *Psittacosaurus*

4. What did *Triceratops* eat?
a) Fruit and nuts
b) Ferns and horsetails
c) Grass

Did dinosaurs eat grass?

Grasses did not develop on Earth until 25 million years after the dinosaurs died out. Instead, herbivorous dinosaurs ate other plants that were around at the time. Long-necked sauropods such as *Shunosaurus* used their simple peg-like teeth to munch on leaves, pine needles and juicy shoots. A hadrosaur such as *Saurolophus* ate leaves from flowering plants and crunchy pine cones. It chopped off the leaves with its horny beak, then chewed them with its flat back teeth. Horned dinosaurs like *Triceratops* sliced up tough ferns and horsetails with their sharp beaks and teeth.

Leaves, pine needles and shoots

Pine cones and shrub leaves

Ferns and horsetails

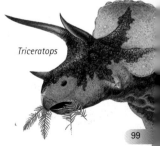
Saurolophus

Triceratops

Meat-Eaters

All meat-eating, or carnivorous, dinosaurs were theropods. (Theropod means 'beast foot'.) They walked on two legs and their three toes were armed with sharp claws. Some were fierce hunters, chasing and killing their prey. Others were scavengers, feeding on dead animals.

Did dinosaurs have sharp teeth?
The sharp, backward pointing teeth of *Megalosaurus* are typical of many large meat-eating dinosaurs. They were good for gripping and ripping their prey. Other carnivorous dinosaurs had small sharp teeth or crushing beaks.

Deinonychus   Owl

Did meat-eaters have sharp eyesight?
Many hunters such as *Deinonychus* had good eyesight. It may have had forward-facing eyes and good binocular (overlapping) vision like modern owls. This would have given it a single view of its prey and helped it judge distances.

Did all meat-eaters look the same?
Meat-eating dinosaurs came in all shapes and sizes. They ranged in size from chicken-sized *Saltopus* (60 centimetres) to huge *Tyrannosaurus* (12 metres long). Big theropods like *Tyrannosaurus*, *Allosaurus* and *Dilophosaurus* hunted large plant-eaters, while speedy *Troodon* killed small reptiles and mammals. *Struthiomimus*, *Avimimus* and *Oviraptor* used their strong beaks to catch and crush insects and eggs.

Tyrannosaurus

Troodon

Allosaurus

Avimimus

Oviraptor

Dilophosaurus

Struthiomimus

Did dinosaurs eat fish?

Experts believe that dinosaurs such as *Baryonyx* snapped up fish with their long crocodile-like jaws. *Baryonyx* may also have speared fish with the huge hook-like claw on its front feet, just as brown bears do today.

Which dinosaurs used claws to kill?

Deinonychus ('terrible claw') and its relatives specialized in using their claws to kill animals much larger than themselves. *Deinonychus* leapt at its victims, slashing them with the deadly 12 centimetres long claw on the second toe of its back foot.

Did dinosaurs hunt in packs?

Like today's wolves, some small meat-eating dinosaurs, such as *Deinonychus*, hunted in packs. This would have allowed them to hunt larger prey such as a young *Diplodocus*, separating it from the rest of its herd.

Wolf pack

Quick-fire Quiz

1. Which dinosaur was a cannibal?
a) *Diplodocus*
b) *Dilophosaurus*
c) *Coelophysis*

2. Which dinosaur ate fish?
a) *Oviraptor*
b) *Allosaurus*
c) *Baryonyx*

3. Which dinosaur name means 'terrible claw'?
a) *Troodon*
b) *Deinonychus*
c) *Tyrannosaurus*

4. What did scavengers eat?
a) Dead animals
b) Bark
c) Leaves

Were any dinosaurs cannibals?

Fossil remains of *Coelophysis* found in New Mexico, United States, had skeletons of young ones inside them. The bones were too big to belong to unborn *Coelophysis*. Experts believe that adult *Coelophysis* would eat young of their own kind if food was short. Other dinosaurs may have been cannibals, too.

Did dinosaurs eat eggs?

Small speedy meat-eaters such as *Troodon* would snatch unguarded eggs from other dinosaurs' nests. Eggs were a good source of food — a complete meal in a shell! *Troodon* could sprint at about 50 kilometres an hour, so few lumbering plant-eaters could catch it.

The Fiercest Dinosaur

Tyrannosaurus rex ('king tyrant lizard') lived about 70 million years ago. At more than 12 metres long and three times as tall as a man, it was one of the largest and deadliest creatures that has ever lived on land.

Has a whole *Tyrannosaurus* skeleton ever been found?

Complete fossil skeletons are very rare, but in 1990 two almost complete *Tyrannosaurus* skeletons were found in America. Experts studying these and other *Tyrannosaurus* skeletons believe that, unlike meat-eaters of today such as lions and tigers, the female *Tyrannosaurus* was probably bigger than the male.

Did *Tyrannosaurus* grasp prey with its front legs?

Tyrannosaurus' arms and hands were too small to grasp its prey. They couldn't even reach its mouth. Its head and teeth were so strong and deadly that it did not need its arms to catch its prey.

Tyrannosaurus skeleton

Dilophosaurus

Allosaurus

Albertosaurus

How big were *T rex* teeth?

Tyrannosaurus had teeth up to 18 centimetres long. These teeth had a razor-sharp point to stab prey, and rough, saw-like edges to rip through flesh. An adult had between 50 and 100 teeth and if one fell out, it simply grew another!

Were there other big meat–eaters?

These three meat-eaters were related to *Tyrannosaurus*, but were not as big. Two huge, 2.6-metre long fossil arms with clawed hands were found in Mongolia and named *Deinocheirus* ('terrible hand'). They may be from a version of *Deinonychu*s that was even bigger than *Tyrannosaurus*.

Quick-fire Quiz

1. How long ago did *Tyrannosaurus* live?
a) 200 million years
b) 70 million years
c) 150 million years

2. How long were its teeth?
a) Up to 5cm
b) Up to 30cm
c) Up to 18cm

3. Which dinosaur was related to *Tyrannosaurus*?
a) *Triceratops*
b) *Albertosaurus*
c) *Deinocheirus*

4. What does *Tyrannosaurus rex* mean?
a) Big bad lizard
b) King tyrant lizard
c) Emperor reptile

Was *Tyrannosaurus* fast or slow?

Experts used to think that *Tyrannosaurus* stood upright and lumbered along, dragging its tail on the ground. By studying the more complete skeletons, they now think it leaned forward, with its tail sticking out as a balance, and that it could run fast. Judging from its skull and the size of its brain, experts think it also had good eyesight and hearing and an excellent sense of smell.

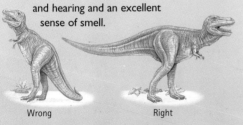

Wrong   Right

Was the fiercest dinosaur a scavenger?

Some experts think *Tyrannosaurus* was a scavenger that ate dead animals and stole prey from other predators. Others think it could run as fast as a racehorse (50 kilometres an hour) and was a fierce hunter. The latest finds show it probably did both.

Attack and Defence

Meat-eating dinosaurs were built to kill, attacking their victims with sharp teeth and slashing claws. Plant-eaters defended themselves in many different ways. Some lived in herds, some relied on speed to escape, while others developed armour and horns for fighting off enemies.

Did huge sauropods fight?

Like elephants today, the giant sauropods mostly relied on their size to protect them. Some, like *Diplodocus*, could lash their long, whip-like tails to frighten off attackers.

Which dinosaurs had armour?

Plant-eating ankylosaurs protected themselves with armour-like skin and bony spikes. *Ankylosaurus* was the size of a tank. If attacked, it crouched down to protect its soft belly and lashed out with the bony club on the end of its tail.

What use were plates and spikes?

Stegosaurus was well protected from its enemies with huge bony plates along its back and four long, sharp spikes on its thick tail. A blow from its tail could seriously injure, or even kill, an attacker.

Armour or radiators?

The plates along the back of *Stegosaurus* were covered with skin and had lots of blood vessels in them. Some experts think they may have helped the dinosaur warm its body when it basked in the sun, and to cool down by losing heat quickly in the shade. Other scientists think the plates were armour to protect it from carnosaurs (meat-eating dinosaurs such as *Tyrannosaurus*).

Did plant-eaters have claws?

Most didn't but the plant-eater *Iguanodon* had two sharp thumb spikes. Perhaps it used them to stab attackers. Or maybe the males used them to fight each other.

Which dinosaurs had horns?

Some plant-eating dinosaurs, called ceratopians, developed horns and bony frills to protect themselves. They may have charged at enemies like a rhinoceros, or maybe rival males fought by locking horns.

Quick-fire Quiz

1. Which dinosaur had plates and spikes?
   a) *Stegosaurus*
   b) *Diplodocus*
   c) *Tyrannosaurus*

2. Which dinosaur had a tail club?
   a) *Velociraptor*
   b) *Ankylosaurus*
   c) *Diplodocus*

3. How did *Iguanodon* protect itself?
   a) With armour
   b) With thumb spikes
   c) With its horns

4. Which dinosaur died fighting with a *Velociraptor*?
   a) *Diplodocus*
   b) *Stegosaurus*
   c) *Protoceratops*

Triceratops

Centrosaurus

Chasmosaurus

What evidence is there?

An amazing fossil was dug up in Mongolia in 1971. A *Protoceratops* had charged a fierce *Velociraptor* like a rhino, smashing into it with its bony beak. The *Velociraptor's* sharp claws had pierced the stomach and throat of the *Protoceratops*. Neither survived.

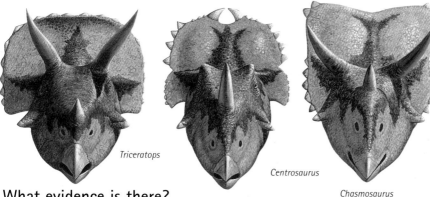

Which dinosaur used its head?

Pachycephalosaurus males had very thick tops to their skulls. Rival males may have had head-butting contests to win a mate, just as some wild sheep do today.

105

All Over the World

Maiasaura

Stegosaurus

This map shows where dinosaur fossils have been found. Experts have divided the dinosaur age into three main parts – the Triassic, Jurassic and Cretaceous Periods. Different dinosaurs lived in each of these periods, so some fossils are older than others.

Deinonychus

Diplodocus

What dinosaurs have been found in North America?

Hundreds of fossil dinosaurs, including *Diplodocus*, *Deinonychus* and *Stegosaurus*, have been found in North America. The famous *Tyrannosaurus* and *Triceratops* have been found only there, and nowhere else.

Cretaceous

Jurassic

Triassic

What was the fiercest dinosaur in South America?

One of the biggest South American meat-eaters found so far is *Piatnitzkysaurus*, which was about 6 metres long and 3 metres high. It chased and killed prey in the same way as its larger North American relative, *Allosaurus*.

Piatnitzkysaurus

Did some dinosaurs live all over the world?

Some dinosaurs, such as *Brachiosaurus*, have been found in North America, Africa and Europe. Other dinosaurs have only been found on one continent.

Iguanodon

Camptosaurus

Which was the first dinosaur to be named in Europe?

Megalosaurus ('great reptile'), a fierce meat-eater, was named in 1824. Since then hundreds of fossil dinosaurs have been found in Europe, including large plant-eaters such as *Camptosaurus* and *Iguanodon* which have also been unearthed in North America.

Megalosaurus

Which dinosaurs lived in Asia?

Hundreds of dinosaur remains have been found throughout Asia. The wolf-sized *Oviraptor*, was found in the remote Gobi Desert in Mongolia. *Shantungosaurus*, a duck-billed dinosaur about 12 metres tall, comes from China.

Oviraptor

Protoceratops

Shantungosaurus

Kentrosaurus

Tuatara

Have fossils been found in Australia?

Few dinosaur fossils have been found in Australia, but thousands of fossil dinosaur footprints were uncovered in Queensland. The most complete dinosaur find is an iguanodon, *Muttaburrasaurus*. A few dinosaur fossils have also been found in New Zealand. The tuatara, a reptile that still lives there today, looks almost exactly the same as its ancestors that lived in the dinosaur age.

Elaphrosaurus

Which is the biggest fossil site in Africa?

One of the biggest fossil sites in Africa is Tendaguru in Tanzania. Over 200 tonnes of dinosaur bones were found there between 1909 and 1912. Many dinosaurs were dug up, including the stegosaur *Kentrosaurus* and the small bird-like *Elaphrosaurus*.

Quick-fire Quiz

1. What is Tendaguru?
a) A city
b) A fossil site
c) A type of dinosaur

2. Which was the first dinosaur to be named in Europe?
a) *Velociraptor*
b) *Megalosaurus*
c) *Iguanodon*

3. How tall is *Shantungosaurus*?
a) About 50m
b) About 12m
c) About 5m

4. Where does the tuatara live?
a) North America
b) Australia
c) New Zealand

Living in Herds

Clues, such as footprints and the mass dinosaur graves, show that some dinosaurs lived in groups. Plant-eating dinosaurs probably herded together for safety, like antelopes do today. Some meat-eaters may have hunted in packs.

Which dinosaurs probably lived alone?

Large meat-eating dinosaurs such as *Albertosaurus* were excellent hunters and had few enemies. They could have lived and hunted alone, just as tigers do today. However, the bones of 40 young and adult *Allosaurus* were discovered in a mass grave in the United States, so perhaps they hunted in packs like lions.

Why did dinosaurs live together?

Many plant-eaters like these *Edmontosaurus* hadrosaurs lived in herds for protection. Lots of pairs of eyes keeping watch for a predator are better than one pair. It is also more difficult for a predator to attack a large moving herd. These hadrosaurs probably hooted and honked to signal to each other if there was danger, such as a carnosaur, nearby.

Did herd members look after each other?

Fossil footprints show some dinosaur herds travelled with their young in the middle and the adults on the outside. If attacked, horned dinosaurs like *Triceratops* may have formed a circle round their young, with their horns pointing out towards the enemy, as musk oxen do today.

How do we know about dinosaur herds?

Vast tracks of fossilized dinosaur footprints all going the same way were discovered in North America. Experts believe they belonged to herds of dinosaurs. Huge numbers of dinosaurs have also been found buried together. One of these burial sites contained 10,000 duck-billed *Maiasaura*. This evidence shows sauropods probably lived in groups.

Why did some herds die together?

In 1947, the fossil remains of a large herd of *Coelophysis* were found at Ghost Ranch in New Mexico in the United States. The bones came from young and old animals. Some experts think they probably all died together in a flash flood. Their bodies were carried along by the water and eventually dumped in a heap on a sandbank where they fossilized.

Quick-fire Quiz

1. Where were a fossilized herd of *Coelophysis* found?
a) Ghost Ranch
b) Ghost Valley
c) Mexico Ranch

2. Which meat-eating dinosaur was found in a mass grave?
a) *Tyrannosaurus*
b) *Allosaurus*
c) *Diplodocus*

3. Why did *Edmontosaurus* herd together?
a) For company
b) For protection
c) To hunt

4. How many *Maiasaura* were found in a mass grave?
a) 40
b) 1,000
c) 10,000

Did dinosaurs travel far?

Like many animals today, such as caribou and wildebeest, some dinosaurs, such as these iguanodons, probably travelled huge distances in search of food.

Did herds migrate?

Fossil dinosaurs have been found in the Arctic and Antarctic. There would have been plenty of food in the summer but little in winter. Experts think that dinosaur herds migrated away from the Poles in the winter, as modern-day caribou do.

Did dinosaur herds have look outs?

No-one knows for sure, but in large herds of animals some adults keep watch for predators. Dinosaurs probably did the same.

Which dinosaurs hunted in packs?

Carnivores like wolves and hyenas hunt in packs. Many small meat-eating dinosaurs, such as *Elaphrosaurus*, probably hunted in packs too. This would have allowed them to hunt and kill larger prey than if they hunted alone.

Fast and Slow

A dinosaur's shape, size and the speed at which it moved was determined by how it lived. Hunters had to be fast to catch their prey. They ran on strong back legs, using their tails to balance. Huge plant-eaters could only move slowly. They did not need to chase food and their huge size kept them safe.

Iguanodon

Megalosaurus

How can we measure a dinosaur's speed?

Experts work out the speed a dinosaur moved from the space between its footprints and the length of its legs. The wider apart a dinosaur's tracks are, the faster it was moving. If the footprints are close together, it was probably walking slowly.

Which was the fastest dinosaur?

Ostrich-sized *Struthiomimus* was one of the fastest. It had no armour or horns to protect it and had to rely on speed to escape. It was as fast as a racehorse, reaching speeds of over 50 kilometres an hour.

What can footprints tell us?

Fossilized footprints can show how dinosaurs moved. *Iguanodon* walked on all fours, but could run on its back legs. The huge three-toed prints of *Megalosaurus* show that it was a meat-eater and always moved on its back legs.

How fast did dinosaurs move?

1 Just like animals today, dinosaurs moved at different speeds at different times. *Tyrannosaurus* walked at 16 kilometres an hour but ran much faster when attacking.

2 *Hypsilophodon* was one of the speediest dinosaurs. This plant-eater could race along the ground at up to 50 kilometres an hour to escape from enemies.

3 *Apatosaurus* weighed 40 tonnes – as much as seven elephants. It walked at 10 to 16 kilometres an hour. If it had tried to run, the impact would have broken its legs.

4 *Triceratops* weighed as much as five rhinos and could also charge like a rhino at speeds of over 25 kilometres an hour. Few predators would risk attacking it.

Quick-fire Quiz

1. How fast could *Triceratops* charge?
a) Over 50km/hr
b) Over 25km/hr
c) Over 5km/hr

2. Which dinosaur could reach over 50km an hour?
a) *Apatosaurus*
b) *Struthiomimus*
c) *Brachiosaurus*

3. Which of these show how fast dinosaurs moved?
a) Their heads
b) Their footprints
c) Their tails

4. Which legs did *Megalosaurus* use?
a) Its front legs
b) All four legs
c) Its back legs

Which was the slowest dinosaur?

The huge sauropods like *Brachiosaurus* were the slowest moving dinosaurs. At over 50 tonnes, they were too heavy to run and so plodded along at about 10 kilometres an hour. Unlike smaller dinosaurs, these huge creatures were probably too big ever to have reared up on their hind legs.

Warm or cold blood?

Mammals and birds are warm-blooded – they make their own body heat. Reptiles are cold-blooded and have to warm up in the sun. To give them the energy to heat their bodies, warm-blooded animals need about ten times more food than a cold-blooded animal of the same size. Studying how much dinosaurs ate may show if any were warm-blooded.

111

In the Sea

While dinosaurs ruled the land, other giant reptiles took over the seas. Mosasaurs, plesiosaurs and pliosaurs were fierce predators, snapping up fish and other sea creatures. Giant turtles and crocodiles also hunted in prehistoric oceans.

Are all prehistoric sea reptiles extinct?

Most kinds of large sea reptiles died out with the dinosaurs, but turtles and crocodiles still exist. Prehistoric *Deinosuchus*, a 16-metre long crocodile, was, however, much bigger than any crocodile living today.

Deinosuchus

Kronosaurus

What did sea reptiles eat?

Sea reptiles ate fish, shellfish and even each other! A *placodont* picked up shellfish with its long front teeth. It crushed them with its back teeth, spat out the shells and swallowed the rest.

Mosasaurus

Teleosaurus

Ammonite (swimming shellfish)

Placodont

Why is Mary Anning famous?

Mary Anning was born in 1799 in Dorset, England. She grew up to be a great fossil hunter and was so good that she earned her living by selling fossils. She found the first complete fossil skeleton of a giant marine ichthyosaur when she was only 12 years old. Another of her amazing finds was the first complete skeleton of a plesiosaur.

Elasmosaurus

Tanystropheus

Did sea reptiles have teeth?

Most sea reptiles had large jaws full of sharp teeth to spear slippery fish or break open tough shells.

Ichthyosaurus

Did any sea creatures come on to the land?

Long-necked *Tanystropheus* hunted on both land and in the sea. It snapped up flying insects as well as slippery fish. Most sea reptiles had to come on land to lay their eggs.

How did prehistoric sea reptiles swim?

Pliosaurs like Kronosaurus and plesiosaurs like Elasmosaurus had four strong paddles instead of feet. They moved them up and down to 'fly' through the sea in the same way penguins do today. Mosasaurus, Ichthyosaurus and crocodiles such as Teleosaurus swam by beating their tails from side to side. Sea reptiles could not breathe under water, so they had to come to the surface to gulp in air.

Kronosaurus skeleton

How big were the sea reptiles?

One of the biggest sea reptiles was the pliosaur *Kronosaurus*. It was nearly 17 metres long with a huge head the size of a car. *Mosasaurus* was 10 metres long, the largest lizard ever. Prehistoric turtles were much bigger than their modern relatives. The largest, *Archelon*, was almost 4 metres long. Its huge front paddles powered it through the water at up to 15 kilometres an hour.

Archelon

Did sea reptiles lay eggs?

Most sea reptiles laid their eggs on land, like turtles today. But *Ichthyosaurus* gave birth to live young in the same way as sea mammals like this dolphin do today.

113

In the Air

When dinosaurs took over the land, other reptiles took to the air. The first reptiles to become masters of flight were the pterosaurs. They ruled the skies for 166 million years but died out at the end of the dinosaur age.

How big were pterosaurs?

Pterosaurs came in many sizes. *Quetzalcoatlus* was the biggest. It had a human-sized body and a wingspan of over 12 metres — bigger than a hang glider! *Rhamphorhynchus* was the size of a crow with a wingspan of 40 centimetres.

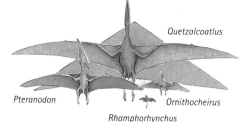

Quetzalcoatlus

Pteranodon

Ornithocheirus

Rhamphorhynchus

What did pterosaurs eat?

Pterosaurs' jaws and teeth help show what they ate. Most fed on fish, while some snapped up insects. *Pterodaustro* may have filtered tiny animals from the water with its sieve-like bottom jaw. *Dzungaripterus'* pincer-like beak could prise shellfish from rocks. *Dimorphodon*'s strong jaws were ideal for catching fish.

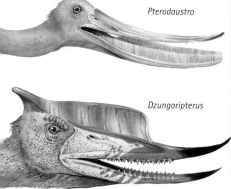

Pterodaustro

Dzungaripterus

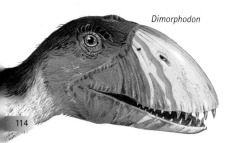

Dimorphodon

Pteranodon

Did pterosaurs build nests?

No-one knows, but scientists think pterosaurs probably laid eggs. They may have laid these in nests, and sat on them to keep them warm. Fossils show that baby pterosaurs were not well developed, so perhaps the adults fed them, as baby birds are fed today.

Furry and active?

Fossil evidence shows that some pterosaurs were covered with fur, which probably means they were warm-blooded like birds. They also had big brains with large areas to control balance and sight.

When did reptiles first fly?

Reptiles first took to the air about 250 million years ago. Early flying reptiles, such as *Coelurosauravus*, were lizard-shaped with four legs. Their wings grew out from the sides of their body and were held rigid on long ribs. These reptiles used their wings to help them glide from tree to tree, but they could not flap them. One of the earliest gliding reptiles, *Longisquama*, had tall crests along its back. The crests may have opened out like wings to help it glide.

Longisquama

Coelurosauravus

Quetzalcoatlus

Bat

Did pterosaurs have tails?

All pterosaurs had tails. Early kinds, such as *Dimorphodon*, had long tails to increase lift and help them steer. Later types, such as *Pteranodon*, were called pterodactyls. They had much bigger wings and tiny tails.

Did pterosaurs have feathers?

Most pterosaurs had furry not feathered bodies and their wings were made from sheets of leathery skin. In this way, they were more like bats than birds. The wings stretched from the pterosaur's body along its arm to the tips of its long fourth fingers. Their long wings were ideal for soaring on air currents.

Quick-fire Quiz

1. Which was the biggest pterosaur?
a) *Pteranodon*
b) *Quetzalcoatlus*
c) *Pterodaustro*

2. What were pterosaurs wings made of?
a) Feathers
b) Hair
c) Skin

3. What did most pterosaurs eat?
a) Fish
b) Dinosaurs
c) Insects

4. What were pterosaurs?
a) Dinosaurs
b) Reptiles
c) Birds

Death of the Dinosaurs

Dinosaurs died out about 65 million years ago. Studies show that they disappeared slowly in some places, but more suddenly in others. There are many theories to explain their death, but no-one knows for sure which is right.

Did a meteorite hit Earth?

One of the main theories is that a huge rock falling from outer space hit the Earth. This meteorite threw up a cloud of dust, blocking out the Sun's light and heat. The Earth became much colder and animals that could not cope with this died out. A huge crater that probably formed around this time has been found off the coast of Mexico. This evidence could mean that a meteorite caused the end of the dinosaurs.

Crater caused by a meteorite

United States

Gulf of Mexico

✳ Impact site

Did mammals eat dinosaur eggs?

One explanation for the death of the dinosaurs is that the number of small mammals increased. The mammals ate so many dinosaur eggs that few babies hatched. There are many strange theories and this is one of the more unlikely ones.

Did plant life change?

The extinction of dinosaurs and other animals may have been gradual. Towards the end of the dinosaur age, the tropical climate in North America became cooler and more seasonal and tropical plants were replaced by woodland plants. The dinosaurs seem to have migrated south, so perhaps they could not adapt to these changes in climate and plant life.

Did volcanoes make a difference?

Fossilized plant remains suggest that by 65 million years ago the Earth's climate had become cooler. Some scientists think this was caused by several huge volcanic eruptions that took place over a period of half a million years. Volcanoes send up gases and dust that can first heat the atmosphere, then cool it down, killing off life.

Quick-fire Quiz

1. How long ago did dinosaurs die out?
a) 650 million years
b) 6 million years
c) 65 million years

2. Which other animals died out?
a) Pterosaurs
b) Mammals
c) Birds

3. Where was a huge meteorite crater found?
a) Europe
b) Mexico
c) Africa

4. Which of these reptiles survived?
a) Plesiosaurs
b) Turtles
c) Pterosaurs

Were there other mass extinctions?

The end of the dinosaurs was not the first mass extinction. About 440 million years ago almost half of the animal species died out, and again 370 million years ago. Over 95 per cent of all living things died out about 345 million years ago, and 210 million years ago, at the end of the Permian Period, many land vertebrates died out. When these events happen, new species can take over the world.

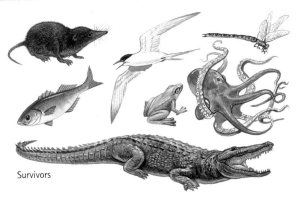

Survivors

Which animals died with the dinosaurs?

When the dinosaurs died out, so did many other reptiles, including mosasaurs, plesiosaurs, pliosaurs and pterosaurs. So did swimming shellfish like ammonites. Most other plants and animals, such as mammals, birds, frogs, fish and other kinds of shellfish survived. Not all reptiles died out either: turtles, crocodiles, snakes and lizards still exist today.

Timescale

The Earth formed about 4,600 million years ago and life developed about 1,000 million years later. The oldest known fossils, which are of shellfish, are 600 million years old. Dinosaurs arrived 230 million years ago and the first true humans about two million years ago.

First life: 3,500 million years ago

When did dinosaurs live?

The dinosaur age, the Mesozoic Era, lasted from 250 to 65 million years ago. Scientists split this time into three main periods. Dinosaurs first appeared in the **Triassic**, about 230 million years ago. The continents were a single land mass called Pangaea ('All-Earth') and dinosaurs could roam all over the world at that time. During the **Jurassic**, about 145 million years ago, Europe and Africa began to move away from the Americas. In the **Cretaceous**, the land masses were separated and different dinosaurs developed on the different continents.

Triassic

Early Jurassic

Early Cretaceous

When did animals move on to land?

Life began in the sea. The first animals moved on to land about 380 million years ago. Amphibians like Eryops could breathe air but, like frogs and toads today, they had to return to water to lay their eggs and to keep their skin moist. Eryops was the size of a pig. Its thick skin protected it and helped support its body weight on land.

DEVONIAN

CARBONIFEROUS

Eryops

Which animals first lived on land?

Although amphibians could live on land they were not true land animals as they had to return to the water to breed. The tiny tadpoles that hatched had to stay in the water until they developed into adults. Reptiles were the first vertebrates (animals with backbones) that could live completely on land. They laid their leathery eggs on land and the baby developed inside the egg, feeding on the yolk. The newly hatched baby was fully formed and active.

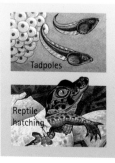
Tadpoles

Reptile hatching

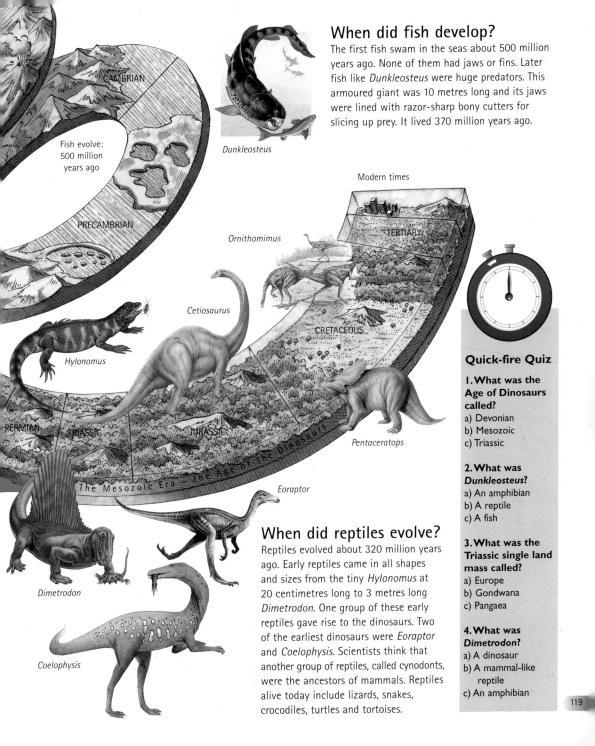

When did fish develop?

The first fish swam in the seas about 500 million years ago. None of them had jaws or fins. Later fish like *Dunkleosteus* were huge predators. This armoured giant was 10 metres long and its jaws were lined with razor-sharp bony cutters for slicing up prey. It lived 370 million years ago.

Dunkleosteus

CAMBRIAN

Fish evolve:
500 million
years ago

PRECAMBRIAN

Modern times

Ornithomimus

TERTIARY

Cetiosaurus

CRETACEOUS

Hylonomus

PERMIAN   TRIASSIC   JURASSIC

Pentaceratops

The Mesozoic Era – The Age of the Dinosaurs

Eoraptor

Dimetrodon

Coelophysis

When did reptiles evolve?

Reptiles evolved about 320 million years ago. Early reptiles came in all shapes and sizes from the tiny *Hylonomus* at 20 centimetres long to 3 metres long *Dimetrodon*. One group of these early reptiles gave rise to the dinosaurs. Two of the earliest dinosaurs were *Eoraptor* and *Coelophysis*. Scientists think that another group of reptiles, called cynodonts, were the ancestors of mammals. Reptiles alive today include lizards, snakes, crocodiles, turtles and tortoises.

Quick-fire Quiz

1. What was the Age of Dinosaurs called?
a) Devonian
b) Mesozoic
c) Triassic

2. What was *Dunkleosteus*?
a) An amphibian
b) A reptile
c) A fish

3. What was the Triassic single land mass called?
a) Europe
b) Gondwana
c) Pangaea

4. What was *Dimetrodon*?
a) A dinosaur
b) A mammal-like reptile
c) An amphibian

119

After the Dinosaurs

After the dinosaurs died out, other animals developed to take their place. Warm-blooded mammals took over as the ruling animals. They dominated the land and even took to the air. A few even went to live in the place where life first developed – the sea.

What are the dinosaurs' nearest surviving relatives?

Many scientists now agree that birds are the closest living relatives of the dinosaurs. The first fossil bird to be found was *Archaeopteryx*. It had a reptile-like skeleton similar to that of *Deinonychus* and feathered wings like a bird. *Archaeopteryx* had a long bony tail, three clawed fingers on each hand, and teeth. Modern birds have lost their teeth and their clawed wing fingers. Their small tail stumps hold their tail feathers.

Deinonychus

What were early birds like?

Very few fossils of early birds have been found. Several almost complete skeletons of *Hesperornis,* a diving bird that lived at the end of the dinosaur age, were found in the United States. *Hesperornis'* wings were so small that it was almost certainly flightless, but its large feet may have been webbed to help it swim. It looked much more like today's birds than *Archaeopteryx* but it still had teeth in its beak and a fairly long bony tail.

Why were mammals so successful?

There are several reasons. Early mammals had bigger brains and were more intelligent than reptiles. They were hairy and warm-blooded, so they could live in colder places. Most of them cared for their young for a long time, so perhaps more young survived. Also, different mammal groups had different kinds of teeth so they could feed on a huge range of food without competing with each other.

What were the first mammals like?

The first mammals evolved about 215 million years ago. One of the earliest known mammals is *Morganucodon*. This mouse-sized hunter was warm-blooded but probably laid eggs like the Australian platypus. *Zalambdalestes* lived at the same time as the last of the dinosaurs, and gave birth to live young.

Morganucodon

Zalambdalestes

Smilodon

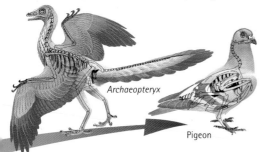

Archaeopteryx

Pigeon

When did mammoths die out?

The huge woolly mammoths died out about 10,000 years ago. The giant North American mammoth was as tall as a double-decker bus. These huge beasts were preyed on by *Smilodon*, a sabre-toothed cat with fangs as long as your hand (15 centimetres). When the mammoths died out, so did *Smilodon*.

Mammoths

Late arrivals?

The first humans evolved about two million years ago, but modern humans or *Homo sapiens* ('wise person') only arose about 100,000 years ago. In the Stone Age, 20,000 years ago, people lived in caves and hunted with stone tools.

Quick-fire Quiz

1. Which of these have no teeth?
a) Birds today
b) *Archaeopteryx*
c) *Hesperornis*

2. Which was the earliest known mammal?
a) *Mammoth*
b) *Smilodon*
c) *Morganucodon*

3. How long ago did modern humans evolve?
a) 20,000 years
b) 100,000 years
c) 5,000,000 years

4. Which animals dominated after the dinosaurs?
a) Mammoths
b) Amphibians
c) Mammals

Web addresses

www.enchantedlearning.com/subjects/dinosaur
Visit Zoom dinosaurs, designed for students of all ages and
levels. This site offers information and activities, jokes, puzzles
and games. Take the opportunity to write your own story and
see it online.

dsc.discovery.com/guides/dinosaur/dinosaur.html
Visit this lively, well-designed site where you can read
interesting features on dinosaurs, prehistoric beasts, fossils
and human origins. Pick up lots of facts and check out the
video gallery.

www.thinkquest.org/library/index.html
The ThinkQuest Library is a collection of over 5,500 educational
websites designed by participants in the ThinkQuest
competitions. To see what they have produced on dinosaurs,
check out subjects such as Dinosaurs and Fossils.

www.bbc.co.uk/dinosaurs
This is the UK website for the television programme *Walking
with Dinosaurs* – the story of Big Al, the Allosaurus. Visit this
site to find lots of dinosaur facts, games and pictures.

www.abc.net.au/dinosaurs/default.htm
This is the US site for the television programme *Walking
with Dinosaurs*.

www.nmnh.si.edu/paleo/dino
Follow a virtual tour of the dinosaurs in the Smithsonian
Museum of Natural History.

www.ology.amnh.org/paleontology/index.html
This is a kids' site at the American Museum of Natural History.

It offers a fascinating insight into dinosaurs and how we find
out about them. Play games and collect 'ology' cards as well as
finding out lots of fun things to do away from your computer.

www.nhm.ac.uk/science
This is the official website for the UK's Natural History
Museum in London, home to one of the best displays of
dinosaur skeletons in the world.

www.nationalgeographic.com/dinoeggs
An online museum of dinosaur hatchlings, displaying the
work of model-makers who recreate them. Join the search
for dinosaur eggs and watch them hatch.

www.kids.net.au/kidscategories/Kids_and_Teens/
School_Time/Science/The_Earth/Dinosaurs
Extensive information about dinosaurs. A search engine
for children, educators and teachers.

www.indyrad.iupui.edu/public/jrafert/dinoart.html
A site dedicated to dinosaur art and modelling. It features
reader art, galleries, books and kits.

www.dinofun.com
This is an interesting dinosaur site covering dinosaur facts and
figures as well as offering games, clip art, homework help and
useful resources for parents and teachers, including a list of
museum exhibitions related to the subject.

www.acnatsci.org
This is the site for the Academy of Natural Sciences in
Philadelphia. Visit their Dinosaur exhibition and learn all about
dinosaurs and the paleontologists that research them.

Quick-fire Quiz ANSWERS

1000
QUESTIONS
& ANSWERS
FACTFILE
ANCIENT
CIVILIZATIONS

Contents

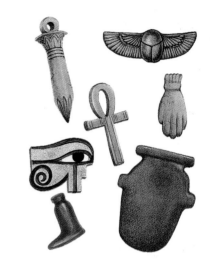

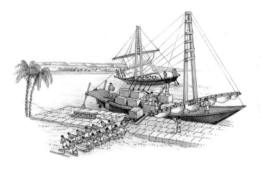

The First Peoples

Early humans lived in caves and tents, moving from place to place in search of food. Around 8000BCE people began to grow crops and keep animals. These early farmers settled down and lived in small villages, which later grew larger and became towns and cities.

Who painted caves?

Over 100 cave paintings have been discovered in Europe, some dating back to about 25,000BCE. Rock paintings have been found in Africa and Australia. They were painted by prehistoric people, who used natural pigments to draw animals and hunting scenes.

Which was the largest ancient city?

The largest known ancient city is Çatal Hüyük in present-day Turkey. By 6250BCE, over 6,000 people lived there. The mud-brick houses were one storey high, but they did not have front doors. People entered by climbing a ladder and crawling through a hole in the roof.

What did the first people hunt?

Stone Age people hunted wild animals for food. One of the largest animals they hunted was the mammoth, a kind of prehistoric elephant. No part of a mammoth was wasted. The flesh fed a group of prehistoric people for weeks. Its furry skin was used to make clothes and tents, and the tusks and bones were used to build huts and carved to make jewellery.

What sort of gods did ancient people worship?

The early city-dwellers built religious shrines, but little is known about their gods. This clay figure, found at a decorated shrine in Çatal Hüyük, may have been a mother goddess.

Quick-fire Quiz

1. What was Çatal Hüyük?
   a) A country
   b) A kind of house
   c) A city

2. What was a mammoth?
   a) A prehistoric elephant
   b) A prehistoric tiger
   c) A prehistoric person

3. When were wolves tamed?
   a) 2000BCE
   b) 10,000BCE
   c) 40,000BCE

4. What was made from palm leaves?
   a) Rope
   b) Paper
   c) Bread

What did they eat?

People in Çatal Hüyük ate meat, fruits such as apples, and nuts and vegetables. They also made great use of date palms. They ate the fruit, the tree trunks provided timber, and the leaves were used to roof their houses or were plaited and woven into rope, mats and sandals.

Did the first people keep animals?

People tamed wolves as long ago as 10,000BCE. These were the first domesticated dogs and were used to herd other animals. In time, wild sheep, goats, cows and pigs were kept as farm animals.

Early farm animals

What crops did they grow?

Early farmers sowed wild wheat and barley seeds. A new form of wheat with plumper seeds developed when wild wheat was cross-bred with a kind of grass. The farmers ground these seeds between stones, mixed the flour with water and made a new food — bread!

What were early villages like?

In Europe, the first villages were groups of houses in a fenced enclosure. The walls of the wooden houses were covered with mud, and the roofs thatched with dry grass. Vegetables were grown in one part of the enclosure, and farm animals were kept in another.

River Valley Civilizations

The first great civilization, Sumer, developed in about 5000BCE between the Tigris and Euphrates rivers. The area was later called Mesopotamia (now Iraq). Sumer lasted 3,000 years. In that time, other civilizations grew up along the River Nile in Egypt and the River Indus in Pakistan.

Did the Indus people build cities?

In the 1920s, two cities – Mohenjo-daro and Harappa – were found in the Indus valley. They dated from about 2000BCE, and were built in a grid pattern like modern American cities.

Who invented the wheel?

No-one knows when the wheel was invented. The potter's wheel was used in Mesopotamia about 6,000 years ago. By about 3500BCE the Sumerians were using simple carts like this. Later they had wheeled war chariots which were pulled by donkeys or wild asses.

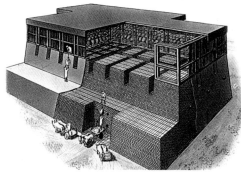

Granary in Mohenjo-daro

Who invented writing?

Writing was probably invented by the Sumerians about 5,000 years ago. At first they drew pictures, but later these were turned into wedge-shaped symbols, which we now call cuneiform writing.

What crops did they grow?

Farmers in the Indus valley grew many crops, including wheat, barley, melons, dates and cotton. Each city had a huge, well-aired granary to store the grain between harvests.

Did they build temples?

The Sumerians built a temple at the centre of each city-state. By 2000BCE, the temples had developed into big towers called ziggurats, like this one at Ur. The king, who was also the high priest, carried out religious ceremonies and sacrifices in the temple at the top of the tower.

Quick-fire Quiz

1. What was a ziggurat?
a) A house
b) A tower
c) A palace

2. What kind of writing did the Sumerians use?
a) Cuneiform
b) Hieroglyphs
c) Letters

3. Where was Harappa?
a) Sumer
b) Egypt
c) Indus valley

4. What did early Sumerians use to build their houses?
a) Wood
b) Stone
c) Reeds

What were river valley homes made from?

Most ancient peoples built homes from the materials around them. The Sumerians had no stones or trees, so they built houses from reeds and, later, sun-dried mud bricks. The Indus people lived in mud-brick houses built around courtyards. Each house had several rooms, a toilet and a well. The Indus civilization lasted 800 years. It came to an end in about 1800BCE.

Did they play games?

Rich Sumerians did not have to work all the time, so they relaxed by listening to music or playing games. This game board, found in a royal grave at Ur, dates from between 3000 and 2000BCE. No-one knows how it was played.

Did the Sumerians have money?

The Sumerians traded at huge markets. Each trader had his own cylinder seal for signing contracts. Sales were recorded on clay tablets. By about 3300BCE, Sumerians were using clay tokens to buy goods. They may have had different sorts of tokens for different kinds of goods.

Who ruled Sumer?

Each Sumerian city-state had its own king. A king sometimes took over other cities, but none ever ruled all of Sumer. The royal families were very rich and wore fine clothes. A Sumerian princess wore a long dress with gold and silver jewellery.

129

Ancient Egypt

Over 5,000 years ago, two Egyptian kingdoms – Upper and Lower Egypt – grew up by the River Nile in North Africa. In 3100BCE, King Menes united Egypt. It became a very powerful empire which lasted until 30BCE, when Egypt fell to the Romans.

How do we know about ancient Egypt?

The remains of tombs, written records and wall paintings have helped build up a picture of ancient Egypt. Wall paintings show religious rituals, royal conquests and scenes of everyday life.

Did Egyptians play games?

Like most ancient peoples, wealthy Egyptians spent their leisure time listening to music or playing board games. Their children played with toys including balls, spinning tops, dolls and model animals.

Scribe

Who wrote letters?

Not all Egyptians could read and write. Men called scribes wrote letters for them. Scribes used hieroglyphs (picture writing) for royal and sacred writing, and simplified symbols for business letters. They used reed pens and a kind of paper called papyrus.

How did Egyptians make bread?

Bread was the main food for poor Egyptians. Wheat and barley were ground into flour. They mixed this with water to make a dough, added flavouring such as garlic or honey, and baked it in clay pots.

Did they wear wigs?

Yes, the ancient Egyptians thought that hair was dirty, so they shaved their heads and wore elaborate wigs. They also wore make-up. They mixed powdered minerals such as lead, copper and iron oxide with water or oils to make bright lipstick, eye shadow and blusher.

Were pharaohs rich?

Egyptian kings, called pharaohs, were worshipped and treated like gods. They owned the whole country, and everybody and everything belonged to them, so they were very rich and powerful! The royal family lived in luxury, waited on by hundreds of servants.

Quick-fire Quiz

1. Who united Egypt?
a) King Nile
b) King Menes
c) King Egypt

2. When did Egypt fall to the Romans?
a) 300BCE
b) 30BCE
c) 3BCE

3. What did a scribe do?
a) Make wigs
b) Build tombs
c) Write letters

4. What crop was swapped for goods?
a) Peas
b) Grain
c) Garlic

Was grain used like money?

Grain was one of the most important crops in ancient Egypt. It was used to pay taxes, and was exchanged for other goods. For this reason, the Egyptians developed an accurate balance to weigh grain and other costly goods.

Why was the River Nile important?

The Egyptian empire grew up along the River Nile because it was good farming land. Hardly any rain fell in Egypt, but every July the River Nile flooded, covering the surrounding ground with water and rich black mud. This mud was great for growing crops. The ancient Egyptians learned how to store enough of the flood water in canals to irrigate (water) the fields in the dry season. This meant they produced enough crops to feed their own people and to sell some to other traders. Almost all Egypt's wealth came from farming.

Priests and Mummies

The ancient Egyptians worshipped many gods and believed in life after death. To make sure their spirits could enjoy the afterlife, the Egyptians embalmed (preserved) the bodies of the dead. The priests were very powerful, helping people with sacred works.

Why were tombs robbed?

Robbers plundered tombs for the treasures they contained. Rich Egyptians were buried

with everything they would need in the afterlife – food, clothes, jewellery and even models of servants. Lucky amulets like these were often placed among a mummy's bandages to ward off evil spirits.

Who was mummified?

Making a mummy was expensive. Only the royal family, top officials and priests were mummified. The poor were buried in reed coffins or in holes in the sand. Animals that represented gods and goddesses, such as cats, dogs, crocodiles and baboons, were sometimes mummified. Cats, for example, represented the goddess Bastet.

What is a mummy?

A mummy is a body that has been preserved. The people who made mummies were called embalmers. After being dried out and rubbed with oils, the body was wrapped in bandages as much as five kilometres long! A priest watched over the embalmers as they worked.

Coffin

Embalmer

Priest

Amulets

Bandages

Canopic jars for the body organs

Which pharaoh's tomb survived?

Most pharaohs' tombs were robbed, but in 1922, archaeologists found the tomb of the young Tutankhamun, who was only 18 when he died. His tomb was still intact and full of priceless treasures, including his mummy and this fabulous golden face mask.

How was a body preserved?

The soft body organs were removed, dried, and placed in vessels called canopic jars. The spaces were packed with rags or sawdust, and the body was stitched up. It was then covered in a kind of salt called natron, which dried it out.

Quick-fire Quiz

1. Who was Anubis?
a) A priest
b) A god
c) A pharaoh

2. What did the Egyptians put in a mummy's bandages?
a) Amulets
b) Natron
c) Hieroglyphs

3. When was Tutankhamun's tomb found?
a) 1912
b) 1922
c) 1932

4. Who preserved a mummy?
a) Priests
b) Pharaohs
c) Embalmers

Coffin-painter

What was painted on the coffin?

A body was placed in a nest of two or three coffins, each painted with hieroglyphs (word pictures), gods, pictures of the person's life and spells to keep away evil spirits.

What was a death mask?

A death mask was a portrait of the dead person. It was put over the mummy's face, so that the soul would recognize its body. Death masks were often made of painted wood, but most pharaohs had death masks of beaten gold.

How was the brain removed?

An embalmer removed the brain by pulling it out through the nostrils with a hooked knife. They did not think the brain was important so they threw it away!

Who wore a jackal's head?

When the priest said the final prayers over a body, he wore a mask to look like the jackal god, Anubis, god of the dead. At the tomb, the priest held the mummy during the 'Opening of the mouth' ceremony, to give the dead person the power to eat, move and breathe.

133

Pyramids and Tombs

Egyptian pharaohs of the Old and Middle Kingdoms (3,500 to 5,000 years ago), were buried under pyramids. In the New Kingdom (3,000 to 3,500 years ago), pharaohs were buried in tombs in a valley on the west bank of the Nile at Thebes.

How was a pyramid built?

Plumb line

Chisels and hammers

It took at least 4,000 craftsmen and thousands of labourers to build a pyramid. The labourers were mostly farmers who worked as builders to pay their taxes. They cleared the site, laid the foundations and dragged the stones into place. Stone masons used an assortment of tools to cut the hard blocks of limestone used to cover the outside of the pyramids. They cut the stone into blocks that fitted together perfectly.

Stone masons

Which temple was moved?

In 1964, the temple at Abu Simbel was moved so that it would not be flooded when the Aswan dam was built. The temple had been carved out of solid rocks on the banks of the River Nile.

Why did Egyptians have funeral barges?

The mummified bodies of Egyptian pharaohs were placed on highly decorated boats so that they could travel to the next world. The boat was dragged to the tomb on a sledge pulled by oxen.

Where did the stones come from?

The inside of a pyramid was built from soft stone found locally. The outside was covered with smooth limestone from quarries up to 800 kilometres away. Huge blocks of stone, up to 50 tonnes in weight, were loaded onto barges in the flood season and shipped to the building site.

Where were the pyramids built?

The pyramids were all built on the west bank of the Nile. The Egyptians believed this was the land of the dead because it was where the Sun set. They built their homes on the east bank, the land of the living, where the Sun rose.

What is the Great Pyramid?

The Great Pyramid at Giza was built for King Khufu (c. 2575BCE) from over two million stone blocks. The pharaoh was buried in a central chamber.

Quick-fire Quiz

1. Where was the Great Pyramid?
a) Thebes
b) Giza
c) Abu Simbel

2. During which Kingdom were the pyramids built?
a) The Old Kingdom
b) All the time
c) The New Kingdom

3. What was built on the west bank of the Nile?
a) Egyptian homes
b) Pharaohs' palaces
c) The pyramids

4. When was the last pyramid built?
a) About 2575BCE
b) About 1570BCE
c) About 570BCE

Temple for daily ceremonies

Temple where body was mummified

Why did pyramids have temples?

Religion was very important to the Egyptians. Temples were the gods' homes on Earth. The priests performed special ceremonies before and after the pharaoh was put in the tomb, so temples were built in the pyramids.

Why did pyramid-building stop?

About 90 pyramids were built – the last one in 1570BCE. But they were easy for robbers to get into, so pharaohs of the New Kingdom were buried in tombs carved in the cliffs in a hidden valley at Thebes instead. This is known as the Valley of the Kings. Although most of these tombs were also robbed, it was here that archaeologists Howard Carter and Lord Carnarvon, found the untouched tomb of the boy-king, Tutankhamun.

135

Crete and Mycenae

The first European civilization began about 4,500 years ago, on the island of Crete. The Minoans, named after a famous king, Minos, were traders who ruled the Aegean Sea. In 1450BCE, this civilization ended and the Mycenaeans, from mainland Greece, took over.

What was the minotaur?

The Minoans told how King Minos kept a minotaur, a monster that was half-man and half-bull, in a labyrinth (maze of tunnels) below his palace. Each year, he sacrificed 14 young Greeks to this terrible creature. The Greek hero, Theseus, was determined to kill the minotaur. With the help of King Minos's daughter, Ariadne, he found a way into the labyrinth, killed the monster and escaped from the maze by following a thread he had unwound on his way through it.

Did Minoans build cities?

The Minoans built several cities, connected to each other by paved roads. Each had a fine palace. The grandest was at Knossos, in the north of Crete. It had over 1,000 rooms, including luxurious apartments, workshops and a school.

Minoan palace

What goods did the Minoans trade?

Craftsmen made beautiful pottery and carved ornaments. Goldsmiths made fine jewellery, such as this bull's head pendant. Minoan goods have been found in many surrounding countries including Egypt.

Who went hunting?

The Mycenaeans loved to hunt wild animals, including lions, which roamed Greece until about 3,000 years ago. This fresco shows a boar hunt. Nobles hunted boar with spears and shields, and had dogs to help them. Hunters cut off the tusks from dead boars, and used them to decorate their helmets.

Did Minoans play sports?

Frescoes (wall-paintings) show the Minoans were very sporty. Boys and girls enjoyed boxing and the dangerous sport of bull-leaping. One person held the bull's head, while the bull-leaper somersaulted between the horns of the bull. A friend stood at the back to catch the acrobat.

Mycenaean palace

What were Mycenaean palaces like?

The Mycenaeans were the ruling Greeks from about 1450BCE until 1100BCE. The remains of the palace of the Mycenaean king Nestor at Pylos, in southern Greece, show that it had richly decorated rooms built around a series of courtyards.

Were the Mycenaeans warriors?

The Mycenaeans, unlike the Minoans, were warriors as well as traders, and built fortified towns. The walls around their city of Mycenae were built from huge stone blocks. At the only entrance, the Lion Gate, a pair of stone lionesses stood guard. Warriors attacked their enemies from the walls.

The Lion Gate

Quick-fire Quiz

1. Which of these civilizations began in Crete?
a) Egyptian
b) Mycenaean
c) Minoan

2. What was the minotaur?
a) Half-man, half-lion
b) Half-man, half-bull
c) Half-man, half-boar

3. Who killed the minotaur?
a) King Minos
b) King Nestor
c) Theseus

4. What was the main gate in Mycenae called?
a) The Lion Gate
b) The Bull Gate
c) The King Gate

Babylon

The Mesopotamian city-state of Babylon rose to power in 1900BCE. Hammurabi the Great increased its power in the 1700sBCE. It collapsed in 1595BCE, but grew great again under Nebuchadnezzar, 1,000 years later. In 539BCE, Babylon fell to the Persians.

Who made Babylon rich?

Nebuchadnezzar made Babylon one of the richest cities in the world. The main entrance, the Ishtar gate, was covered with glazed blue tiles. He brought plants and trees from Persia for the famous Hanging Gardens, which were one of the 'Seven Wonders of the Ancient World'.

Did the Babylonians go to war?

The Babylonian army was well trained and had good leaders. Both Hammurabi the Great and Nebuchadnezzar waged wars against surrounding lands. Skilled archers helped Nebuchadnezzar conquer lands, including Phoenicia, Syria, Judah and Assyria.

What were their houses like?

About 4,000 years ago, most people in Babylon had simple homes. However, rich people built large, flat-roofed houses with wooden balconies around a central courtyard. They lived in great comfort, with many servants to cook and clean for them.

Who lost the secret of eternal life?

Legend tells how the Babylonian hero and king, Gilgamesh, was given the secret of eternal life – a plant from under the sea. He dived and picked the plant but he fell asleep on his way home. A snake gobbled up the plant and Gilgamesh lost the chance to live forever.

Did they have gods?

The people of Babylon had many gods. Ishtar, the mother goddess, and Marduk, the dragon god, were the most powerful. One myth tells how the hero Gilgamesh's pride angered the gods, who sent a Bull of Heaven to destroy him – but Gilgamesh survived.

Quick-fire Quiz

1. Who was the mother goddess?
a) Marduk
b) Ishtar
c) Gilgamesh

2. How many laws did Hammurabi make?
a) 282
b) 272
c) 262

3. What ate the secret of life?
a) A snake
b) A bull
c) A genie

4. Who conquered Babylon in 539BCE?
a) The Greeks
b) The Egyptians
c) The Persians

What were genies?

The Babylonians believed that winged gods, or genies, protected royal palaces from demons and disease. This genie is holding a bucket and a pine cone, which were symbols of purification.

Who made good laws?

Hammurabi made 282 laws for his people to follow. Most were good laws, to protect the weak from the strong. They covered everything from fair rates of pay to rules for trading.

Did they keep pets?

Some Babylonians probably had domesticated cats and dogs, but rich people kept more exotic pets. The first zoos were owned by wealthy princes, who gave each other presents of wild animals such as lions and leopards.

Did Babylonians do maths?

Like earlier people in the region, the Babylonians used cuneiform writing, which can still be seen on clay tablets. Babylonian mathematicians worked out a system of counting based on the number 60. This was especially useful as 60 can be divided in many different ways. We still use this system today when we record the time (60 minutes in an hour, 60 seconds in a minute), and in measuring (there are 60 x 6 degrees in a circle). Babylonians recorded details of royal grants of land on boundary stones which deterred land disputes between neighbours. The Babylonians were also great astronomers.

Assyrians and Hittites

The Hittites from Anatolia (now in Turkey) conquered most of Syria, Mesopotamia and Babylon in the 1500sBCE. Their empire fell in 1200BCE and the Assyrians, from northern Mesopotamia, took over. In 609BCE, the Assyrian empire fell to the Babylonians.

Who used battering rams?
Both the Hittites and the Assyrians were skilled at using siege warfare to defeat their enemies. Their armies would surround the enemy's city to stop food getting in. Then they used huge battering rams to knock holes in the city walls.

What did they build?
The Assyrians built magnificent cities, temples and palaces. The king often supervised the building from his chariot. Stones were brought from distant quarries, and oarsmen in skin boats towed laden rafts up the Tigris.

Who last ruled Assyria?
King Ashurbanipal was the last and greatest ruler of Assyria. He was a ruthless king, but he also built a great library where records and literature from Sumer and Babylon were stored on clay tablets. His palace at Nineveh had gardens stocked with plants from all over the world.

The Assyrian royal court

Who carved in stone?

The Hittites and Assyrians were great stone masons. The Hittites carved huge pictures of their gods and goddesses into the rock face near their temples. The Assyrians left many finely carved stone sculptures which tell us about their history and how they lived. Most of them show the kings and their conquests, but this one shows scenes of everyday life such as people preparing and cooking food.

Carved stone being dragged to a new temple

Quick-fire Quiz

1. Who was Ashur?
a) A god
b) A king
c) A goddess

2. Where were the Hittites from?
a) Syria
b) Egypt
c) Anatolia

3. Where was Ashurbanipal's palace?
a) Babylon
b) Nineveh
c) Sumer

4. What animals pulled a war chariot?
a) Bulls
b) Lions
c) Horses

What gods did the Assyrians worship?

Winged lion

The Assyrians believed in many gods. Their chief god was Ashur whose name was used for their capital city. Ishtar was the Assyrians' goddess of war. The Babylonians also worshipped Ishtar, but believed that she was a mother-goddess who helped protect their city. To ward off evil spirits, huge stone sculptures of winged lions with human heads were placed on each side of important doors and gateways.

Who drove war chariots?

Both the Hittites and the Assyrians used war chariots in battle. The two-wheeled chariots were drawn by horses, and the skilled archers would fire at the enemy as they raced along. The Assyrians were fierce warriors, fighting with swords, slings, shields and bows.

Assyrian war chariot

141

Ancient Sea Traders

The Phoenicians were the best sea traders of the ancient world. They lived in city-states on the coast of the Mediterranean Sea (now Lebanon) from about 1200 to 146BCE. Their culture died out after the area was conquered by Alexander the Great.

Were the Phoenicians explorers?

The Phoenicians were skilled sailors and had fine ships. Around 600BCE, the Egyptians paid the Phoenicians to explore West Africa. They also sailed to Britain, where they traded goods for tin and silver.

What goods did Phoenicians trade?

Phoenician craftsmen made fine cloth as well as pottery, ivory and metal goods to sell. They also traded in the wood from cedar trees.

Who blew glass?

The Phoenicians were the first people to produce see-through glassware on a large scale. They also invented the process of glass blowing, which allowed them to make fine glassware like this.

Letters from the Phoenician alphabet

Could Phoenicians read and write?

The Phoenicians must have been able to read and write because they were among the first people to use an alphabet for writing words, rather than pictograms. Their alphabet was made up of 30 consonants — there were no vowels. These letters became the basis for all modern alphabets.

How did the Phoenicians get their name?

The name came from the Greek word 'phoinos' meaning 'red'. They were called this because they made a rich reddish-purple dye from a sea snail called a murex. Cloth dyed with this was expensive. In Roman times, only emperors were allowed to wear murex-dyed robes.

Murex

Quick-fire Quiz

1. What was made from a murex?
a) A dye
b) A food
c) A drink

2. Where was Carthage?
a) Spain
b) Africa
c) Greece

3. Who was the Phoenicians' main god?
a) Dido
b) Baal
c) Alexander

4. Where did Phoenicians explore?
a) America
b) Australia
c) Africa

Who founded the city of Carthage?

Carthage was the largest Phoenician city. According to legend, the founder of Carthage was the Phoenician princess Dido. After landing on the coast of North Africa, Dido asked the local ruler for land to build a city. He said she could take an area of land that could be enclosed by an ox-hide. Clever Dido had the hide cut into thin strips so that she could mark out a large plot of land. Carthage became one of the most important trading cities in the area.

Did they build temples?

The Phoenicians built many temples and shrines to their gods. Their main god was the warrior god Baal. There were priests and priestesses, who occasionally, in times of trouble, sacrificed children to the gods.

Phoenician priestess

Where were Phoenician colonies?

The Phoenicians spread throughout the Mediterranean, setting up colonies in many foreign lands including Marseilles (France), Cadiz (Spain), Malta, Sicily, Cyprus and Carthage (now Tunisia) in North Africa. From Carthage they traded with local Africans, buying precious ivory, animal skins and wood.

Phoenicians trading with Africans

Ancient Greece

By 500BCE, ancient Greece was made up of small, independent city-states around the Mediterranean. Each city-state had its own government and laws. The most important of these city-states were Athens and Sparta.

Who were the Spartans?

The city-state of Sparta in southern Greece was a mighty military power. All Spartan men were in the army, and boys left home at seven to start training as soldiers. Women did not fight, but they had to be very fit so their babies would be healthy and strong.

What was an acropolis?

Each Greek city-state had a walled city with an acropolis (fort) and an agora — a large open space used for meetings and markets. In time the acropolis became a religious centre.

Who left Athens?

Criminals or unpopular politicians could be banished (ostracized). Each year, Athenians could write the name of a person they wanted banished on bits of pottery called 'ostraka'. Anyone with more than 6,000 votes had to leave for 10 years!

Did Greeks play sports?

The ancient Greeks enjoyed competitive games. The Olympics – the most famous – were first held in 776BCE, and took place every four years. At first, there was just one race. By 500BCE, the Games lasted five days.

Who won an olive wreath?

On the final day of the Olympic Games the winners received their prizes – crowns of laurel leaves or wild olives cut from a special grove near the temple of Zeus. Afterwards they were guests of honour at a victory feast.

Who played outdoors?

Greek plays were performed in large open-air theatres. The semicircular theatre in Athens held over 10,000 people. All the actors were male, and they wore brightly painted masks to show which characters they were playing.

The Acropolis in Athens

Did they enjoy music?

The Greeks enjoyed singing and dancing, and music was played on most social occasions. Poetry was chanted, accompanied by music, or sung. The main stringed instrument was the lyre, which was sometimes made from a tortoise shell.

Who read the future?

The Greeks had many gods. The chief was Zeus who lived on Mount Olympus, the highest mountain in Greece. If the Greeks wanted to ask the gods about the future, they visited oracles. Priests and priestesses at an oracle spoke on behalf of the gods. The advice from the gods was usually so vague that it always seemed to be right. The most famous oracle was in the temple of the sun god, Apollo, at Delphi.

Whose speeches were timed?

In Athens, all men who were not slaves were citizens, and could speak at the Assembly. At this meeting they could give their opinions on political matters. Each speaker was timed with a water clock, so he could not talk for too long!

Quick-fire Quiz

1. What foretold the future?
a) The Assembly
b) An acropolis
c) An oracle

2. What was a lyre?
a) A bird
b) A musical instrument
c) An Olympic sport

3. How often were the Olympic Games held?
a) Every year
b) Every four years
c) Every ten years

4. Who could speak at the Assembly?
a) Citizens
b) Slaves
c) Everyone

145

Greek Life

Greek architecture, the arts, sport and science flourished during the Golden Age (600 to 300BCE). Athens became the centre of Greek culture. In 338BCE, King Philip of Macedonia conquered Greece. His son, Alexander the Great, spread Greek learning to North Africa and the Middle East.

Where did people shop?

In the agora, or marketplace, you could buy everything from food to fabrics, silverware to slaves. Fast-food sellers supplied tasty snacks, and you could even visit a doctor.

What were Greek houses like?

Greek houses were made of sun-dried, mud bricks built round a central courtyard. Most houses were single storey, but some wealthier homes had bedrooms on a second floor. Greek men, women and slaves all lived in separate quarters.

How do we know about ancient Greek life?

Archaeologists have found marble and bronze statues and pottery bowls, vases and cups decorated with scenes from Greek life. These tell us what the Greeks wore and how they lived.

What did Greeks wear?

Everyone wore a chiton – a large cloth rectangle fastened at the shoulders. Saffron yellow was a favourite colour, but purple, red and violet were also fashionable. Wealthy women piled their hair into elaborate styles, and wore make-up, earrings, necklaces, bracelets and rings.

What did ancient Greeks eat?

Basic foods were bread, olives, figs and goats' milk cheese. Meat was expensive but fish was cheap along the coast. Women prepared the food, and everyone ate in the courtyard.

Did Greeks have baths?

Few homes had baths, but the gymnasium, a public sports ground in Athens, had plunge pools and steam baths. Women and children washed using bronze basins, and some homes had terracotta hip baths. Slaves helped their masters to wash.

Quick-fire Quiz

1. What was an agora?
   a) A school
   b) A marketplace
   c) A temple

2. Who went to school?
   a) Boys
   b) Girls
   c) No-one

3. What was a chiton?
   a) A stool
   b) A book
   c) A robe

4. Who conquered Greece in 338BCE?
   a) Philip
   b) Alexander
   c) Socrates

Where did people relax?

The agora was a place to relax and meet friends. Men met there to listen to storytellers recounting tales, or to hear philosophers such as Socrates discuss politics.

Did they have furniture?

Wealthy Athenians lived in heated homes with fine furniture. They lounged on padded couches and ate from small tables inlaid with ivory. Their wooden beds had leather thongs to support a mattress, and lots of cushions.

Did Greek children go to school?

Rich Athenian boys went to school between the ages of seven and 18. They studied maths, reading, writing, music and poetry in the morning and did athletics and dancing in the afternoon. The girls stayed at home, learning to spin, weave and run a household.

The Persians

About 3,000 years ago, Persia (Iran) was ruled by two powers, the Medes and the Persians. In 550BCE, Persian king, Cyrus the Great, seized power. He made Persia the centre of a huge empire, which lasted until 330BCE, when Alexander the Great took control.

Who was Alexander the Great?
Alexander the Great became king of Greece in 336BCE, and set out to conquer the Persians. He was a great soldier and a clever leader. Within 12 years he had taken over Persia, and built an empire stretching from Egypt to India.

Who made Persia great?
King Darius I ruled Persia from 521 to 486BCE. His powerful empire included Egypt and the Indus Valley. He taxed all the people he conquered, and the tributes they brought him included food, animals, fine cloth, gold and jewels. He built roads to link the empire, and introduced a standard currency to increase trade.

Who were the Parthians?

The Parthians moved into Persia in about 1000BCE and lived under Persian rule. After the death of Alexander the Great, the Parthians took over the area. A favourite trick of Parthian archers was to pretend to retreat, then turn in their saddles to fire back at the enemy – the origin of the saying 'a Parthian shot'.

What sort of religion did the Persians have?

Many Persians worshipped Mithras, the god of light, truth and justice. There was a legend that he killed a magic bull, and that every animal and plant sprang from its blood. Later, Mithras was popular with Roman soldiers, who built temples to him. A Persian prophet called Zoroaster, who lived around 600BCE, founded a new religion, Zoroastrianism, which is still followed today in parts of Iran and India.

Quick-fire Quiz

1. Who founded the Persian empire?
a) King Cyrus
b) King Darius
c) King Philip

2. When was the Battle of Salamis?
a) 380BCE
b) 480BCE
c) 580BCE

3. Who or what was Zoroaster?
a) A palace
b) A city
c) A prophet

4. What was a trireme?
a) A god
b) A sword
c) A ship

Did Persia have an army?

The Persians had a large, well-trained army. The soldiers were armed with spears, daggers and bows and arrows. They wore leather tunics strengthened with scales to protect them in battle.

Did the Persians and Greeks fight?

The Greeks and Persians were at war for many years. At the Battle of Salamis, in 480BCE, the Persian fleet was forced to retreat by the might of the Greek triremes. A trireme was a swift ship powered by more than 150 oarsmen grouped in threes on either side of the ship.

Was Persia rich?

Persia became very rich under Darius I, who lived in a huge palace in Persepolis. The Great Hall alone held 10,000 people. When Alexander the Great invaded, he is said to have taken 4,500 tonnes of gold from the Persian cities of Persepolis and Susa.

Ancient China

The first emperor of China was King Zheng of Qin. In 221BCE, he defeated the rulers of all the states that made up China, and founded the Qin dynasty, from which China gets its name. The Han dynasty (206BCE to CE220) opened up trade with the West.

What is a dynasty?

China was governed by a series of ruling families, called dynasties. The Zhou dynasty ruled China for over 800 years from 1122BCE. Zhou society was divided into nobles, peasants and slaves. Iron was first used at this time, and farming methods improved.

Who was Confucius?

Confucius, or K'ung Fu-tzu, was born in China in 551BCE. He was a great thinker who believed that the emperor should care for his people like a father, and that the people should love and obey him. For over 2,000 years his teachings influenced the way China was ruled.

Who invented paper?

Chinese inventors discovered many useful things. Around CE100, a man called Tsai Lung rolled a paste of hemp and wood into a sheet which he stretched and dried. He had invented paper! About 800 years later, the Chinese printed the first banknotes.

What are Yin and Yang?

The Chinese believe everything in nature is in harmony. Confucius depicted this by the Yin and Yang symbol. The dark Yin interlocks with the light Yang, and each one contains a tiny bit of the other.

What was the terracotta army?

When King Zheng became emperor, he changed his name to Shi Huangdi ('first emperor') and ordered a splendid tomb to be built. His tomb was guarded by a terracotta army – 7,000 life-size clay soldiers. The soldiers had real crossbows and spears, with life-size clay horses and chariots.

Who invented the compass?

The ancient Chinese were great scientists and inventors. During the Han dynasty, scientists invented the first magnetic compass with a dial and a pointer. At first, they did not use it for navigation, as we do now, but to make sure that their temples faced the right way. The Chinese were very skilled sailors. Hundreds of years before the Europeans, the Chinese built sea-going ships with lots of sails and steered by rudders. Chinese sailors travelled as far as Africa to trade. They were also skilled mathematicians and astronomers. The Chinese were the first to make maps using a grid system, and to work out that a year has 365.25 days.

Who built the Great Wall?

The Great Wall of China was built for Shi Huangdi between 214 and 204BCE, by thousands of poor farmers. Short bits of wall were joined up to make the longest wall in the world, stretching over 2,200 kilometres. The wall is up to 15 metres high, and is wide enough for a bus to drive along the top.

Who defeated an emperor?

Life was hard for most peasants during the Qin dynasty. They had to pay taxes and work for Shi Huangdi. After his death, the peasants rebelled against the new emperor, his son. They raised a large army and, in 209BCE, the emperor was defeated.

Peasants during the Qin Dynasty

Quick-fire Quiz

1. What did the terracotta army guard?
a) A palace
b) A tomb
c) A city

2. Who invented paper?
a) K'ung Fu-tzu
b) Shi Huangdi
c) Tsai Lung

3. How high is the Great Wall?
a) 25m
b) 15m
c) 5m

4. When was Confucius born?
a) 551BCE
b) 151BCE
c) 51BCE

The Celts

Between 750 and 50BCE, the Celts were the most important tribes in Europe. There were many different Celtic tribes, but they all spoke the same kind of language and had similar lifestyles. Eventually, the Romans conquered most of their lands.

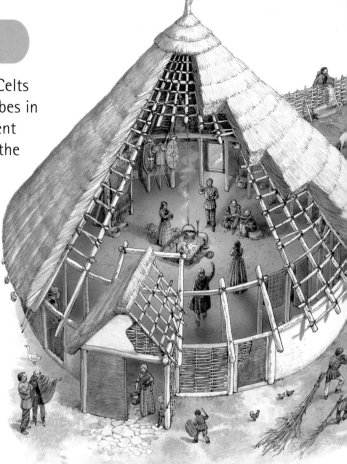

What were Celtic homes like?

A Celtic house often had walls made of branches covered with clay, and a thatched roof of straw or reeds. Most homes had one large room, where the family cooked, ate and slept. There were no windows. A central fire provided heat and light.

Were the Celts warriors?

Celtic men and women were renowned fighters and battles between tribes were common. Many warriors painted their faces and bodies blue to look as fierce as possible. Some went into battle naked but others wore tartan tops, capes and trousers, and carried fine bronze shields.

Were the Celts interested in arts and crafts?

The Celts were great poets and musicians and made beautifully decorated metalwork. Wealthy warriors carried fine shields, and often wore an armband made from gold and a delicately carved neck ring, called a torque. Celtic jewellery and weapons were decorated with abstract or geometrical designs.

Shield

Armband

Were cattle important?

The Celts were farmers. They depended on meat to get them through the winter, so cattle were very important. At the feast of Beltane on May 1, which marked the start of summer, Druids (priests) chased cattle through bonfires to expel evil spirits and disease.

A bull's head decoration from a cauldron found in Denmark

Quick-fire Quiz

1. What was a torque?
a) An earring
b) A neck ring
c) A belt

2. When was Beltane celebrated?
a) November
b) February
c) May

3. What was a Druid?
a) A priest
b) A warrior
c) A king

4. What is Stonehenge?
a) A feast
b) A city
c) A monument

What are Celtic myths about?

Very few Celtic myths and stories have survived. Some of the best known come from Ireland and Wales. The Welsh Mabinogion tells the mythical history of early Britain. In this scene from an Irish myth, a giant brings a king a magic cauldron, which represents plenty, fertility and rebirth.

Who built Stonehenge?

Stonehenge in England was built by Stone Age people in around 2750BCE, long before the Celts. The layout of the huge circle of standing stones marked the midsummer sunrise and the midwinter moonrise. Historians think this monument was used as a place of worship and to study the stars. Later, Celts may have used it as a meeting place for worship and to make sacrifices to their gods.

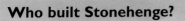

Could Celts read and write?

Celts did not read or write. Their myths, laws and religion were passed down by word of mouth. Druids taught poetry, history and the law. At feasts, musicians and storytellers called bards told tales of brave heroes.

Life in Ancient Rome

At first, ancient Rome was ruled by kings, but in 509BCE the Romans set up a republic with elected leaders. Rome gradually took over other lands, and by CE150 the empire stretched across Europe into Africa.

Who were looked after by wolves?

According to Roman legend, a king named Numitor had two baby grandsons, called Romulus and Remus. They were thrown into the River Tiber, but a wolf rescued them and brought them up. When they grew up, the brothers built Rome.

Where did rich Romans live?

Many rich Romans had a country home (a villa) and a town house (a domus). Houses were built around a courtyard and had lots of rooms, running water, a kitchen, central heating and sometimes even a bathroom.

Did Romans wear make-up?

A rich Roman lady powdered her face with chalk or white lead and painted her lips with red ochre. She took a long time to get ready for the day, even though slave girls helped her dress and style her hair.

Who ruled Rome?

The Roman republic was ruled by the Senate – a group of elder citizens. Each year, the Senate elected two consuls to lead Rome. The Senate met to decide how Rome was to be run and to advise the consuls, who were the most powerful people in Rome.

Where did the poor live?

Romans with little money lived in tiny flats in high-rise buildings. Many buildings were not very stable, and sometimes fell down with the people still inside. The flats had no kitchens or gardens, so people had to buy hot food from take-aways, and string washing between the buildings. They threw their rubbish into the streets, making the city dirty and smelly. Water had to be collected from a public water trough. Only rich people had piped water in their homes.

Did rich Romans have feasts?

Rich Romans really enjoyed having friends round for a feast. They served dozens of tasty dishes such as oysters, stuffed dormice, roast peacock and boiled ostrich. The Romans did not sit on chairs to eat, instead they lounged on couches. They ate with their fingers or with a spoon. Some rich Romans were so greedy they tried every dish and, in order to make room for more, they made themselves sick. They even had a special room for people to be sick in. It was called the vomitorium!

Who fought for sport?

The Romans loved to go to the amphitheatre to watch violent shows, which they called 'games'. At the amphitheatre, gladiators fought each other, often to the death. Some gladiators had to fight wild animals, such as lions, with spears, flaming torches or even their bare hands.

Quick-fire Quiz

1. When did Rome become a republic?
a) 509BCE
b) 409BCE
c) 309BCE

2. Who ruled the republic?
a) The emperor
b) The Senate
c) The king

3. What was a gladiator?
a) A public bath
b) A country house
c) A fighter

4. Who brought up Romulus and Remus?
a) Rich ladies
b) A wolf
c) The consuls

Gladiator

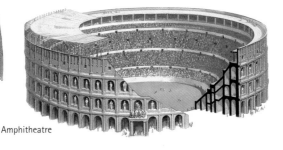

Amphitheatre

Where did Romans relax?

Most Romans went to the public baths to relax. These were more like leisure centres than places to wash. You could play games, read, chat to friends, work out in the gym or take a stroll in the gardens. You could even get your hair cut or have a massage.

The Roman Empire

The Roman republic ended in 27BCE, when Emperor Augustus set up a Roman empire. However, in CE395 the empire was split into two. The western part (based in Rome) fell to tribes the Romans called 'barbarians' in CE476. The eastern part, ruled from Constantinople (now Istanbul) lasted until CE1453.

Did the Romans build bridges?

The Romans were very clever builders and engineers. They built huge stone bridges called viaducts to carry roads, and aqueducts (stone channels to carry water) across valleys. They also built many fine cities, linking them with long, straight roads.

Which Roman leader was murdered?

Julius Caesar was a great general who made himself dictator (sole ruler) for life. Although he brought peace and passed good laws, the Senate thought he was too powerful. So on March 15, 44BCE, a group of them stabbed him to death.

Julius Caesar

What did the Romans trade?

Roman trade routes spread throughout Europe and into China and India. Their ships took many goods such as wine, olive oil and farm products as well as works of art to distant ports. They brought back exotic goods such as wild animals, ivory and silk.

Roman ship

Where did Roman soldiers live?

Soldiers on the move lived in leather tents. At other times, they lived in large forts with workshops, stables and hospitals. The men shared simple rooms, but the officers had houses.

How did Romans protect their cities?

In later times, the Romans needed to protect their cities from attack by the barbarian tribes that swept across Europe. They built thick walls around their towns and forts which could be defended easily by armed soldiers.

What did Roman soldiers wear?

Roman soldiers wore armour of metal strips joined together with straps, over a woollen tunic. They carried a shield to protect the lower body. On the move, they carried everything on their backs – weapons, tools and a kit bag.

Why was Rome so successful?

A well-organized, full-time army was the key to Rome's success. Highly trained soldiers were split into legions of 6,000 men made up of ten cohorts, and then into centuries of 100 men, under the command of a centurion (officer).

Who met in the catacombs?

Early Christians were persecuted by the Romans who thought they were plotting against the emperor. The Christians met in secret in the catacombs (underground burial chambers) beneath Rome. Many Christians were put to death in the arena to entertain the crowds. Some were made to fight unarmed against gladiators or lions. Emperor Constantine was converted to Christianity in CE313, and about 60 years later it became the empire's official religion.

How were soldiers like a tortoise?

When they attacked an enemy fort, Roman soldiers protected themselves by forming a 'testudo' (tortoise). They held their shields over their heads so that they overlapped.

Who attacked Rome with elephants?

In 218BCE, Hannibal, a military leader from Carthage in North Africa, led 10,000 soldiers and 38 elephants through Spain and across the Alps to attack Rome. Hannibal won three important victories but only 12 elephants survived.

Quick-fire Quiz

1. Who attacked Rome on elephants?
a) Augustus
b) Hannibal
c) Caesar

2. What was a centurion?
a) An officer
b) A politician
c) A senator

3. What does an aqueduct carry?
a) Oil
b) Wine
c) Water

4. What are catacombs?
a) High-rise flats
b) Public baths
c) Burial chambers

The Mayan Empire

The Maya Indians built a vast empire that covered parts of Mexico, Guatemala and Honduras in the jungles of Central America. It reached its peak from CE300–800 but, over the next 200 years, it collapsed and was taken over by the Toltecs.

What clothes did Mayans wear?

Mayan men wore simple loin cloths. If it was cold they also wore a cloak called a 'manta'. Men dressed up in elaborate headdresses decorated with quetzal or macaw feathers. The more important the person, the bigger his hat! Women wore simple smock-like dresses.

God-king   Noble   Warrior   Priest

What were Mayan cities like?

The Maya were the first people in America to build big cities. These cities, which lay deep in the jungle, were full of grand pyramids, temples and palaces built of local limestone. The walls were covered with plaster and sometimes painted red. This colour was especially important to the Maya, for religious reasons. Walls were sometimes decorated with paintings of gods and hieroglyphs.

Who ruled the Maya?

Every Mayan city-state had its own royal family. They were ruled by a warrior god-king who led his people into battle. Next in importance were nobles, warriors and priests. Then came craftsmen and merchants, and last were peasants and labourers. The Maya worshipped the jaguar and noble Mayan warriors wore jaguar skins and headdresses. They thought that this would help to make them as fierce and brave in battle as a jaguar.

Did the Maya build pyramids?

The Maya built huge, stone-stepped pyramids with temples and an observatory at the top. The Castillo, the main pyramid in the Mayan city of Chichen Itza, has four stairways, each with 91 steps. These, together with the step at the temple entrance, add up to 365 – the number of days in a year.

Did Mayans study the stars?

The Maya were expert astronomers and studied the moon, stars and planets. They were also skilled mathematicians, and had a complicated calendar for counting the days and years. They used their knowledge to predict special events such as an eclipse.

Could Mayans read and write?

The Maya wrote in hieroglyphs (picture writing). They carved important inscriptions on huge stone monuments called stelae. They also wrote detailed accounts of important events in books made of bark or on animal skins. When the Spanish conquered the area in the early 1500s, they burned most of these books.

Did the Maya play ball?

The Maya played a religious ball game called Pok-a-tok. The players, who were bandaged to prevent injury, bounced a solid rubber ball to each other using their elbows, hips and thighs. The game was won by the first team to hit the ball through a stone ring mounted on the wall.

What gods did they worship?

The Mayans had over 150 gods. The most important was the sun god, who went down into the Underworld at sunset and became the jaguar god. They sometimes sacrificed captured enemies to their gods.

159

Timeline

Key dates in the development of ancient civilizations are recorded here – from the first cave paintings, through the creation and establishment of great empires to the sacking of Rome by the Vandals.

25,000BCE to 2000BCE

c.25,000BCE Stone Age people painted cave walls
c.10,000–9000BCE Start of agriculture in Near East
8000–7000BCE First permanent houses built; walled cities developed in Near East and Turkey
6000–5000BCE Looms used for weaving in Near East
5000BCE People began farming in Nile Valley in Egypt
4000–3000BCE Sumerian civilization in Mesopotamia; invented cuneiform writing; used ploughs and wheel
3372BCE First date in Mayan calendar
3000BCE Lower and Upper Egypt united under a single pharaoh
3000BCE Troy flourished as a city-state in Anatolia
c.2800BCE Stonehenge built in England
2800–2400BCE City-states of Sumer at their most powerful
2500BCE Rise of Indus Valley people
2700–2200BCE Old Kingdom in Egypt; first step pyramids built
2690BCE Huang Ti (Yellow emperor) ruled in China; according to legend, silk was discovered by his wife Hsi-Ling Shi
2600BCE Sphinx and Great Pyramids built in Egypt
2500BCE First European civilization, the Minoans, grew up on Greek island of Crete
2360BCE Arabians migrated to Mesopotamia and set up Babylonian and Assyrian kingdoms

2250BCE Hsai dynasty in power in China
2050BCE Start of Middle Kingdom of Egypt
2000BCE Hittites arrived in Anatolia (now Turkey)
2000BCE Mycenaeans invaded Greece

1999BCE to 1000BCE

1925BCE Hittites conquered Babylon
1830BCE First dynasty of Babylonian empire founded
1814–1782BCE Assyria extended empire
1792–1750BCE Hammurabi the Great ruled Babylon; empire declined after his death
1760BCE Shang dynasty founded in China
1750–1500BCE Hittites spread throughout area; invaded Syria

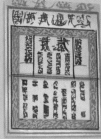

1650–1450BCE Mycenaean power centred on Mycenae and Pylos
1550–1050BCE New Kingdom in Egypt; Valley of Kings used for pharaohs' tombs
1500–1166BCE Egypt at peak of power
1500BCE Aryans invaded Indus Valley
c.1500BCE Mayans farm land in Central America; developed a calendar and writing
1450BCE Minoan civilization collapsed and Mycenaeans took over
1350–1250BCE Assyrian empire extends
1200BCE Trojan Wars: Mycenaeans invaded and destroyed Troy in Anatolia
1200BCE Hittites' empire collapsed after invasion of Phoenicians; Phoenicians became the world's most powerful sea traders
1150BCE Israelites arrived in Canaan
c.1122BCE Zhou dynasty in China came to power after defeating armies of Shang dynasty
1100BCE Mycenaean civilization collapsed
1050BCE Phoenicians developed alphabet (basis for all modern alphabets)
c.1000BCE Dorians invaded Greece; start of Dark Ages
c.1000BCE Kingdom of Kush in Africa began
1000BCE Israel ruled by King David

999BCE to 500BCE

900–625BCE Assyria and Babylon at war
900–700BCE Etruscans flourished in upper Italy
c.814BCE Carthage founded
800BCE Greek poet Homer wrote about Trojan Wars and Greek legends
800BCE Olmecs in Mexico built temples
753BCE Traditional date for founding of Rome
750–600BCE Celts appeared in Central Europe and spread throughout western Europe
c.750–682BCE Kingdom of Kush defeated Egypt; Nubians rule over Egypt
729BCE Assyrians ruled Babylon
700BCE Assyrians took over Phoenicia and Israel
700–500BCE Rise of Athens and other Greek city-states
689BCE Assyrians destroyed Babylon
671–664BCE Assyrians ruled Egypt
668–627BCE Assurbanipal increased power of Assyria
609BCE Assyrian empire ended
605–562BCE Nebuchadnezzar rebuilt Babylon
c.600BCE Zoroaster reforms the ancient Persian religion
590BCE Babylonians took over Jerusalem
c.550BCE Persian empire became powerful
551BCE Confucius was born in China
539BCE Persians took over Babylon and Phoenicia
525–404BCE Persians ruled Egypt
509BCE Roman kings replaced by Roman republic
508BCE Athens became a democracy
500BCE Italian Etruscan empire very powerful

499BCE to CE1

490–480BCE Persian wars between Greeks and Persians; Greeks defeated Persians in 479BCE
c.477–405BCE Golden Age of Athens
463–221BCE Time of warring states in China
450–400BCE Etruscan empire declined
431–404BCE Peloponnesian wars between Athens and Sparta; Sparta won in 404BCE
390BCE Celts attacked Rome
338BCE Philip of Macedonia conquered Greece

336BCE Alexander the Great became king of Macedonia and Greece
333–323BCE Alexander the Great conquered Phoenicia, Egypt, Persia and parts of India
321–184BCE Mauryan empire founded in India
300BCE Mayans started to build stone cities
275BCE Romans took over all Italy
265BCE Romans started to conquer Europe
264–146BCE Carthage at war with Rome (Punic Wars)
250BCE Celtic tribes at peak of power
221BCE Emperor Qin united China in first dynasty
206BCE–CE220 Han dynasty in China
218BCE Hannibal invaded Rome on elephants
202BCE Hannibal defeated by Romans
146BCE Carthage defeated; North Africa became part of Roman empire
55BCE Julius Caesar invaded Britain but had to retreat
52BCE Caesar conquered Celtic Gaul (France)
45BCE Caesar became dictator of Rome
44BCE Caesar assassinated
30BCE Egypt taken over by the Romans
27BCE Octavian becomes first Roman emperor, Augustus

CE1 to CE800

CE43 Romans conquered Britain
CE61 Celtic Queen Boudicca led revolt against Romans in Britain
CE64 Rome destroyed by fire
CE79 Mount Vesuvius erupted covering Pompeii (Roman city) in ash
c.CE150 Roman empire most powerful
CE250 European barbarian tribes attacked Rome
CE284 Roman empire split into east and west
CE268 Goths sacked Athens and Sparta
CE330 Constantinople (now Istanbul) became capital of eastern Roman empire
CE300–700 Mayan civilization at height
CE406 Tribe called Vandals overran Gaul
CE410 Rome sacked by Visigoths; Romans left Britain
CE455 Rome sacked by Vandals
CE476 Last western Roman emperor deposed; eastern empire continued until CE1453 as Byzantine empire
CE800 Mayan cities abandoned; civilization collapsed; Toltecs took over

Web Addresses

www.bbc.co.uk/history/forkids

This history website, aimed at children between 7 and 9, offers lots of games, videos, animations and activities. It covers various topics, including the Romans, Ancient Greeks and the Vikings.

www.cultures.com

Devoted to living and ancient cultures, this site also features the *Illustrated Encyclopedia of Greek Mythology* and the *Illustrated Encyclopedia of MesoAmerican Cultures.*

www.pbs.org/nova/pyramid/explore

The American television and news pbs website also offers information on the Vikings, the Roman Empire and the Greeks.

www.bbc.co.uk/history/topics

This site covers a multitude of topics including the Egyptians, Romans and the Greeks.

www.historychannel.com

This site offers a variety of topics related to ancient civilizations.

www.thebritishmuseum.ac.uk

Explore the museum's collection of artefacts belonging to other cultures, ancient and modern, in Africa, the Americas, Asia, Britain, Europe, Greece, Japan, the Near East, Pacific Rim and Ancient Rome.

www.louvre.fr/louvre.htm

Investigate the Louvre's fine collection of artefacts from Egypt, Greece and Rome.

www.eduweb.com

Play fun, educational web adventures on this site.

www.thinkquest.org/library/index.html

This library of over 5,500 entries has been created by teachers and pupils worldwide. To see what's available on ancient civilizations check out Rome, Egypt, Greece, Incas and Mayans.

www.civilization.ca/civil/egypt/egypte.html

This is a clearly written informative site on Egyptian civilization – with links to lots of relevant topics such as religion, archaeology and architecture.

touregypt.net/kids

This is a kids' site featuring the history of Egypt, an ABC of Egypt, Egyptian colouring book and galleries of childrens' Egypt-inspired drawings and paintings.

www.historyforkids.org

This site covers many eras of history. Either search the site or click on an icon to find information on an ancient civilization.

members.aol.com/donnclass/Chinalife.html

A fun site about daily life in ancient China, which includes a 'cheat sheet' summary of 11,000 years of Chinese history.

www.andes.org

A cultural site featuring songs, dances, jokes and pictures of the Andean people living in the Cusco region in Peru.

www.ancientsites.com

Site for all history lovers. Most of it is free, although it does include extended features that are available on subscription.

www.civilization.ca/civil/maya/mminteng.html

Lots of historical and social information about Mayan culture.

Quick-fire Quiz ANSWERS

1000
QUESTIONS
& ANSWERS
FACTFILE
KNIGHTS
AND CASTLES

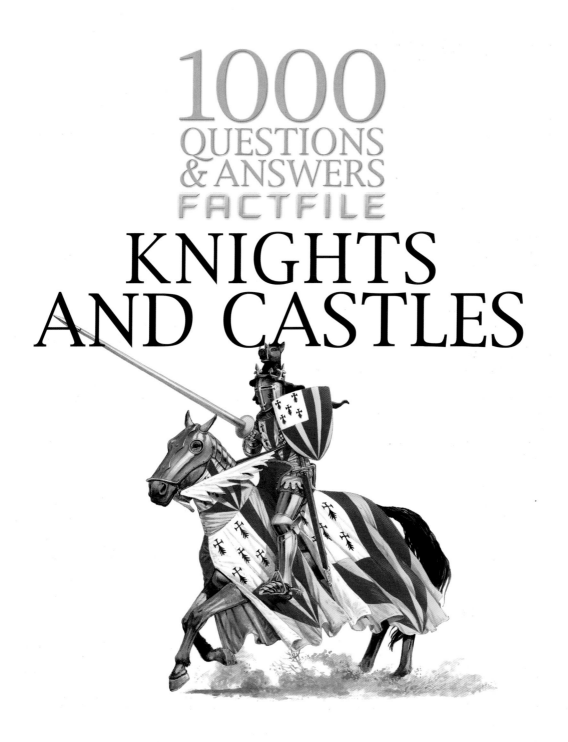

Contents

First Knights

The king

Knights were noblemen who fought on horseback and often lived in castles. This lifestyle began in the early Middle Ages (see page 200) in France, and spread across Europe. Knights were successful because they were part of a system that helped kings win wars and govern their kingdoms. It was known as the feudal system.

Roman cavalryman

Goth horseman

How did the feudal system work?

In a country with the feudal system, the king owned all the land, but he distributed some of the land to his lords – who were knights. This 'gift' provided a knight with an income, but in return he had to fight for the king and help run the kingdom. In turn, the knight allowed peasants to make a living from his land as long as they also worked for him.

Who were the first knights?

Knights and feudalism arrived when Charlemagne (right) created his empire in the ninth century. Earlier, the Romans had used mounted soldiers, but their role in battle was limited. Some of the European peoples ruled by the Romans, such as the Celts and Goths, were good horsemen and fought on horseback. But they had no feudal system and so were not true knights.

Who was Charlemagne?

Charlemagne was the king of the Franks, a people who occupied France and western Germany. From his base at Aachen, he built up a huge empire. He set up local lords as governors of each area, giving them land in return for service – creating an early feudal system. In the year 800, he was given the title of Roman emperor, although the true Roman empire had fallen 300 years earlier.

Why were the Normans so powerful?

The Normans (left) were people who originally came from Scandinavia and settled in northwestern France. They were good builders and erected many strong castles. Like their Viking ancestors, they were skilled soldiers, sailors and boat-builders. Unlike the Vikings, they also had a feudal system. All these factors helped them to create a kingdom in France and England and to rule it effectively. The Normans also carved out dominions in southern Italy and the Middle East.

What were mottes and baileys?

Mottes and baileys were the first true castles. When the Normans conquered England they needed castles quickly as bases for their lords. They made an earth mound, called a motte, and built a wooden tower on top as a stronghold. Next to this they fenced off a yard, called a bailey, where they built a hall, stables, a chapel and other buildings. A ditch or moat surrounded the castle.

Motte

Bailey

How could you tell a high-ranking Norman?

A high-ranking Norman (above) rode a horse, carried a kite-shaped shield and wore mail armour. He wielded a sword and lance, and on his lance he tied a small flag, called a pennon, which showed he was a noble.

Were wooden castles weak?

Wooden castles were well protected by their earth mounds and moats, but they were easy to knock down or to attack with fire. Most of them were eventually replaced by stronger stone buildings.

Building a Castle

Skilled craftsmen were needed to build a castle, including masons to work stone, carpenters to build floors and roofs and metalworkers to make bars and fastenings for doors. The master mason, who designed the castle, supervised all these activities, and made sure the building was extremely strong.

How quickly could you build a castle?

The Normans could put up a wooden castle in a few days, but a big stone castle (right) could take years to construct. Castle builders had no modern tools. They had to rely on simple aids like treadmills for lifting heavy loads, together with wooden scaffolding and ladders to reach to the tops of high walls.

How did stone masons cut large blocks of stone?

Stone masons (above) used large, two-man saws to cut stone roughly. They then marked the stone with dividers and set-squares before shaping it more precisely with chisels. They did as much work as they could at the quarry in order to save time and energy. By removing all the unwanted stone, the masons did not have to cart too much extra weight to the building site.

Why do the stairs wind up to the right?

With the stairs going this way, a right-handed defender could easily use his weapon. The attacker coming up the stairs found it harder to swing his sword.

How did they build the walls?

Castle builders liked to use neat, rectangular stone blocks for the walls – if they could get them – shaped with a mallet and chisel. These would be bonded together tightly with cement (right) so that an attacker would find it difficult to break them down. Laid carefully, these blocks could even be used for the curves needed for round castle towers. For extra strength, rubble and cement were packed into the main walls (see page 171).

(see page 171)

How did workers lift large stones into position?

Carrying heavy lumps of stone up to the castle battlements was hard work. Masons used a rope and pulley, which they linked to a simple wooden winch (left), to haul up the stone. At the end of the rope they could attach either a basket for small stones, or a pair of pincer-like metal grabbers, for a larger block.

Why did they turn timber?

Carpenters used a tool called a lathe to make rounded items like posts. Powered by a long, springy pole (right), the lathe could spin a piece of wood at speed. The carpenter held his chisel on the wood, removing the corners and giving it a round shape. This process was called turning.

How were planks cut from massive tree trunks?

Medieval carpenters used a pit and a long, two-handled saw (above) to cut right along the length of a tree trunk. One man stood inside the pit, pulling the saw downwards, while the other held the top end of the saw, guiding it carefully along. Once they had begun to saw away, the workers drove wooden wedges into the gap to keep the cut open. One large trunk could make several planks.

169

Castle Designs

Castle builders tried all sorts of different designs to make their buildings stronger. One of the simplest was the square stone tower, or keep. But a keep was not enough on its own and was usually surrounded by extra walls. Later, builders added towers, gatehouses and more walls.

Why were some towers round?

Round towers were stronger than square towers, because they did not have weak corners. In addition, defenders could fire arrows in many different directions from a round tower, giving them more chance of hitting their enemies. Not all towers were round, but their importance for defence made them increasingly popular.

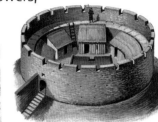

What was a shell keep?

A shell keep was a circular stone wall on top of an earth mound. Many of these were built on the site of old motte and bailey castles. Around the inside of a shell keep was a wall walk, where defenders could stand to shoot through the battlements. Below this were structures such as the hall set against the outer wall.

Why have extra sets of walls?

Early castles had just one set of walls. This made it fairly easy for an attacker to break inside, so builders began adding extra sets of walls (right). This slowed attackers down. It also meant that defenders could trap their enemies between two walls, making them sitting targets for defending archers.

Where was the castle strongest?

In early castles, the stronghold was usually the keep. But when keeps went out of fashion, the gatehouse (above) became the strongest part. Gatehouses had thick walls, twin towers, and one or more strong gates, called portcullises (see page 189). Outside the main walls, lords sometimes built a barbican, a strong outer courtyard that an enemy would have to take before attacking the main castle.

Outer bailey

Ditch

Wooden hoardings

How thick were the walls?

Stone castle walls could be several metres thick. The thicker they were, the harder they were for attackers to knock down. If they were really thick, enemies might not even bother to attack them. Sometimes, a castle wall was actually made up of two parallel walls. The gap between them could be filled with rubble for extra strength.

What was a concentric castle?

A concentric castle was a castle with two parallel sets of walls, one inside the other. As well as giving an enemy two barriers to get through, these twin walls provided defenders with two firing platforms. The outer wall was often lower than the one on the inside, so that one group of defending archers could fire safely over the heads of the others.

Battlements

Chateau Gaillard (begun 1196)

Keep

Inner wall

Inner bailey

Round tower

Outer wall

Quick-fire Quiz

1. Where did archers stand in a shell keep?
   a) In the courtyard
   b) On the wall walk
   c) On the catwalk

2. Why did archers like round towers?
   a) They gave more lines of fire
   b) They were warm
   c) They were spacious

3. What was a portcullis?
   a) A type of tower
   b) A strong gate
   c) A thick wall

4. What were extra walls for?
   a) To accommodate more soldiers
   b) To prevent mining
   c) For defence

Parts of the Castle

A castle had one or more courtyards, with main rooms in buildings along the insides of the courtyard walls. Near the great hall, where everyone ate, were the pantry and kitchen. Stables, workshops and extra living rooms were located in wall towers or in buildings separate from the great hall.

Where were the stables?

Stables were usually built in one of the castle courtyards. Like many buildings inside the walls, they could be large but were often built of timber. Near the stables was a workshop for the farrier, the craftsman who made and fitted horseshoes.

What was in a keep?

As the keep was one of the strongest parts of the castle, everything of value was kept in its basement. The lord's hall was above this, with the family's private rooms on the upper floor. Further floors were used by members of the lord's household.

Were dungeons really prisons?

The basement rooms in castle towers, now called dungeons, were storerooms, not prisons. Weapons, equipment and food would be kept here. Prisons were rare in the Middle Ages and the only people held prisoner for long periods were nobles captured in battle. These people could then be set free in return for money (right) from their families.

Where was the bathroom?

Castles did not have bathrooms like those in modern houses! When people washed they used a bowl of water. For toilets there were garderobes. A garderobe consisted of a wooden seat above a stone drain which emptied through the castle wall directly into the moat. Garderobes were smelly and must have been cold, as the drain usually led straight out into the open air.

How was the food cooked?

Castles had no modern kitchen appliances, so most food was cooked over the fire (left). The cook roasted meat on a spit, which could be turned with a handle so that the food was cooked all round. Other foods were boiled in a large iron pot over the flames. Castle kitchens also had ovens for baking the bread that everyone ate with their meals.

How were wall towers used?

Wall towers (left) were used in all kinds of ways. Guards could get the best view of the surrounding country from the top of the stair turret, and could fire at an enemy from the battlements around the roof. In the rooms below, there were more windows to shoot out from. In peacetime, these rooms, which often had fireplaces, provided accommodation for the soldiers or members of the lord's family.

Did castles have gardens?

Many castles had gardens where vegetables and herbs were grown for cooking. In the later Middle Ages, when castles became more luxurious, some even had ornamental gardens. Here the flowers, herbs, shrubs and trees were arranged in neat patterns.

Quick-fire Quiz

1. What was in the keep basement?
a) The hall
b) The storeroom
c) The kitchen

2. What did a farrier make?
a) Castles
b) Horseshoes
c) Bread

3. When might you be imprisoned?
a) For a minor crime
b) For a serious crime
c) For ransom

4. Why were garderobes cold?
a) They were used only in winter
b) They drained into the open air
c) They had large windows

Castle Life

During peacetime, the lord and his followers collected rent from tenants and made sure the castle was in good repair. Knights went hunting to bring extra food for the table. Women and girls spun wool, cooked, and mended clothes. In the evening, everyone came together for a meal in the great hall.

Where did everyone sleep?

Medieval castles had no bedrooms. The lord and his family usually slept in the solar (right), a private room next to the hall. Most of the rest of the household slept in the hall itself. After the evening meal, they took down the tables and leaned them against the wall, and put straw-filled mattresses on the floor. Others slept where they worked. Cooks, for example, slept in the kitchen.

What was on the menu?

People ate whatever farmers could provide – plus what could be hunted. If food was plentiful, the diet included meat such as venison and boar together with beef, pork and mutton from the farm. Bread and vegetables were served with the meat, often on a *trencher* – a dinner plate of firm bread. This was washed down with ale or wine (right). In lean times, people ate meat preserved with salt and flavoured with herbs to hide the salty taste.

Trencher

What sort of music entertained the guests?

Minstrels (right) played instruments and sang songs. The fiddle was popular but after the crusades, many minstrels took up an Arab instrument, the lute. In Wales, musicians played the harp, while the harp-like psaltery was played all over Europe.

Did women have rights?

Medieval women had few rights. Few were educated and most had to endure a life of household chores. If a woman had property, it passed to her husband when she died. For the lady of the manor, things could be different. She helped run the manor if her husband was away, and might even have to defend the castle.

Who was the boss?

The lord was the boss, and everyone had to obey him. His power covered almost every aspect of life, from how his land should be farmed to who rode into battle with him. The only area that the lord did not control was religion, when his power was second to that of the local bishop and clergy.

Who helped the lord?

A host of servants, from the steward to the reeve, helped run the lord's manor (see page 192). Others performed menial duties in the castle (above). Pages served at the lord's table while grooms looked after his horses. He might have a clerk – who could also be the chaplain – to keep records and write letters. But the lord's constant companion and most important personal servant was his squire (see pages 176–177).

Quick-fire Quiz

1. What was used to take away the saltiness of meat?
a) Dairy products
b) Herbs
c) Wines

2. Which musical instrument came the Arab world?
a) Lute
b) Fiddle
c) Drum

3. How did people prevent draughts?
a) By building fires
b) By fitting carpets
c) By using tapestries

4. What were mattresses filled with?
a) Straw
b) Cotton
c) Springs

How did people keep warm?

Compared with houses today, castles and manor houses were cold and draughty, even when heated with blazing log fires. To keep down the draughts, the lords lined their walls with tapestries. People wore several layers of thick woollen clothing in the winter, and the rich added garments trimmed with fur (right) when the weather was really cold.

Becoming a Knight

To become a knight, a young man had to belong to a noble family. As a boy, he began his training as a page and learned how to behave in a noble household. As a teenager, he became a squire – learning knightly conduct and how to handle weapons and horses. Finally, in a ceremony known as dubbing, he became a knight.

Serving at table

Practising with a lance

How did you become a page?

If you were the son of a noble family, you did not go to school. Instead, when you were about seven years old, you were sent away to be a page in the household of another lord. Here you learned good manners and such skills as carrying food to the table (right), and serving your lord and lady.

What did a squire do?

A squire was a knight's personal servant and helper. His duties included looking after all the weapons and tending the horses. Before a battle the squire helped his master put on armour. He may even have had to fight beside his lord, providing aid if the knight was wounded. By doing all these things, a squire learned how to behave as a knight.

Did knights pray?

In the Middle Ages, religion played a big part in most people's lives. When a squire was to be made a knight, he often spent the whole night before the dubbing ceremony at prayer in the castle chapel (left). This vigil was a sign that he would take his vows seriously to serve his king faithfully for the rest of his life.

How did squires practise sword play?

For practice, knights and squires often used a sword and a small round shield called a buckler. To build up strength, squires were sometimes given swords that were heavier than those actually used in battle. Pages or young squires might even be given wooden swords with which to practise.

Exercising

Helping the knight

Practising swordplay

Dubbing

Quick-fire Quiz

1. At what age did a boy become a page?
a) At about 4
b) At about 7
c) At about 17

2. Why could being a squire be dangerous?
a) Lords were cruel
b) You may have had to fight in battle
c) You had no shield

3. What was a tiny round shield called?
a) A buckler
b) A helm
c) A hand shield

4. What was used to dub a knight?
a) A shield
b) A lance
c) A sword

How did squires exercise muscles?

Squires kept fit by practising sword play, wrestling, throwing the javelin, and all sorts of other sporting activities. They made sure that they were fit in case they had to go into battle.

Were knights and squires well mannered?

Knights and squires were supposed to behave with good manners. They were meant to be considerate to women and courteous to all. But they did not always live up to this ideal. Sometimes squires got together in rowdy gangs and went around causing mischief. On one occasion they even burned down part of a town.

What was dubbing?

Dubbing was the ceremony at which a squire was made into a knight. The squire kneeled in front of his lord or the king, who tapped him on the shoulder with his sword. The new knight was then presented with a sword and spurs. There was often a celebration afterwards.

Heraldry

In the Middle Ages every noble family had a coat of arms that acted as its badge. A knight wore his coat of arms into battle and when competing in a tournament so that he could be easily recognized. Coats of arms were always designed in a similar way, using the same range of colours and basic patterns.

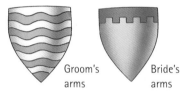

Groom's arms

Bride's arms

Combined coat of arms

How was a coat of arms designed?

The herald chose the colours, shapes and other designs that were suitable for the family who were to bear the arms. He made sure that the design was different to all others – every coat of arms had to be unique. When two noble families were united by marriage, the couple could have their two coats of arms combined (above), with the bride's and groom's arms on opposite sides of the shield.

What did heraldic symbols mean?

Many of the symbols used in heraldry have special meanings. Designs such as the diagonal bar (left) showed that the bearer's parents were not married. This was important in the Middle Ages as an illegitimate son would not be able to inherit his father's title or lands.

What were a herald's duties?

A herald was an officer in the household of the king or great lord. As well as designing coats of arms (above), it was his job to organize ceremonies and tournaments. In war, the herald carried messages between opposing armies (left). Therefore, it was essential that he could recognize every coat of arms, and so deliver the message to the right person.

How could you recognize an eldest son?

An eldest son used his father's coat of arms but with an added element. While the father was alive, the son's coat of arms were marked with a symbol called a label. The label ran across the shoulders and looked like a horizontal line with three thicker downward-pointing lines joined to it. When the father died, the eldest son removed the label.

How were knights identified on the battlefield?

A knight's shield and his surcoat – a loose robe worn over the armour – were decorated with his coat of arms. This made it easy to see who was who in the confusion of battle. Heralds also used coats of arms to identify casualties after the battle (below).

Quick-fire Quiz

1. Which of these was a herald's job?
   a) Carrying messages
   b) Fighting
   c) Looking after the horses

2. Where were the supporters placed?
   a) Above the shield
   b) Below the shield
   c) On either side of the shield

3. What was red called in heraldry?
   a) Or
   b) Scarlet
   c) Gules

4. What mark denoted an eldest son?
   a) Bar
   b) Label
   c) Chevron

What was the language of heraldry?

Coats of arms were described in a special language based on Old French. Each of the colours has its own name in this language, for example red was called gules and black was referred to as sable. Experts on heraldry still use this language to describe coats of arms today.

What were supporters?

The supporters were a pair of figures that stood either side of the shield in a coat of arms, as if they were holding it up. These figures were often animals and could be real beasts, such as lions or antelopes, or mythical ones, such as unicorns or griffons. Supporters were not normally shown on a knight's surcoat, but were included in the full coat of arms.

179

Horsemanship

Destrier was the usual name for a warhorse. Destriers were large, powerful stallions that could carry their owners swiftly into battle. The best and costliest destriers were said to come from southern Europe, especially from Italy and Spain. The name destrier comes from the Latin word for right, perhaps because the horse led with its right leg, swerving away from an opponent in battle.

Whether fighting, hunting or travelling, a knight spent much of his time on horseback. A horse was the knight's most valued possession. As a page or squire, he was shown how to ride and how to care for his mount. As he got older, he learned how to fight on horseback using a sword and lance so that he could fight for his king and take part in tournaments.

How many horses did a knight own?

Most knights had several horses, which were used for different tasks. A knight would have one or two warhorses (destriers) together with a powerful horse for hunting (a courser) and perhaps another animal for travelling. Knights also kept packhorses in their stables. These were used to carry luggage when the knight and his household were travelling or when items had to be sent across country.

How could you stop a horse in its tracks?

If footsoldiers were going into battle against mounted knights, they might scatter fearsome looking spiked objects called caltrops on the ground. A caltrop had four metal spikes, and these were arranged so that whichever way the caltrop landed, one spike pointed upwards. A caltrop could injure a horse that stepped on it.

Caltrop

How did a knight control his horse?

A knight controlled his horse with both his feet and his hands. He placed his feet in a pair of stirrups, and used them to grip his mount. This meant that the knight's hands were free to hold the reins or wield a sword or lance. The leather reins were connected to a bit that was placed in the horse's mouth. By changing the tension of the reins, the knight could make his horse speed up (right), slow down or turn a corner.

Stirrup

Were spurs cruel?

A good rider would use his spurs only sparingly, for example when urging his horse to give an extra turn of speed. Even so, a jab from the single long metal spike of a prick spur must have hurt; rowel spurs, with their rings of shorter spikes, did less damage.

Rowel spur

Armoured horse

How could a knight protect his horse?

Some knights had armour made for their warhorses because it was just as dangerous for a horse in battle as it was for the animal's rider. Horse armour was usually made up of a shaffron, or head-piece, and a crinet, a series of metal plates that covered the neck. Because plate armour was expensive, the rest of the horse sometimes went unprotected into battle.

Weapons and Fighting

The most feared sight on a medieval battlefield was a line of enemy knights charging directly at you. Well armoured, mounted on warhorses and wielding weapons that they had spent years training to use, knights were fast, powerful and difficult to stop. A knight's favourite weapon was the sword, which could be used either on foot or from a horse, but he was adept with other weapons.

What was a double-edged sword used for?

A two-edged sword was used for cutting and slashing blows. This type of weapon was very effective against an enemy who was not wearing armour, especially if it was a 'great sword' with a large grip that the knight could hold in both hands. He could then use all his strength to deliver powerful, cutting blows.

Mace

Shield

Sword

Dagger

Crossbow

Battle-axe   Arrows

Longbow

How did the Normans use their shields?

Norman soldiers held their large, kite-shaped shields in front of them to give plenty of protection. If a group of men were fighting in a row, they moved their shields together (below), to form a wall that archers or even mounted warriors found difficult to break through.

Did knights use only swords and daggers?

In addition to the sword, the knight used several other hand weapons (above and right) including the battle-axe and the mace. The mace was especially fearsome because its raised metal ridges or spikes concentrated the power of the blow, knocking the enemy sideways.

How did you use a flail?

A flail consisted of a wooden handle linked by a chain to a spiked metal ball. A knight normally used the flail when fighting on foot. He aimed to strike at an enemy's head, knocking him out or piercing his armour.

How could you injure someone who was wearing mail?

To do serious injury to an opponent in mail, a knight needed a sword or dagger with a narrow, sharp point, to get through one of the gaps between the metal rings. Archers (right) also found that they could pierce mail by using narrow metal heads on their arrows.

When was a lance used?

A lance was a long, heavy weapon like a pole, which was most effective at the start of a battle. Wielded by mounted knights charging at speed, it could kill a man with a single thrust. After the charge, the knight discarded the lance and drew his sword – a better weapon for close-quarters fighting.

How were swords made stronger?

Armourers gave blades extra strength by altering their shape. A blade with a cross-section like an elongated diamond was the strongest. Both cutting and stabbing swords (below) were made with blades in this shape.

Quick-fire Quiz

1. How did you hold a great sword?
a) Close to the chest
b) With one hand
c) With two hands

2 Which blade shape gave greatest strength?
a) Diamond
b) Rounded
c) Hollow

3. What did a weapon need to pierce mail?
a) A narrow point
b) Extra power
c) Plenty of weight

4. Where was a knight most likely to use a flail?
a) On horseback
b) On foot
c) In a boat

Armour

Every knight wanted to go into battle well protected. In the early Middle Ages, knights wore mail, but armour made up of metal plates became more popular. Knights liked plate armour because it protected them well from arrows and sword blows, while allowing them to move with great freedom. But only a rich man could afford a full suit of plate armour.

What did the armourer do?

Armourers (below) were skilled craftsmen who made both armour and weapons and could beat pieces of metal into sturdy breastplates or helmets. They did this by hammering a sheet of metal on an anvil or on a rounded object called a former. This gave the piece the right curve. Suits of armour often came back damaged from battle, so armourers also spent a lot of time on repairs.

How could you 'knit' with metal?

By making mail! Mail, or chain mail as it is sometimes called, was a form of armour made up of thousands of tiny linked metal rings. By varying the number of rings in a row, the armourer could shape mail into garments such as shirts, head-coverings, leg-guards and even mittens. Mail was popular until plate armour became fashionable in the late thirteenth century.

Single ring

Linked mail

Conical helmet

Basinet

Great helm (jousting)

Frog-mouthed (jousting)

Barbute

Why were there so many types of helmet?

Fashions in helmets changed just like fashions in clothes. Late fourteenth-century knights often wore the basinet, a helmet with a pointed visor and a collar of mail, which offered excellent protection. By the mid-fifteenth century, they were wearing lighter helmets, called barbutes. For jousts and tournaments, a rich knight might wear a highly decorated great helm.

What did a knight wear under his armour?

Under his armour a knight wore a padded jacket called an arming doublet. The doublet had sections of mail sewn under the arms and in other places to protect areas where there were gaps between the plates.

Helmet

Bevor

Breastplate

Was plate armour heavy?

Plate armour was the strongest armour of all. It looks very heavy, but a full suit weighed little more than 20 kilograms. This compared well with mail, because a mail shirt alone could weigh 14 kilograms, and when a helmet and mail leg-guards were added, the suit could weigh more than a suit of plates. A knight in plate armour could move about or mount a horse with ease.

Plate armour

Pauldron

Besagew

Vambrace

Gauntlet

Tasset

How was plate armour attached to the body?

Some of the sections were tied to the leather thongs on the padded undergarment. The other pieces were attached with leather straps and buckles, which fitted around the knight's legs or waist.

A knight needed his squire to help with the tricky business of attaching all the plates.

Quick-fire Quiz

1. Which was the strongest armour?
a) Plate
b) Mail
c) Leather

2. What was an arming doublet?
a) A helmet
b) A padded jacket
c) A coat of mail

3. How were plate sections fixed together?
a) By welding
b) With chains
c) With leather thongs and rivets

4. A popular 14th century helmet was called a...?
a) Barbute
b) Basinet
c) Great helm

How could the plates move?

Many of the main sections of a suit of plate armour, such as the part protecting the arm, were made up of several smaller pieces of metal (below). These small pieces were joined together by flexible leather links or sliding rivets, so that they could move backwards and forwards. This gave the knight lots of freedom of movement as he walked, rode and fought.

Cuisse

Greave

Sabaton

Siege

When an enemy arrived in force to attack a castle, the castle's owner and his men pulled up the drawbridge and got ready for a siege. The siege could end peacefully, especially if the defenders ran out of food and were forced to surrender. But if there was a fight, the attackers could use all sorts of powerful weapons to force their way in.

How effective were archers?

The longbow was one of the medieval soldier's most awesome weapons. Its deadly arrows could fly some 300m and a skilled archer could fire up to 12 arrows per minute. Castle defenders were forced to hide behind the battlements to avoid the arrows' sharp metal points.

What were siege engines?

The devices used by medieval armies to attack castles were known as siege engines. These were fearsome weapons for hurling missiles at the enemy or knocking down walls. The trebuchet and mangonel were catapults powerful enough to fling rocks. The ballista, a giant crossbow, shot bolts that were often tipped with blazing rags. Weapons on wheeled platforms could be moved into position to find their target. Reloading very large devices was slow work, but their devastating power struck fear into the enemy.

How could an attacker get through walls?

One way was to batter down the walls using a ram, a huge tree trunk mounted on wheels. A group of men, protected by the ram's roof, pushed the weapon repeatedly at the walls. Alternatively, attackers could try wheeling a wooden siege tower up to the walls and climbing over. Both ram and tower were covered with animal skins to protect their wooden structures from flaming arrows.

Siege tower

Ram

What was mining and how was it done?

Mining was another way of bringing down castle walls. The miners dug a tunnel under the walls, holding everything up with wooden props. Once they had finished digging, they lit a fire in the tunnel. This set the props alight, so that the walls above no longer had anything to support them. If all went according to plan, a section of the castle walls collapsed and the attackers swarmed into the castle. If the defenders could see a mine being dug, they could retaliate by digging their own tunnel into the mine and fighting off the attackers.

Tunnel entrance far outside the walls

Miners set fire to wooden props

Workers bring wood for the fire

Removing vital foundation rocks

Trebuchet

How did a catapult work?

Catapults worked like giant slings to launch missiles. Trebuchets used counterweights; the mangonel's sling was held in place by ropes, which were then released. It took many men to reload the largest catapults.

187

Defence

Everything about a castle was designed to make it easy to defend. The walls were thick to withstand attacks from siege engines, while windows were small to keep out arrows. Battlements, towers and hoardings all gave good lines of fire.

What was a moat?

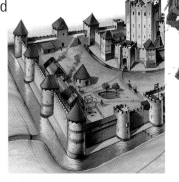

A moat was a barrier between the castle and its attackers. Many castles were surrounded by dry ditches, but a water-filled moat gave more protection. An attacker could walk across a dry ditch and start mining – digging holes under the walls to make them fall down. With a moat, it was virtually impossible for the enemy to undermine the castle walls.

What were murder holes?

Murder holes were small openings in the ceiling, usually within a castle gatehouse. They enabled defenders to look down on anyone passing through the gate below. If the person below was an enemy, the defender could shoot arrows or pour boiling liquid through one of the holes.

How was an embrasure used?

An embrasure was a hole in the wall where an archer could stand. The hole was splayed on the inside, so that the archer could stand to one side of the opening, out of reach of enemy fire. When the archer was ready to shoot, he moved quickly to the opening, fired his arrow, and then ducked back out of range.

How could you pour boiling oil on your enemies?

Castle defenders sometimes emptied boiling oil or water straight over the battlements on to their enemies below. Another method was to use the machicolations, which were holes in the floor right next to the battlements. Anything poured through these would land on an opponent who was attacking the base of the wall or trying to climb it.

How did you make a sortie?

To make a sortie (left), defenders left the safety of the castle and launched an attack on the besieging enemy. The defenders would burst out, trying to take their enemies by surprise before the walls of their stronghold were destroyed. A sortie would often target the powerful siege engines and their trained crews.

What were hoardings?

Wooden hoardings (right) were often built over the battlements to protect archers while providing them with a wide field of fire. Sometimes hoardings also had holes in the floor, for pouring boiling oil or firing at attackers directly below.

What was a portcullis?

A portcullis was a barred gate controlled by ropes and pulleys. It was closed by dropping it down from above. If a portcullis was dropped down on an enemy, he could be caught between its spiked bars (right).

The Crusades

In the late eleventh century, Christian rulers tried to take control of the Holy Land – the part of the Middle East where Jesus had lived. At that time, the Holy Land was ruled by the Muslims – followers of Islam – to whom the area was also sacred. It was the start of a bitter conflict – the Crusades.

Who went on the Crusades?

All sorts of people went on the Crusades. Some were kings, such as Richard I of England and Philip II of France. Others were nobles, and many were men-at-arms who went with their lords to the east. A large number of poor peasants also went on crusade, inspired by leaders such as the French monk Peter the Hermit.

Why did they go?

Many crusaders were men who genuinely believed that it was right to fight for control of the Christian sites in the Holy Land (right). But others went just for the adventure or because they thought that they could benefit themselves, either by looting after battles or by setting themselves up as lords in the east. Many of the latter were the younger sons of nobles, who would not inherit any of their parents' wealth back home.

What was the Children's Crusade?

In 1212, Nicholas, a 12-year-old boy from Cologne, Germany, led thousands of children across the Alps and into Italy on their way to the Holy Land. Another boy, Stephen, from France, led a further group of children. Both groups failed. Stephen and his followers were captured and sold as slaves, the followers of Nicholas died in Italy.

Who were the 'fighting monks'?

The fighting monks were groups of men who took religious vows but were still allowed to fight the Muslims. There were several groups, or orders, of fighting monks – the Knights Templar (named after their headquarters near the Temple in Jerusalem), the Knights of St John (famous for their work healing the sick), and the Teutonic Knights (who originally came from Germany).

What did the crusades achieve?

Although the crusaders set up states in the Middle East, these were soon reconquered. Only the ruins of their great castles, such as Krak des Chevaliers (below), survive. But they brought useful knowledge back to Europe as well as new medicines and eastern inventions such as the windmill.

Who was Saladin?

Saladin was a twelfth-century Muslim leader who ruled Egypt and part of Syria. He defended his lands from crusaders and defeated the Second Crusade. When the Third Crusade began, Saladin fought Richard I of England. Again Saladin was victorious, and greatly reduced the crusaders' power.

Saladin

How many Crusades were there?

There were eight separate Crusades from Europe to the Holy Land between the eleventh and thirteenth centuries. The most successful was the first (1096–99), which was led by a group of French and Norman barons. It ended with the capture of Jerusalem. In 1271, the last crusader territory in the Holy Land was lost to the Muslims.

Quick-fire Quiz

1. Which French king led a crusade?
a) Philip I
b) Philip II
c) Richard I

2. Who led the First Crusade?
a) French and Norman barons
b) Richard I
c) German lords

3. Which was the most successful crusade?
a) The fourth
b) The second
c) The first

4. What were the Knights of St John known for?
a) Healing the sick
b) Helping the poor
c) Fighting for St John

The Knight's Manor

A manor consisted of a lord's castle, church, houses for the peasants and farmland. The lord was the most important person. He was the landlord, boss and judge, and the peasants had to do what he told them. These peasants were known as serfs or villeins; they had no freedom.

Who looked after the money?

The person who kept the accounts on the manor was the steward (left). He had to be educated, although most accounting systems were primitive. Later, a group of merchants in Italy invented the system of 'double-entry' book-keeping, which is still used by accountants today. As well as looking after the money, the steward managed the lord's farm, and also acted as judge in the manorial court if the lord was away.

What did the bailiff do?

The bailiff was a peasant farmer who had his own land. As well as his own fields, he looked after the day-to-day running of the lord's personal land, making sure that all the jobs were done properly and at the right time. In addition, the bailiff was responsible for repairs and building work on the manor, bringing in any workers, such as stone masons or carpenters, to get these jobs done. He was second in importance to the steward.

What was life like for the workers?

Life was hard for peasants. Men spent nearly all their time working in the fields. Women had to cook, look after the house and make the family's clothes. For children there was no school. Boys helped in the fields while girls learned how to spin, sew and cook. Sunday and religious holidays were the only days off. For some, local markets (below) offered a welcome break from the hardships of daily life.

Who kept watch on the peasants?

The reeve (right) was the person who kept an eye on the peasants. He was a peasant himself, chosen by his peers, and he worked closely with the bailiff. He was most often seen out in the fields, making sure that everyone was working hard. But if any of the workers had a problem, the reeve could tell the bailiff, who would then decide what to do, or whether to report the matter to the lord.

Reeve

Who worked the lord's land?

The lord's land was divided into two sections. Most was allotted to the peasants who worked the land in return for services to the lord and a share of the produce. The rest of the lord's land was called the demesne. This was farmed by the lord with the help of the peasants, who owed him some of their labour each week.

Who dealt with criminals?

The lord held his own court in his hall for minor crimes. Punishments included whipping, beating, fines or being locked in the stocks. Serious offences were judged by the county sheriff and could be punished by death by hanging. The church had its own laws and courts (above) for dealing with law-breakers among the clergy.

What happened when people were ill?

Medieval medicine was basic. Some herbal medicines worked well, but other remedies, such as blood-letting, did no good. As a result, many people died of minor illnesses, and few lived beyond the age of 40. Life was especially hard for women, many of whom died in childbirth. The most feared illness was bubonic plague or the Black Death (right). It killed a third of the population of Europe in the mid-fourteenth century.

Quick-fire Quiz

1. Who was judge in the court when the lord was away?
a) The bailiff
b) The reeve
c) The steward

2. Who farmed the demesne?
a) The lord
b) The sheriff
c) The reeve

3. How many years did a peasant spend at school?
a) 10
b) 6
c) None

4. What caused so many women to die young?
a) Overwork
b) The Black Death
c) Childbirth

Peacetime Pursuits

In the Middle Ages, people had to make their own entertainment. Poor families filled their limited spare time with simple games and story-telling. For noble families, life was easier, but even knights had to mix some of their pleasure with work. Many liked to hunt, but the main reason for hunting was to provide food.

What was chivalry?

Chivalry was a code of conduct that all knights were meant to follow. A knight was expected to be considerate, especially towards women, and to treat enemies with respect. Many did not live up to this, but the Middle Ages are often known as the 'Age of Chivalry'.

What were the favourite games?

Peasant children usually played games, such as leapfrog and tag, that did not need any equipment, since ordinary families could not afford toys. Noble families had more money, and a knight's children were sometimes given toys, such as wooden swords and shields, or miniature models of men-at-arms.

What about pastimes for adults?

Some people liked to play board games, such as chess (above), which appealed to noblemen because chess is like a battle. Otherwise, knights and their ladies looked forward to visits from musicians and actors who arrived from time to time and performed in return for board and lodging.

How did a falconer exercise his birds?

Falconers trained their birds to hunt and bring back prey. One way to exercise a falcon was to let it hunt for animals as it would in the wild. An alternative was to use a lure – a dummy bird on the end of a long string. The falconer twirled the lure around in the air, encouraging the bird to pounce on to it.

Why did girls learn to spin?

In the Middle Ages most manors kept sheep for meat and also for wool. It was the job of the women and girls to spin the wool into yarn, which was then woven into cloth. A simple spindle or wooden spinning wheel was all that was needed, so almost every medieval girl learned to spin to produce yarn.

How did people like to be entertained?

One of the favourite pastimes was telling stories. Few people could read, but popular tales were handed down from one generation to the next by word of mouth. People liked to listen to stories about the exploits and loves of knights in times gone by. Some of the favourites were about the adventures of the mythical English king, Arthur (right), and his knights of the round table.

Which creatures did knights most enjoy hunting?

Knights hunted animals that they could eat. They liked best to chase large creatures that provided plenty of meat – and offered a challenge to the hunter. Deer and wild boar were favourites. When these animals were scarce, smaller creatures like hares were hunted. Poorer people might hunt birds or rabbits. In the Middle Ages, there were few imported foods, and everyone had to eat what could be grown on the local land. So hunting made the diet more varied. Hunting also offered knights useful riding practice for war.

Quick-fire Quiz

1. What animals did knights hunt?
a) Falcons
b) Dogs
c) Deer

2. Which king was a favourite of storytellers?
a) King Alfred
b) King Arthur
c) King Albert

3. What are the Middle Ages sometimes called?
a) Age of Innocence
b) Age of Chivalry
c) Bronze Age

4. Which board game was popular with noblemen?
a) Chess
b) Drafts
c) Solitaire

Tournaments

Knights needed to practise fighting, so they often engaged in mock combat as a rehearsal for war. Many people liked to watch the knights fighting, so tournaments soon became great festivals to which spectators came from far afield. As well as mock-battles, knights also fought one-to-one on horseback in the joust and with swords in foot combat.

How was jousting done?

In a joust (right), two mounted knights hurtled towards each other and tried to knock one another off their horses as they passed. The weapon they used was the lance – either a pointed lance for the 'joust of war', or a safer, blunt lance for the 'joust of peace'. Both types of joust were stunning spectacles. Knights wore special armour for the joust. Their breastplates had metal rests for their lances, and they wore helmets that covered the entire head. Only a narrow slit was left in the helmet to allow the knight to see his target.

How did squires practise for the joust?

Jousting was dangerous, so knights invented a safer way for themselves and their squires to practise. They rode towards the quintain, a device with two moving arms attached to a wooden post. One arm held a shield, the other a heavy weight. The squire had to hit the shield with his lance and then ride past at speed to avoid being hit by the swinging weight, which would be spinning quickly round towards him.

What if you weren't a knight?

If you were not a knight you could train for war by practising archery. Archers organised competitions, with everyone trying to hit the gold disc at the centre of the target. To protect others, there was a barrier or mound of earth – the butts – behind the targets.

Quick-fire Quiz

1. A quintain had a weight on one arm, what was on the other?
a) A helmet
b) A sword
c) A shield

2. Which weapon was used in joust?
a) The sword
b) The lance
c) The mace

3. Who took part in tournaments?
a) Knights
b) Squires
c) Common soldiers

4. In archery, what was the earth mound called?
a) The knoll
b) The butts
c) The bumps

What drew spectators to the tournament?

Many people liked the pageantry seen at the tournament. This included the knights' shields decorated with their coats of arms, the banners, and the brightly patterned cloths – known as caparisons – on the horses. As the knights rode through the streets to the tournament, onlookers could easily recognize those they supported from all the badges and heraldry.

Who took part in tournaments?

It was mostly knights who took part, and they were usually members of the country's powerful families. Large-scale mock-battles, called mêlées (right), involved many knights and sometimes also foot soldiers. Tournaments were hosted by the king or one of his highest-ranking lords. As well as giving battle practice, tournaments showed people how strong the king was and how many knightly followers he had.

The Last Castles

After the fifteenth century, nobles stopped building castles as secure strongholds. Instead, they built elegant houses in which to enjoy a life of comfort. This came about because of changes in the way nobles lived and how battles were fought. Some families still lived in buildings that looked like castles from the outside, but would have been of little use in war.

Were cannons effective against castles?

The first cannons (above), used from the fourteenth century onwards, did not always work very well. They made lots of noise, but damaged few castles. But as time went on, cannons became larger and more reliable and could blow huge holes in castle walls. This meant that, by the sixteenth century, castles were no longer as secure from attack as they had been.

Was armour bullet-proof?

Yes. Armourers normally tried to make their plates thick enough to stop a bullet. As firearms became more common from the fifteenth century onwards, people were anxious to be protected by their armour. So armourers often fired bullets at their breastplates before they left the workshop. The mark left by the bullet reassured the wearer that he would be safe.

How did leather replace armour?

By the seventeenth century, light cavalry soldiers (left) were doing the jobs of knights on the battlefield. Many of these horsemen found that a jerkin of pale leather – called a buff coat – gave them enough protection from sword cuts. Buff coats were worn with a metal breastplate and helmet, to shield the most vulnerable parts of the body.

Why did knights stop building castles?

In 1453, the Ottoman Turks laid siege to Constantinople (modern Istanbul), the capital of the Byzantine Empire (left). When their firearms battered down the walls and the Turks swarmed into the great city, it seemed to be the end of an era. Lords realised that there was little point in building stone castles for defence. At the same time, the feudal system was breaking down. Knights were no longer powerful and other people – especially merchants – were getting richer. The age of castles was at an end.

Are there 'new' castles?

Many nobles in the late eighteenth and nineteenth centuries wanted to revive the Age of Chivalry. They designed their homes in the style of castles by adding towers, gatehouses, thick walls and pointed windows, to create buildings like Schloss Neuschwanstein in Germany (above).

Why are so many castles ruined?

A castle could be damaged in a siege, and 'slighted' by an enemy to make it unusable. Some lords abandoned their castles because they wanted a more comfortable home. Local people would use much of the stone to build new houses.

Quick-fire Quiz

1. Who might wear a buff coat?
a) Lady of the manor
b) Squire
c) Cavalry soldier

2. How did armourers test plate armour?
a) By firing bullets at it
b) By hammering it
c) By heating it

3. How did castle windows change over the centuries?
a) They got smaller
b) They got bigger
c) They were filled in

4. Which weapon was the greatest threat to castles?
a) Siege tower
b) Cannon
c) Catapult

How did castles change?

Lords still lived in castles after the fifteenth century, but these castles were no longer built to withstand a siege. Nobles added features that gave them more comfort, such as luxurious bedrooms. Inside walls were lined with wooden panelling and decorated plasterwork adorned the ceilings. Castle owners also put in bigger windows, so that the rooms were much more light and airy than in medieval castles.

Timeline

This timeline records the key dates in the history of castles and knights. Most of the story takes place in a period known as the Middle Ages, or the medieval era. This period is called the 'Middle' Ages because it is midway between the end of the Roman Empire (in the fifth century) and the Renaissance (in the fifteenth century). The period does not have precise dates, but many historians say that the Middle Ages lasted from 500 to 1500.

CE1 to CE800

1–500 Romans use light cavalry troops to support footsoldiers. They build forts throughout Europe to defend their empire.

350–550 Western Roman Empire disintegrates.

410 Goths sack Rome.

622 The Islamic religion is established.

634 Omar I, caliph of the Arab Muslims, conquers Holy Land from Byzantines.

771 Charlemagne becomes king of the Franks. He uses mounted warriors to defend his lands.

790s Vikings begin raids on Britain and mainland Europe.

CE800 to CE1000

800 Charlemagne is crowned Holy Roman Emperor by Pope Leo III.

800–1000 Rulers in western Europe begin to grant land to their nobles in return for services – the feudal system is established.

800–1150 The current style of architecture is the Romanesque, featuring rounded arches, thick walls and tunnel-like barrel vaults.

911 The Viking leader Rollo settles with his followers in northwestern France. They become known as the Normans and their territory Normandy.

950 The stone keep at Doué-la-Fontaine, France, is built. This is now the oldest stone keep to survive.

987–1040 Foulques Nerra of Anjou builds 27 castles as part of his war with the Count of Blois.

CE1000 to CE1100

1000 The Normans spread the fashion for castle-building around many areas of Europe. They begin by building wooden motte-and-bailey castles but later construct castles using stone.

1000–1200 Many Italian towns become independent states, each defended with its own stone walls and castle. Italian lords each build their own stone tower, and some cities have many towers, with lords competing to build the tallest.

1066 William of Normandy invades England and defeats King Harold II at the Battle of Hastings. As his nobles take over, they build castles all over the country to increase their power.

1071 William of Poitiers, said to be the first troubadour (medieval poet and singer), is born.

1090 Christian writers lay down rules of conduct for knights. The rules become the code of chivalry.

1095 Pope Urban II preaches the First Crusade.

1096–1099 The First Crusade. Jerusalem is captured from the Muslims.

1100 Tower keeps become popular in many areas. In England and France, stocky, square towers are common; German knights prefer more slender towers surrounded by strong curtain walls.

ce1100 to ce1200

1100–1200 Many crusader castles are built.

1113 The Knights of St John are founded in Jerusalem.

1118 The Knights Templar build their first headquarters near the Temple in Jerusalem.

1142 Crusaders take and rebuild Syria's greatest castle, the Krak des Chevaliers.

1147–49 The Second Crusade.

1150 The Gothic style replaces the Romaneqsue as the favoured building style.

1160 Castle builders experiment with different shaped keeps. Round keeps and many-sided designs are tried.

1170 Many Norman mottes with wooden towers are converted into stone shell keeps.

1180 Philip Augustus, one of the greatest French kings, comes to the throne; he will build many castles in his kingdom.

1188–92 The Third Crusade.

1190 The Teutonic Knights are founded. They build many castles in Europe.

1190 The keep goes out of fashion. Builders concentrate on courtyard castles with strong gatehouses.

1196 Richard I begins work on Château Gaillard, France. One of the strongest castles, it will withstand a siege for over a year.

ce1200 to ce1300

1200 Rounded wall towers become popular.

1202–04 The Fourth Crusade.

1212 The Children's Crusade.

1217–22 The Fifth Crusade.

1228–29 The Sixth Crusade.

1220 Frederick II, one of the greatest castle builders, becomes Holy Roman Emperor.

1248–54 The Seventh Crusade.

1270 Rise of the concentric castle.

1270 The Eighth Crusade.

1272 Edward I comes to the throne of England. He launches military campaigns against the Scots and Welsh, and builds many castles to control the population.

1291 Sultan Baybars storms the Christian city of Acre, and the crusading movement comes to an end.

ce1300 to ce1400

1302 Battle of Courtrai. Flemish peasants armed with pikes defeat mounted French knights, proving that knights are not invincible in battle.

1312 The Knights Templar are dissolved.

1320s Cannons are first used in Europe.

1330 Plate armour becomes more fashionable.

1337–1453 The Hundred Years' War between England and France.

1347–51 The Black Death kills around one third of the population of Europe.

1380 Castle builders start to use gun loops, so that defenders can fire out safely.

ce1400 to ce1600

1400 Decline of castles begins.

1415 Battle of Agincourt. Henry V of England defeats army of French knights.

1450 Thicker walls are built to protect castles from pounding by cannon.

1453 The city of Constantinople, capital of the Byzantine Empire, falls to the Ottoman Turks, ending the Byzantine Empire.

1476–77 France fights wars with the Duchy of Burgundy; the widespread use of pikes and hand guns shows that the age of the knight is coming to an end.

1500s Lords convert their castles into more comfortable residences or build palaces.

1509 Henry VIII builds forts (strongholds designed for guns where no one lives permanently) rather than true castles.

ce1600 to ce2000

1650 Star-shaped forts used to defend many towns in France.

1800 People begin to be interested in castles as symbols of the 'Age of Chivalry'.

1854 French architect Eugène-Emmanuel Viollet-le-Duc begins to publish books about medieval building, renewing interest in castles and showing how they were built.

1869 Work is started on Neuschwanstein, the fairy-tale castle built for King Ludwig II of Bavaria.

Web Addresses

www.castlesontheweb.com
This site offers an extensive database of links to all things castle-related, including sites such as castles for kids, with free software for building a castle of your own and online heraldry games involving roleplay.

www.nationalgeographic.com/features/97/castles/enter.html
This is a charming interactive site for younger children, based around exploring a medieval castle and meeting all its ghostly inhabitants who address you by name.

kotn.ntu.ac.uk/castle
A fun, fictional, but historically accurate, rendering of a castle based on Nottingham Castle as it was in about 1480. Move around the castle, learning what happened where – listen to music in the great hall, write recipes in the kitchen and dress a knight ready for a tournament.

library.thinkquest.org/10949
The ThinkQuest Library is a collection of over 5,500 educational websites designed by participants in the ThinkQuest competitions. This is an informative site treating a variety of related medieval topics, covering fortifications, war and buildings, society and how people lived.

www.castlewales.com/life
www.medieval–castles.net
Useful websites describing all aspects of a medieval castle, including its design, defences and domestic life.

www.castles-of-britain.com
This site is dedicated to the study and promotion of British castles and offers lots of information on all aspects of castle life, including unexpected topics such as bathing and washing.

www.tower-of-london.com
This is the official site for the Tower of London – home and prison to many of England's medieval monarchs. Play games, take a virtual tour and read about its history, ghosts, traditions and ceremonies.

tayci.tripod.com/boy2knight.html
Among other things, this website explains how a young boy may have become a knight in medieval times.

www.stemnet.nf.ca/CITE/medieval_castles.htm
This is a useful site for a list of castle-related websites for both children and adults.

score.rims.k12.ca.us/activity/castle_builder
Find out why castles were such an important part of medieval life and learn how they were built and who lived in them. This interesting site offers class research projects covering all sorts of medieval topics from feudalism, food and feasting to monks, nuns, knights and weapons.

www.yourchildlearns.com/heraldry.htm
Download free software to make your own coat of arms and learn about the Middle Ages, feudalism, knights and chivalry while you do so.

www.castles.org/kids
This site offers a simple, well-illustrated, straightforward story, suitable for younger children, about King Edward and his castle.

Quick-fire Quiz ANSWERS

Page 167 First Knights
1. c 2. a 3. c 4. b

Page 169 Building a Castle
1. a 2. c 3. b 4. b

Page 171 Castle Designs
1. b 2. a 3. b 4. c

Page 173 Parts of the Castle
1. b 2. b 3. c 4. b

Page 175 Castle Life
1. b 2. a 3. c 4. a

Page 177 Becoming a Knight
1. b 2. b 3. a 4. c

Page 179 Heraldry
1. a 2. c 3. c 4. b

Page 181 Horsemanship
1. a 2. c 3. b 4. b

Page 183 Weapons and Fighting
1. c 2. a 3. a 4. b

Page 185 Armour
1. a 2. b 3. c 4. b

Page 187 Siege
1. b 2. b 3. c 4. b

Page 189 Defence
1. b 2. c 3. a 4. a

Page 191 The Crusades
1. b 2. a 3. c 4. a

Page 193 The Knight's Manor
1. c 2. a 3. c 4. c

Page 195 Peacetime Pursuits
1. c 2. b 3. b 4. a

Page 197 Tournaments
1. c 2. b 3. a 4. b

Page 199 The Last Castles
1. c 2. a 3. b 4. b

1000
QUESTIONS
& ANSWERS
FACTFILE
INVENTIONS

Contents

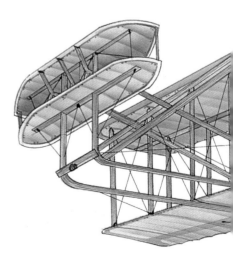

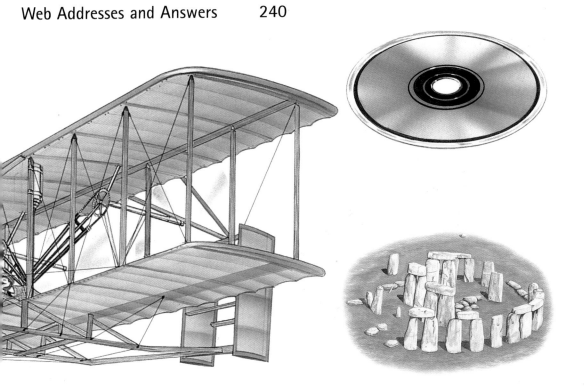

Writing and Printing

The first true writing system was invented by the Sumerians over 5,000 years ago. They used pictures called pictograms to stand for objects, ideas and sounds. Today, the written or printed word is central to human communication.

Who invented printing?

Block printing was invented by the Chinese nearly 2,000 years ago. They carved characters on wooden blocks, covered them in ink and stamped them on to paper. Modern printing, with movable metal type, began in the 1440s when a German, Johannes Gutenberg, developed the printing press.

When were full stops and commas first used?

Medieval monks and scribes produced handwritten, beautifully decorated illuminated manuscripts. To make the manuscripts easier to read, the scribes separated words with spaces, used capital and small letters and introduced a system of punctuation, including full stops and commas.

Why did typewriters make you crazy?

People are often scared of a new inventions. When the first typewriter went on sale in 1874, some doctors said that using one could make you go mad! However, the typewriter was a huge success for its American inventor, Christopher Latham Sholes. The first successful portable typewriter appeared in the early 1900s and electric typewriters whizzed into action in 1901.

Who invented the paper clip?

The paper clip is such a simple and useful design, it is surprising that it is quite a recent invention. It first appeared in 1900, invented by Johan Vaalar, a young scientist who worked for an invention office in Norway. Before the paper clip, people used straight pins or ribbons tied through holes in the corner of the pages to fasten papers together temporarily.

Who was Mr Biro?

Ladislao Biro, a Hungarian journalist, invented the ballpoint pen in 1938. It contained a tube of quick-drying ink which rolled evenly on to the paper thanks to a tiny movable ball at the tip.

What was the first advertisement?

The oldest known piece of publicity is an ancient Egyptian papyrus dating from almost 5,000 years ago. The message is written in hieroglyphs, or picture writing, and offers a reward for finding a runaway slave.

Is there really lead in a pencil?

No! The 'lead' in a pencil is not made from the metal lead at all. It's made from graphite mixed with clay. The modern pencil was invented independently by Frenchman Nicholas-Jacque Conte and Austrian Josef Hardtmuth in 1795. Their invention was a great success – it could be easily sharpened and erased.

How does a mouse draw?

A computer mouse allows you to direct the cursor around the screen to give the computer commands. Using a mouse, designers can draw new details on to a picture. The computer mouse was invented in the United States in 1964 by Douglas Englehart. He also invented a foot-controlled 'rat' but it never caught on.

Why were felt-tip pens invented?

The Japanese inventor hoped that the pen's soft tip would make people's handwriting more graceful – like the brushstrokes in Japanese writing. The first felt-tips went on sale in Japan in 1962.

Medicine

Doctors in the ancient world used herbs, surgery and 'magic' to treat illnesses. Scientific medicine began in the 1600s with the invention of the microscope and an understanding of anatomy. Technical advances in the 1900s led to modern medicine.

Who were the first doctors?
The earliest doctors were physicians in ancient Egypt and China. In Egypt, physicians used drugs and potions. Surgeons treated injuries, and priests dealt with evil spirits. The first known physician was an Egyptian, Imhotep, who lived about 4,600 years ago.

When were bacteria discovered?

The Dutch instrument-maker Antonie van Leeuwenhoek made the first high-powered microscope. It could magnify up to 200 times. In 1683, he published drawings of bacteria – tiny living things that can cause disease. He was building on the work of English scientist Robert Hooke who, 20 years before, had discovered that living things were made up of small cells.

Modern microscope

Who discovered how blood flows?
In 1628, an English doctor, William Harvey, found that the heart pumps blood into the arteries. He showed that it circulates all around the body and returns to the heart along the veins.

Arteries   Veins

Are drugs made from plants?
Most modern drugs are made from chemicals, but many were originally made from plants. For example, the heart drug, digitalis, comes from foxgloves. Quinine from the cinchona tree is used to treat malaria and aspirin is made from the bark of the willow.

Foxglove

Can artificial limbs move?

Back in the Middle Ages, the French surgeon Amboise Paré used springs and cogs to move artificial arms and legs. Today, whole legs and arms can be replaced with computer-controlled plastic or metal limbs. In some cases, nerve-endings in the patient's limb send messages to motors in the artificial limb to make it move.

Artificial arm and hand

Prosthetic hook

How can we 'see' our bones?

We can see the bones in our bodies by taking X-rays of them. In 1895, the German scientist Wilhelm Röntgen first discovered that X-rays could pass through paper, wood and flesh, but not through metal or bone. Within months, doctors were using X-rays to photograph bones in the body.

What is a body scan?

In 1972, British scientist Godfrey Hounsfield developed a Computerized Tomography (CT) scanner to take pictures of the inside of the body. CT scanners take thousands of X-rays of the brain and body and build them up into a kind of 3-D picture for doctors to study.

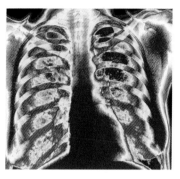

Chromosomes

DNA

Nucleus

Cell

Francis Crick

James Watson

Who made surgery safer?

In 1865, the Scottish surgeon Joseph Lister was the first doctor to use antiseptics during surgery to stop patients dying from infections. He sprayed carbolic acid round the operating theatre and soaked dressings in it to kill germs.

Early carbolic acid spray

What is the double helix?

DNA (deoxyribonucleic acid) is the chemical that controls how cells behave and reproduce. In 1953, two scientists Francis Crick from England and the American James Watson worked out that DNA was made up of a twisted spiral — a double helix.

209

Buildings

The first permanent buildings were put up about 10,000 years ago. At first people used natural materials, such as wood and stone, and most of the work was done by hand with simple tools. Today, hi-tech machines and the latest materials are used to build huge skyscrapers.

What is a Gothic building?

The Gothic style of building began in the mid-1100s in western Europe. It was mainly used for churches and cathedrals, which often had tall spires and towers, pointed arches, carved stonework and decorative windows. The workers had to scramble up and down wooden scaffolding tied up with rope, as there were no cranes to help them.

What was Stonehenge for?

Stonehenge, England, was built about 5,000 years ago. The standing megaliths (big stones) were arranged to mark the midsummer sunrise and the midwinter moonrise. It may have been a religious meeting place or a huge outdoor calendar used to study the movement of the Sun.

Can bridges carry water?

Bridges for carrying water were first built by the Assyrians, around 700 BC. Three hundred years later, the Romans improved the technique and built huge stone aqueducts to supply their cities with running water. Many Roman aqueducts still stand today.

Who designed a sail-like roof?

One of the most stunning modern buildings is the Opera House in Sydney Harbour, Australia. The architect, Jorn Utzon from Denmark, designed it to look like wind-filled sails. The main roof was made from concrete segments covered with thousands of ceramic tiles. The Opera House took 15 years to build. It was finished in 1973.

How are suspension bridges built?

The towers are built first. Steel ropes are suspended from the towers. Special machines spin these into strong steel cables. Next, long steel cables called hangers are attached to the suspending cables. Sections of the deck are lifted into place and fixed to the hangers.

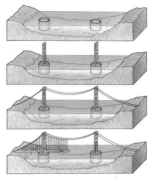

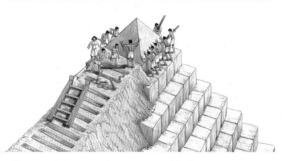

How old are the pyramids?

The first true pyramid was built in Egypt in about 2575 BC. Each of these huge tombs for the dead pharaohs took about 20 years to build. Thousands of workers dragged the huge stones up ramps and levered them into place with wooden poles.

Are there wire bridges?

In 1883, the Brooklyn Bridge in New York, United States, was the first suspension bridge built using steel cables, which can carry huge loads. Its designer, John Roebling, used over 1,900 kilometres of wire anchored with around 90,000 tonnes of masonry.

Do buildings have skeletons?

In the 1880s, architects had the idea of using a skeleton of steel and concrete columns to support the roof, walls and floors of tall buildings. They fixed the outer walls to this framework. The first skyscraper, built in Chicago in the United States, was ten storeys tall. Today many tower over 400 metres high.

211

Food and Agriculture

Farming probably began about 10,000 years ago in the Middle East. Early farmers harvested wild wheat and barley and sowed some of the seeds to grow new crops. Gradually, farmers developed tools and, after the 1700s, farms began to be mechanized.

Did early farmers use ploughs?

Wooden ploughs developed from digging sticks used in Mesopotamia over 5,500 years ago. At first, people pulled ploughs, but then oxen were used. Ploughs with iron blades to break up heavy soil were made about 4,000 years later. More land could be cultivated with these, so farms grew larger.

Who first used windmills?

Windmills were first used in Persia over 1,200 years ago. By the 1200s they were being used in Europe, mainly to grind grain. During the 1700s and 1800s thousands were built to grind grain, power saws, raise materials from mines and pump water.

What is a combine harvester?

A combine harvester reaps, threshes, loads grain on to trailers and bales the leftover straw. The first one, built by an American, Hyram Moore, in the late 1830s, was pulled by horses. Later, tractors were used. By the 1930s, they were diesel-powered.

Who invented the milking machine?

In 1860, American Lee Colvin had an idea to speed up milking. Hoses linked rubber caps on the cow's teats to a bucket and bellows. Pumping the bellows milked the cow. Modern milking machines use a similar idea. Today, many milking parlours are computer-controlled.

Cups fit over a cow's teats

What is organic farming?

Artificial fertilizers were first made commercially by Sir John Bennet Lawes in England in 1842. Now many farmers use them to increase crop yields. In the 1970s, some farmers, worried about the effects of these fertilizers, returned to organic farming, in which only natural fertilizers are used.

Why are crops sprayed?

Crops are sprayed with pesticides to kill unwanted pests that could destroy the crop. The first synthetic insecticide, DDT, was isolated in 1874 by the German, Othmar Zeidler. It was first made commercially in 1939, when a German chemist, Paul Muller, found it could kill insects, including the mosquitoes that carry disease.

Quick-fire Quiz

1. Who first used windmills?
a) The Chinese
b) The Persians
c) The Sumerians

2. When was the seed drill invented?
a) 1501
b) 1601
c) 1701

3. Who invented the milking machine?
a) Lee Colvin
b) Jethro Tull
c) Hyram Moore

4. What is DDT?
a) A fertilizer
b) An insecticide
c) A machine

Who was Jethro Tull?

Seed used to be scattered on the fields by hand. Then, in 1701, English farmer Jethro Tull developed a machine that could drill and sow seeds in straight lines. His machine fed seeds at an even rate into a furrow made by a coulter, or blade.

Can farm animals be cloned?

Scientists can make clones (identical copies) of living things by growing a new organism from a cell taken from the 'parent'. In February 1997, Dolly the sheep made history – she was a clone of her mother. She was grown from one of her mother's cells instead of from an egg. A year later, a cow was produced in the same way.

At Home

The first homes were caves and simple huts. Slowly, people developed new skills to build better homes, preserve food and make their lives more comfortable. Modern homes have electricity, gas, water and drainage and lots of household goods and furniture.

Prehistoric home

Waste tip

Well

Open fire

Preserved fish

Central heating radiator

Sewerage pipe

Water pipe

Who invented furniture?

Simple wooden furniture has probably been around since people began to build permanent homes. In Egypt, beautiful carved furniture was being made over 3,500 years ago. These luxurious articles were found in a tomb for a dead pharaoh to use in the afterlife.

Have homes changed?

In prehistoric times (and in some parts of the world today) people lived in homes built from mud or stones, cooked on open fires and got water from wells. Modern homes are stronger and more comfortable. From the 1880s homes were wired with electricity, giving light and power at the flick of a switch.

When did irons 'go electric'?

The American Henry Seely made the first working electric iron in 1882 and it went on sale in 1885. Before that, people used 'flat irons'. These were solid metal irons that had to be heated up on a fire before they could be used to press their clothes.

How was food kept cool?

Over 4,000 years ago, people stored food in ice pits to keep it cool. Early domestic refrigerators – insulated cabinets for holding ice – first appeared in the United States around 1850. The first mechanical one, powered by a steam pump, was the bright idea of German engineer Karl von Linde in 1879. Within 12 years he had sold 12,000 in Germany and the United States. The first electrical refrigerator, developed by Swedish engineers von Platen and Munters, went on sale in 1925.

How old is the flushing toilet?

Over 5,000 years ago, the Mesopotamians had special seats with holes and water running underneath to take away the waste. This idea was developed further by the English inventor John Harington, who published the earliest design for a flushing toilet with a cistern in 1596. The first practical flushing toilet was made by Alexander Cumming in the 1770s.

Modern home

Television satellite dish

Electrical power

Flushing toilet

Chamber pot

Quick-fire Quiz

1. What did von Linde use to power his 'fridge'?
a) Electricity
b) Microwaves
c) Steam

2. When did light bulbs go on sale?
a) 1780
b) 1880
c) 1980

3. Who made the first working electric iron?
a) Henry Seely
b) Joseph Swan
c) Thomas Edison

4. Who invented central heating?
a) Egyptians
b) Romans
c) Mesopotamians

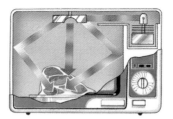

Which waves can melt chocolate?

American Percy Spencer discovered microwave cooking by accident. He'd been working on ways of using invisible microwaves to detect aircraft. When he found that these waves had melted a chocolate bar in his pocket, he realised they could be used to cook food too. In 1946, the first microwave oven was developed and in 1955, commercial ones appeared.

Who lit up homes?

In 1878, the Briton Joseph Swan demonstrated his electric light bulb. A year later, the American inventor Thomas Edison made a long-lasting light bulb with a carbon filament, which went on sale in 1880. The two men eventually set up a joint company to make light bulbs.

How old is central heating?

The ancient Romans first developed a method of heating their houses with hot air nearly 2,000 years ago. Called a hypocaust, warm air, heated by burning fuel in a furnace, flowed through tiled flues in the walls into the spaces beneath the floor, heating the rooms above.

215

Clothes and Fabrics

Early people wore animal skins to keep them warm, but about 10,000 years ago people learned how to make cloth. They used a spindle to spin wool, cotton, flax or hemp into thread, which could be woven into fabric. These fabrics were then made into clothes.

How old are needles?
Bone needles over 20,000 years old were found in Stone Age caves in France. They were probably used to stitch animal skins together. Modern metal needles were not developed until the 1400s.

How do zips work?
Zips have two rows of teeth joined together by a sliding 'key' which locks the teeth together or pulls them apart. The American Whitcomb Judson invented the first zip fasteners in the 1890s. In 1913, Gideon Sundback patented the interlocking zip fastener.

Who wore safety pins?
Ancient Egyptians first invented safety-pin type clasps which they wore like brooches. The modern safety pin was 're-invented' by American Walter Hunt in 1849. He didn't make any money from his invention – he gave the patent away to repay a $15 debt!

Linen weaving in ancient Egypt

Who invented the loom?
Simple looms were used in Turkey almost 7,000 years ago. These early weavers made cloth much as we do today, by interlacing (or weaving) threads together at right angles to one another. Cloth was hand woven until mechanical and power-driven looms were invented in the mid-1700s.

Are shoes made in factories?

Shoes have been around for thousands of years and, until the mid-1800s, they were all handmade. These Native American moccasins were made by hand from soft deer-skin and adorned with coloured porcupine quills. This took many hours. Today a pair of shoes can be made in minutes by a machine in a factory.

Which machine was destroyed?

French tailor Barthélemy Thimonnier developed a sewing machine in 1829. Other tailors destroyed it, fearing it would put them out of work. In the United States, a lock-stitch machine was invented by Walter Hunt in 1833 and Elias Howe made a better machine in 1845. Sewing machines became widely available in the late 1850s.

Early sewing machine

Who tanned leather?

Leather clothing, footwear and household goods were used over 5,000 years ago in Mesopotamia. In the past, people 'tanned' leather by rubbing the hides with the juices of bark and roots that contain the chemical tannin. (This is where 'tanning' gets its name.) Sometimes skins were soaked in salt and the chemical alum to preserve them.

Quick-fire Quiz

1. When were zips invented?
a) 1690s
b) 1790s
c) 1890s

2. Who first made silk?
a) Romans
b) Native Americans
c) Chinese

3. Who invented the spinning jenny?
a) Whitcomb Judson
b) Elias Howe
c) James Hargreaves

4. What did George de Mestral make?
a) Velcro
b) Lock-stitch sewing machine
c) Safety pin

What was a spinning jenny?

In 1764, Englishman James Hargreaves invented an automatic spinning machine, the spinning jenny. It could spin eight reels of thread at once, compared with the one reel made by an ordinary spinning wheel.

What is Velcro?

Swiss engineer George de Mestral spent eight years developing Velcro. It is made from two nylon strips, one covered with tiny loops, the other with tiny hooks. The strips stick to each other when pressed together but can easily be ripped apart. Velcro went on sale in the mid-1960s.

What was China's best-kept secret?

Silk was first discovered by the Chinese over 4,600 years ago. They set up farms to breed silk worms about 3,500 years ago but kept the method a secret for another 2,000 years. Silk was so valuable that the Chinese traded it for gold and silver.

217

Useful Materials

Once, people used natural materials such as wood or cotton to make things. Later, they discovered how to extract metals from ore found in the ground. Today, synthetic materials, such as nylon, plastic and fibreglass, are used to make many goods from cars to clothes.

Pottery-making in ancient China

Is glass made from sand?

Glass is made by heating silica (sand), limestone and soda to very high temperatures. It can then be coloured and shaped. Many medieval churches have windows made of stained glass, like this one. The oldest surviving window, in Augsberg Cathedral, Germany, dates from 1065.

Why do cars rust?

Iron and steel objects rust in damp air because the iron changes into a red-brown iron oxide, a mixture of iron and oxygen. In 1913, the Briton Harry Brearley added the metal chromium to steel to make the first successful rust-resistant stainless steel.

What is steel?

Steel, a strong metal made from iron, was first developed over 3,000 years ago. In 1856, the British inventor Henry Bessemer devised a cheap way of producing steel. Molten iron was poured into a converter and hot air or oxygen was blown over it. Most of the carbon in the iron was burned, turning it into steel.

Steel-making

Where was china made?

Pottery goods have been made for about 9,000 years, but fine china, or porcelain, was only invented about 1,200 years ago in China. The art remained a secret until just over 300 years ago, when fine porcelain goods were taken to the West.

Who first used plants to make materials?

People have made useful materials from plant fibres for thousands of years and many are still used today. About 5,000 years ago, cotton plants were first cultivated in India and the Chinese used the fibrous stems of hemp to make rope. The ancient Egyptians made fine linen fabric from flax stems.

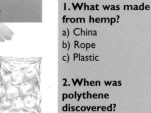

Are plastics oily?

All plastics, such as polyvinylchloride (PVC), polythene, nylon and some paints, are made from chemicals found in oil, natural gas or coal. Polythene was first discovered by accident in 1933 by chemists working at ICI in Britain. Two years later, nylon was made by Wallace Carothers in the United States.

Quick-fire Quiz

1. What was made from hemp?
a) China
b) Rope
c) Plastic

2. When was polythene discovered?
a) 1733
b) 1833
c) 1933

3. Where was rubber discovered?
a) China
b) Brazil
c) India

4. Who made steel cheap?
a) Bessemer
b) Brearley
c) Carothers

Is fibreglass strong?

Fibreglass material is made by mixing glass fibres and plastic. It was developed in the United States in the 1930s. It is flame-resistant, does not rust and is tough enough to make car bodies or boats. It is also used to insulate buildings.

Fibreglass canoe

Bakelite radio

What was Bakelite?

In 1909, a Belgian-American chemist named Leo Hendrik Baekeland made the world's first artificial plastic – Bakelite. As it did not conduct heat or electricity it was ideal for making electrical goods.

Is rubber liquid?

Natural rubber is made from the thick, runny sap, or latex, of rubber trees. The latex is collected, strained, mixed with acid to solidify it and rolled into sheets. Wild rubber was discovered in Brazil in the early 1800s and was first used for waterproofing. Today we mostly use synthetic rubbers, developed about 60 years ago.

Energy

People use energy for all sorts of activities from powering cars to lighting their homes. Most of the energy we use is made by burning fossil fuels such as coal, gas and oil. Renewable energy sources such as solar, water and wind power can be used to generate electricity.

Arkwright's Mill

Did water-power run factories?

Watermills have been used for over 2,000 years to grind corn. In 1771, Richard Arkwright turned a watermill into a cloth-making factory, using the water wheel to power his new spinning machines.

What is a wind farm?

Modern windmills are used to turn machines called turbines which generate, or make, electricity. These wind turbines are grouped together in wind farms. The first large wind generator was built by the American Palmer Putnam in 1940.

Who made engines steam?

An English blacksmith, Thomas Newcomen, built the first practical steam engine in 1712. The Scotsman James Watt came up with an improved design and in 1782 his double-action steam engine was used to power factory machinery.

Crane raises and
lowers equipment
to the seabed

Derrick

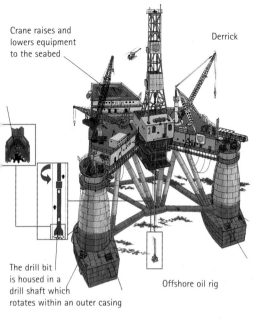

The drill bit
is housed in a
drill shaft which
rotates within an outer casing

Offshore oil rig

Is oil found under the sea?
In the 1970s, large oil deposits were found under
the North Sea. Oil wells were drilled 200 metres
beneath the sea. Offshore oil rigs had to be built
to pump the oil to the surface. These rigs are
supported on steel or concrete structures that
are sunk deep into the seabed.

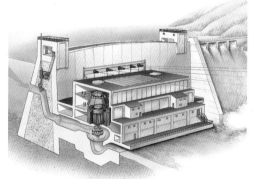

What is a hydrodam?
Hydroelectric power stations are often built inside
dams called hydrodams. Water from a lake behind
the dam gushes down pipes, turning turbines that
drive generators and make electricity. The world's
first major hydroelectric power station opened in
1895 at the Niagara Falls in North America.

Can the Sun heat a home?
A few modern homes have solar panels
in the roof. Some use the Sun's heat to
warm water. Others contain electronic
devices called photovoltaic (solar) cells
to change sunlight into electricity. Solar
power can run machines. The first
practical solar-powered machine, a
steam engine, was developed by
Frenchman Augustin Mouchet in 1861.

Who split the atom?
In 1932, British scientists John
Cockroft and Ernest Walton first
split the atom, releasing huge
amounts of energy. In the United
States, in 1942, Italian-born Enrico
Fermi and his team built the first
successful nuclear reactor to
control this energy. In 1954, the
first nuclear power station was
opened in Russia.

What are
fossil fuels?
Coal, oil and gas are
called fossil fuels.
Coal is the remains
of ancient plants that
lived and died in
prehistoric forests.
Oil and gas are made
from the bodies of
tiny dead sea

creatures. The first coal-fired power station to generate
electricity opened in 1882.

Calculations

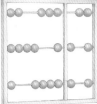

When people first began to count, they could get by using just fingers and toes. But soon they invented tally sticks and number systems to record and calculate measurements. Numbers are the basis of all calculations. Today, most people use a modern version of numbers invented in Arabia (0 to 10).

Who invented the abacus?

A simple abacus dates back to Mesopotamia, 5,000 years ago. The Chinese abacus, designed about 1,700 years ago, is made up of rows of beads representing units, tens, hundreds and thousands. It is a rapid tool for adding, subtracting, multiplying and dividing.

What was an astrolabe?

The astrolabe was originally a circular map of the heavens used by astronomers to measure the height of stars and planets. In the early Middle Ages, Arab scholars developed the astrolabe as an instrument to measure latitude and help them to navigate at sea.

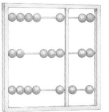

Astrolabe

Moroccan students in the Middle Ages

What was the earliest money?

Long ago, people used to swap goods for the things they wanted. The people of ancient Lydia (now Turkey) were the first to make coins, about 2,700 years ago. They used electrum, a mixture of gold and silver. The Chinese invented paper bank notes about 1,200 years ago.

Who first used weights?

The first known standard weights and scales were used by the Babylonians about 4,600 years ago. The ancient Egyptians also used sensitive scales and weights to weigh precious stones and gold over 5,000 years ago.

The Babylonians used three standard weights.

Who made the first mechanical calculator?

The first mechanical calculator was made by the Frenchman Blaise Pascal in 1642 when he was aged only 19. It had a row of toothed wheels with numbers around them. Numbers to be added or subtracted were dialled in and the answer appeared behind holes at the top. Modern electronic pocket calculators went on sale in 1971. They can do complicated calculations in seconds.

What was a handspan?

The ancient Egyptians and the Romans used parts of the body as measuring units. They used the size of the hand, foot and arm to calculate distances, but these measurements varied according to the size of the person making them. Eventually, standard measurements were adopted.

What were the first clocks?

Sundials and shadow clocks, which use the Sun's passage across the sky to measure time, were first used in ancient Egypt to tell the time. The Babylonians divided the sundial's circle into 360 parts or degrees and divided it into 12 hours. In the Middle Ages, the hour- or sandglass was a popular 'clock'. Atomic clocks were first developed in 1969 and are accurate to one second in 1.6 million years!

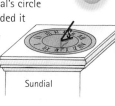

Atomic clock

Sandglass

Sundial

How do we measure temperature?

The first practical sealed alcohol thermometers, in which liquid rose up a tube as it heated, were made around 1660. In 1714, the German Gabriel Fahrenheit made a more accurate thermometer using mercury.

Alcohol thermometer

Who was Einstein?

Albert Einstein was a very clever German scientist who studied many things including energy and time. In 1915 he developed the theory of relativity, which says that time would slow down, length would shorten and mass would increase if you could travel almost as fast as the speed of light.

$E = mc^2$

223

Computers

Modern computers – electronic machines that can store and process masses of information – were first designed in the 1940s. Computers can do billions of calculations a second and we use them to carry out many tasks, from predicting the weather to making other machines.

What are microchips?

In the 1960s, scientists came up with a new way to run computers. They used a tiny slice, or chip, of a material called silicon to make the electronic 'brain' that controls a computer. Today a tiny microchip contains up to 250,000 parts that tell it how to work. A computer uses different microchips to do different jobs.

Who was Mr Babbage?

In 1834, the British mathematician Charles Babbage invented the first mechanical computer that could be programmed, but he did not have the money or technology to build it. His machine was finally made in 1991 – and it worked!

Why were computers as big as a room?

The Americans John Mauchly and J. Prosper Eckert Jr built the first proper automatic computer (ENIAC) in 1945. It filled two whole rooms and weighed as much as five elephants. It was this large because it used 19,000 valves, each as big as a hand, to control the switches that made it work. Computers got smaller in the 1950s when tiny transistors replaced valves.

Who developed PCs?

The first successful personal computer, or PC, was developed by Steve Jobs and Steve Wozniak in 1978. At first only a few people could afford them, but today personal computers are found in schools, offices and homes all over the world.

How do computers work?

All computers change the information they handle into numbers, which are stored as electrical signals. In modern computers these signals are either 'on', which stands for 1, or 'off', which stands for 0. All numbers, letters and pictures are turned into a sequence of 1s and 0s (called 'binary code'). A computer does rapid calculations using these numbers, which are then changed into words and pictures that you can understand.

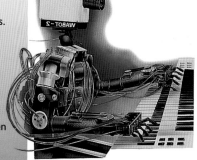

Do computers have disks?

The information used to run computer programs is usually stored as electrical pulses on magnetic disks. Plastic 'floppy disks' were created by the IBM company in 1970. In 1983, compact disks (CDs), plastic-coated metal disks read by laser, went on sale. CDs used by computers can store vast amounts of information.

Can robots see?

The first industrial robot – a computer-controlled machine that carries out tasks – was made in the United States in 1962. In 1980, the first robot that could 'see' using electronic eyes was developed in America. Today, some robots have laser vision systems and can both see and hear.

What is virtual reality?

The computer inside a virtual reality headset creates scenes and sounds that seem real to the wearer. This system was pioneered by Ivan Sutherland in 1965 but was not fully developed until the 1990s. Virtual reality headsets are great for games and for learning different skills.

What is the Net?

Computers anywhere in the world can be linked via a telephone line and a gadget called a modem. This network, called the Internet or Net for short, is used by over 40 million people. The Internet was first developed in the late 1960s by the US government as a safe way to communicate in wartime.

Quick-fire Quiz

1. When was ENIAC built?
a) 1935
b) 1945
c) 1955

2. What are microchips made from?
a) Copper
b) Plastic
c) Silicon

3. What does PC stand for?
a) Personal computer
b) Private computer
c) Plastic computer

4. Who invented a mechanical computer?
a) Eckert
b) Wozniak
c) Babbage

Communications

Before the printing press was invented in the 1450s, people could only swap information by word of mouth or by writing letters. Today we use books, newspapers, radio, television, telephone and e-mail to spread news and views.

Who first recorded sound?

In 1877, the famous American inventor Thomas Edison built a machine to record sound. The sounds were stored as patterns of indented lines on a tin-foil cylinder. The first words to be recorded clearly were 'Mary had a little lamb'.

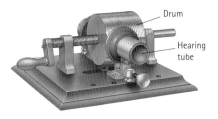

Drum

Hearing tube

Who rang the bell?

In 1875, the Scottish-American inventor Alexander Graham Bell discovered a way to send the human voice along wires. A year later he built the first working telephone and within months hundreds of telephone bells were ringing all over America.

Can glass fibres 'talk'?

Optical fibres are strands of glass twisted into a cable that can transmit light. In 1976, Charles Kao and George Hockham had the idea of using them to carry telephone calls at the speed of light. The first optical fibre telephone link was set up in America in 1977.

Who invented the radio?

The Italian Guglielmo Marconi built the first proper radio set that sent messages using radio waves in 1895. His machine produced radio waves by making a strong electric spark. The system was known as the wireless because the signals were sent through the air, not along a wire. Marconi sent the first signal across the Atlantic in 1901, and public radio broadcasts began about 20 years later.

Who said 'number please'?

The first telephone exchange set up in America in 1878 was manual, with just 21 customers. An operator answered your call, took the number you wanted and plugged in your line to complete the electrical circuit and connect your call. The first automatic exchange was installed in America in 1892.

The Morse Code

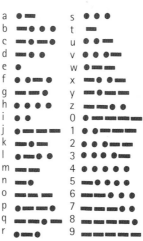

a	•—	s	•••
b	—•••	t	—
c	—•—•	u	••—
d	—••	v	•••—
e	•	w	•——
f	••—•	x	—••—
g	——•	y	—•——
h	••••	z	——••
i	••	0	—————
j	•———	1	•————
k	—•—	2	••———
l	•—••	3	•••——
m	——	4	••••—
n	—•	5	•••••
o	———	6	—••••
p	•——•	7	——•••
q	——•—	8	———••
r	•—•	9	————•

Early telegraph machine

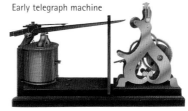

Quick-fire Quiz

1. What was _Telstar_?
a) A radio
b) A satellite
c) A phone

2. What did Marconi invent?
a) The telephone
b) The television
c) The radio

3. What are optical fibres made from?
a) Copper
b) Glass
c) Light

4. When was the telephone invented?
a) 1775
b) 1875
c) 1975

When did phones go mobile?

In the early 1980s, computers allowed the telephone to lose its wires and go mobile. A system of low-powered radio stations link the moving telephone to a computer network that keeps track of the caller.

What is Morse Code?

Before the telephone was invented people sent messages by telegraph. This used a coded series of short and long electrical signals – dots and dashes. It was invented by the American Samuel Morse.

How do telephone calls travel round the world?

Communication satellites orbiting the Earth pick up signals and send them on to a receiver thousands of kilometres away. _Telstar_, the first one, went into orbit in 1962. It could relay 12 telephone calls or one television channel. Satellites today carry thousands of calls and several channels at once.

On Film

Before cameras were developed people could only record images by drawing or painting them. Photography was invented in the early 1800s. At first it was a slow process and all pictures were in black and white. Now we have film and video cameras to record people and places all over the world.

Who first said 'Smile, please'?

The Frenchman Joseph Niépce took the first permanent photograph in about 1827. It took eight hours for the photo of a view to develop on a thin metal plate. In the late 1800s, taking photos was such a lengthy business that people needed a back rest to help them sit still!

What is a Polaroid®?

The Polaroid® camera, invented by the American Edwin Land in 1947, produces 'instant' photos. It uses slim plastic envelopes instead of a roll of film. Inside is a sheet of film and a packet of processing chemicals, which burst as the photo is ejected. The picture develops in about 60 seconds.

Did early cameras use rolls of film?

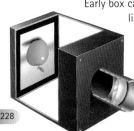

Early box cameras used a lens to focus the light rays on to a metal or glass photographic plate at the back of the camera. The light changed the chemicals on the plate and the picture developed in a few minutes. Rolls of film were first introduced in 1888 by the American George Eastman.

When did movie stars first talk?

Early movies were silent and actors had to be very good mime artists. Words came up on the screen to explain the action and an organist played mood music to liven up the film. The first full-length movie with sound was *The Jazz Singer*, shown in the United States in 1927. It was so popular that silent movies soon lost their appeal and 'talkies', talking pictures, took over.

Who invented television?

The Scottish inventor John Logie Baird first demonstrated the television in public in 1926. His original machine was made from an old box, knitting needles, a cake tin and a bicycle lamp! The first picture of a human face was a blurry image of 15-year-old William Taynton.

Rotating disc

Baird's camera had a mechanical scanner with a rotating disc. This was soon replaced by the electronic scanner developed by the American-Russian Vladimir Zworykin in 1923.

Baird's television, 1930

Quick-fire Quiz

1. When was the first 'talkie' shown?
a) 1917
b) 1927
c) 1937

2. Who invented television?
a) Thomas Edison
b) George Eastman
c) John Logie Baird

3. What did Edwin Land invent?
a) Polaroid® camera
b) Colour television
c) Movies

4. Who was the first photographer?
a) Louis Lumière
b) Auguste Lumière
c) Joseph Niépce

How do colour television cameras work?

The first colour televisions went on sale in the 1950s. Colour television cameras split the light from the scene being filmed into three images – one red, green and one blue. The light from each image is turned into an electrical signal which is recorded with the sound signal on film or tape. A colour television converts these signals back into the coloured picture.

Who made the first movie?

The American Thomas Edison was the first person to film moving pictures, but the French brothers Auguste and Louis Lumière were the first to show a 'movie' to an audience. The brothers made 10 films in 1895 and built a machine to show them on screen to audiences in Paris clubs and cafés.

When did home videos arrive?

Videotape was invented in 1956 and the first camcorder, or video camera-recorder was developed in the 1960s. Modern lightweight camcorders went on sale in the 1980s. A camcorder uses magnetic tapes instead of photographic film to record the images and sound.

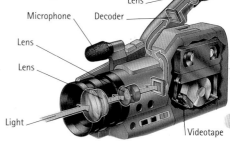

Lens

Microphone   Decoder

Lens

Lens

Light

Videotape

Travel on Land

Prehistoric people had to walk everywhere, carrying their goods or dragging them on sledges. By 3000BCE, people had developed wheeled vehicles pulled by animals. In the late 1800s, the invention of the steam engine and petrol engine changed land travel completely.

What is a TGV?

The French TGV, *Train à Grande Vitesse*, first went into service in 1981. These speedy electric trains can travel at over 300 kilometres an hour on special tracks. The first electric train was demonstrated at an exhibition in Germany in 1879.

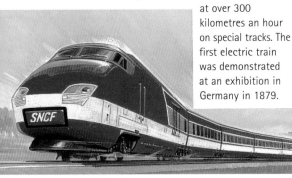

Did cars run on steam?

The first cars ran on steam, but they were noisy and often broke down. Early cars were not allowed to travel faster than walking pace and in some countries a man with a red flag had to walk in front to warn people they were coming!

Who invented the wheel?

The wheel was invented about 6,000 years ago in the Middle East. It was laid on its side and used to make pottery. About 500 years later, the Sumerians living in the same region had turned wheels upright and were using them on horse-drawn chariots. The first wheels were solid, made from three planks of wood pegged together and cut to shape. The plank wheel turned on a fixed axle.

When was the bicycle invented?

The bicycle was invented in the 1790s in France, but you moved by pushing your feet along the ground! A German, Baron von Drais, made a bike with a steerable front wheel in 1817. The first bike with pedals and cranks to turn the back wheel was designed by the Scotsman Kirkpatrick Macmillan in 1839.

Can the Sun power cars?

Engineers are experimenting with a new form of energy to power car engines – energy from the Sun. Several prototypes run on solar-powered batteries. A few of these solar cars have reached speeds of 140 kilometres an hour in races across Australia.

How do trains hover?

'Maglevs', or magnetic levitation trains, hover above the track supported by magnetic fields. They are driven by linear motors with no moving parts. The trains are still being developed – but once in use, they may reach speeds of up to 700 kilometres an hour.

Solar panels

Solar-powered car

Quick-fire Quiz

1. What was a Tin Lizzie?
a) A train
b) A car
c) A bicycle

2. Who built the first petrol-powered vehicle?
a) Daimler
b) Benz
c) Ford

3. Who built the first steam train?
a) George Stevenson
b) Henry Ford
c) Richard Trevithick

4. How fast could the Rocket travel?
a) 56km/h
b) 46km/h
c) 36km/h

Who was Mr Benz?

In 1885, the German engineer Karl Benz built the first vehicle to be powered by a petrol engine. The first true four-wheeled car was developed in 1886 by another German, Gottlieb Daimler.

Which train was a winner?

In 1829, Englishman George Stevenson and his son Robert entered a contest to find the fastest steam train. Their winning engine, the *Rocket,* could pull a train at 46 kilometres an hour – twice as fast as their rivals. The first steam locomotive was developed by the English engineer Richard Trevithick in 1803.

What was a Tin Lizzie?

Hand-built early cars were too expensive for ordinary people. But in 1908, in America, Henry Ford had the idea of mass-producing cars on his other invention –

the assembly line. In the next 20 years, he sold 15 million 'Model T' cars, also known as Tin Lizzies.

On the Sea

Early people travelled over water using rafts and dug-out canoes. About 5,000 years ago the Sumerians and Egyptians built ships with sails and oars. In the 1800s steam engines took over from sails and steel replaced wood. A hundred years later, ships with petrol engines took to the waves.

When were paddle steamers first used?
The Frenchman Jouffroy d'Abbans built the first working steamboat in 1783. Within 20 years paddle steamers were being used to ferry people and goods up and down rivers and across the sea.

How do divers swim underwater?
The ancient Greeks used diving bells to go under water over 2,300 years ago. Divers were not able to swim freely until the aqualung – an air supply carried in tanks on the back – was developed in 1943 by Frenchmen Jacques Cousteau and Emile Gagnan.

What was a trireme?
Triremes were fast galleys powered by three rows of oarsmen on each side. The Greeks first built triremes in about 650BCE. Later triremes were up to 40 metres long with a pointed ram at the front to smash into enemy ships.

How did sailors find their way?
In the mid-1700s, two British inventions helped sailors fix their position at sea. The sextant, invented by John Campbell, determined latitude by measuring the angle of the Sun or stars above the horizon. John Harrison's chronometer – a kind of clock – helped to measure longitude.

Sextant

Why were clippers fast?
The super-fast clipper of the mid-1800s had a new shape of hull and a combination of square and triangular sails with which it could catch and use the slightest breeze. Clippers could maintain speeds of 37 kilometres an hour.

Quick-fire Quiz

1. When was the first steamboat trip?
a) 1683
b) 1783
c) 1883

2. Who designed the hovercraft?
a) Campbell
b) Cockerel
c) Gagnon

3. What was the *Turtle*?
a) A steamship
b) An aircraft carrier
c) A submarine

4. Who first built triremes?
a) Romans
b) Egyptians
c) Greeks

When were submarines invented?

In 1620, the Dutchman Cornelius Drebbel's wooden submarine, rowed by 12 oarsmen, travelled several kilometres up the River Thames in London, England. The *Turtle*, the first submarine that could rise and sink, was designed by the American David Bushnell in 1776. It was used in the American War of Independence.

The *Turtle*

What craft floats on air?

Hovercraft can skim over land or water on a cushion of air blown down by fans and trapped inside a flexible rubber skirt. The hovercraft was designed by the British engineer Christopher Cockerel in the 1950s and made its first test run in 1959.

How do jet aircraft land on ships?

The first carrier for jet aircraft, *USS Forrestal*, was completed in 1955. Aircraft can take off and land on the deck in mid-ocean. During take-off the aircraft is propelled forward by a device called a 'catapult'. When it lands, the aircraft is slowed down by huge 'arrester' wires stretched across the deck.

233

By Air

Over 2,000 years ago the Chinese flew war kites to fire-bomb their enemies, but they did not travel in them. Air transport did not begin until the 1780s, when hot-air balloons took to the skies. Just over 100 years later, powered flight got off to a bumpy start.

How do hang-gliders fly?

Hang-gliders depend on the wind and rising warm air to fly. In 1853, British engineer George Cayley was the first to design a suitably shaped wing. Nearly 100 years later, in the 1940s, the American Francis Rogallo developed a triangular-shaped kite that gave rise to modern hang-gliders.

When was the first flight?

The first flight was made in a hot-air balloon on 21 November 1783 by François de Rozier and the Marquis d'Arlandes. The balloon, made by the French Montgolfier brothers, had a basket for passengers slung beneath the huge paper balloon.

Who was the first hang-glider?

Otto Lilienthal, a German engineer, designed and flew over 15 different hang-gliders. He made the first flight in which the pilot controlled the machine. Lilienthal died in 1896 when his hang-glider crashed.

Who were the Wright brothers?

The American brothers Orville and Wilbur Wright had the idea of fitting a petrol engine and propeller to their glider. On 17 December 1903, Orville made the world's first powered flight. *Flyer 1* flew for 12 seconds and covered 37 metres – less than the length of a jumbo jet!

How do helicopters rise up vertically?

Helicopters have one or two large rotors made up of long, thin wings. When the rotors spin round, they lift the aircraft and drive it along. Helicopters can fly forwards, backwards and sideways. The first single-blade helicopter was built by Russian-American Sikorsky in 1939.

Can aeroplanes land by themselves?

Modern jet liners are controlled from a hi-tech flight deck. They even have computer-controlled autopilot systems to land planes in bad weather when the pilot cannot see the runway clearly. The first autopilot landing of a scheduled airliner was in 1965 at Heathrow Airport, England.

What were zeppelins?

Zeppelins, named after their German inventor Ferdinand von Zeppelin, were giant airships up to 240 metres in length. They were powered by petrol engines and a propeller, and filled with hydrogen gas which is lighter than air but very flammable. The first zeppelin flight was in 1900.

Are helicopters really 500 years old?

The Italian artist and inventor Leonardo da Vinci sketched a simple helicopter (see above) over 500 years ago, but it was never built. The French inventor Paul Cornu built the first helicopter in 1907 – it rose to a height of 30 centimetres and hovered there for 20 seconds. Cornu's helicopter was very difficult to control, and it was not until the 1930s that helicopters became a practical means of flying.

Jet power – when and where?

Gloster
E28/39 jet

In the 1930s, both Britain and Germany were working on a new form of power for aircraft – the jet engine. The British engineer Frank Whittle came up with the idea in 1929, and prototypes were built by Whittle in Britain and by Hans von Ohain in Germany. The first jet aircraft, built by the German Ernst Heinkel, took to the air in 1939. Two years later, Whittle's engine powered the Gloster E28/39 jet. Jet engines allow planes to travel much faster – some military jets can zoom along at 3,200 kilometres an hour!

Into Space

In the early 1950s, the United States and Soviet Union began the space race. In 1957 the Russians launched the first satellite, *Sputnik I*. Four years later, the Russian cosmonaut Yuri Gagarin blasted into orbit in *Vostock I*. His historic trip round the world lasted for under 2 hours, but manned space flight was launched.

Who first saw stars?

In 1609, the Italian scientist Galileo was the first person to look at the stars through a telescope. His studies led him to suggest that the Earth moved round the Sun and was not at the centre of the Universe as people then thought.

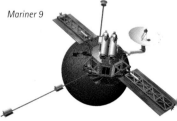

Mariner 9

Why do telescopes detect radio waves?

Stars and other objects in space give out radio waves as well as light. Radio telescopes have huge dish-shaped antennae to pick up these radio waves. Radio telescopes have discovered exploding galaxies, radiation from distant galaxies and spinning neutron stars called pulsars.

Is there life on other planets?

The other planets in our Solar System are probably not able to support life, but scientists are looking further afield. In 1974, astronomers beamed a radio message out into space from a huge radio telescope in Puerto Rico. They aimed it at a dense star cluster, M13, over 25,000 light years away. The message is travelling at the speed of light so we will have to wait 50,000 years for a reply!

What is a space probe?

Space probes are unmanned spacecraft that travel into space. Several have been sent to other planets in the Solar System. *Mariner 9*, launched in 1971, visited Mars. *Mariner 10*, launched in 1973, was the first probe to visit two planets. It flew by Venus and visited Mercury three times, where it found that the daytime temperatures were hot enough to melt lead.

Who was the first man on the Moon?

The American Neil Armstrong was the first man to set foot on the Moon in July 1969. He and fellow astronaut Edwin 'Buzz' Aldrin put up the American flag and a plaque saying 'We come in peace for all mankind'.

When did people first walk in space?

In 1965, the Russian Aleksei Leonov made the first space walk, but he had to remain attached to the spacecraft. In the early 1980s, scientists developed the MMU (manned manoeuvring unit), which let astronauts walk freely in space. The first free space walk took place from the American *Challenger* in 1984.

What is a shuttle?

Early spacecraft used rocket power to blast them into space. Then the Americans came up with the idea of building a re-usable spacecraft. The shuttle still needs rocket power to take off, but it lands like an aircraft and so can be re-used. In 1981, the first space shuttle, *Columbia*, took off.

What is a space station?

Space stations are large spacecraft that spend several years orbiting the Earth. The first space station was the Russian *Salyut I*, which was launched in 1971. Modern space stations like the Russian *Mir* use solar panels to power the station while it is in orbit. The crew can stay up in space for many months carrying out scientific experiments and repairing equipment.

solar panels

Mir

237

Timeline

Hundreds of inventions and discoveries have marked human progress from the Stone Age to the Space Age. Some happened by accident, others took people years to perfect. Here are a few important milestones.

20000BCE to 2000BCE

c.20000BCE Bone needles used
c.8000BCE First permanent houses built
4000–3000BCE Earliest known writing (cuneiform) (Sumeria)
3500BCE Simple ploughs pulled by people (Sumeria)
3200BCE About 300 years after the potter's wheel was invented, people made simple wheeled vehicles (Sumeria)
3000BCE Simple glass beads made (Egypt)
c.2800BCE Stonehenge built in England; first step pyramids built in Egypt
2350BCE First lavatories with pedestals (Mesopotamia)

1900BCE to CE0

c.1900BCE Metal workers began extracting iron from its ore; steel was made c.1200BCE
1000–700BCE First shadow clocks (Egypt); by 700BCE divided sundial was in use
c.690BCE First bridges (aqueducts) used to carry water (Assyria)
c.620BCE First coins made from electrum in Lydia (Asia Minor)
c.450BCE Decimal abacus c.450BCE; early stick and dust tray abacus (Mesopotamia c.2500 BCE)
c.85BCE First water-powered mills used to grind flour (Greece)

CE1 to 1400

105 Tsai Lun made paper from pulp (China)
600 Chess developed (India or China)
c.840 Camera obscura developed (China)
c.868 First printed book Diamond Sutra (China)
c.1000 Spinning wheel used (Asia)
c.1090 Magnetic compass invented (China, Arabia)
c.1300 First mechanical clocks with equal time periods developed (Europe)
c.1300 Astrolabe adapted for sea navigation (Arabia)

1401 to 1700

c.1440 Johannes Gutenberg developed printing press with movable type (Germany); first book printed c.1450
c.1590 Janssen made compound microscope (Netherlands)
c.1592 Galileo made first thermometer (Italy)
1608 Hans Lippershey made working telescope (Netherlands)
1609 Galileo first person to look at stars (Italy)
c.1620 Drebble built first submarine (England)
c.1642 Pascal built calculating machine (France)
c.1683 Antonie van Leeuwenhoek made first high-power (x 200) microscope (Netherlands)

1701 to 1800

1712 Newcomen built steam-powered engine (England)
1714 Fahrenheit developed mercury thermometer (Germany)
1752 Franklin developed lightning conductor (USA)
1757 John Campbell built sextant (England)
1759 Harrison developed accurate chronometer (England)
1764 James Hargreaves built spinning jenny (England)
1765 Watt built condensing steam engine (Scotland)
1769 Richard Arkwright built powered spinning machine (England)
1783 Montgolfier brothers built first practical hot-air balloon (France)
1783 Jouffroy D'Abbans built first steam boat (France)
1785 Cartwright built power loom (England)

1801 to 1900

1803 Richard Trevethick built steam train (England)
1821 Michael Faraday made first electric motor (England)
c.1827 First photograph taken by Niépce (France)
1829 Stevenson's steam train *Rocket* was built (England)
1829 Sewing machine built by Thimonnier (France)
1837 Telegraph developed by Morse (USA) and Cooke and Wheatstone (England)
1839 First practical bicycle built by Kirkpatrick Macmillan (Scotland)
1852 Henri Gifford built first working (steam-powered) airship (France)
1853 George Cayley pioneered glider technology (England)
1856 Henry Bessemer invented cheap steel-making process (England)
1865 Lister first used antiseptics (England)
1867 Joseph Monier developed wire-reinforced concrete (France)
1873 C. L. Sholes made first practical commercial typewriter (USA) (went on sale in 1874)
1875 Scot Alexander Graham Bell invented telephone (USA)
1877 Thomas Edison developed the phonograph (USA)

1878/9 Swan (England) and Edison (USA) made electric light bulb
1882 First power station opened by Edison (USA)
1882 Henry Seely built first practical electric iron (USA)
1884 Gottlieb Daimler made first light-weight petrol engines (Germany)
1885 Karl Benz made first petrol-driven motor car (Germany)
1893 W. Judson made the first slide fastener (USA)
1895 Wilhelm Röntgen discovered X-rays (Germany)
1895 Marconi invented radio communication (Italy)
1895 Auguste and Louis Lumière first showed a 'movie' to an audience (France)

1901 to 2000

1903 Wright brothers flew first powered aircraft (USA)
1907 First helicopter built by Paul Cornu (France)
1925 John Logie Baird invented television and demonstrated it in 1926 (Scotland)
1929 Whittle patented idea of the jet engine (England)
1933 Polythene discovered at ICI (England)
1935 Wallace Carothers made nylon (USA)
1936 Focke made first practical helicopter (Germany)
1942 Enrico Fermi built first nuclear reactor (USA)
1945 Mauchly and Eckert developed first proper computer (USA)
1947 Edwin Land invented polaroid camera (USA)
1948 First atomic clock built (USA)
1953 DNA double-helix discovered by F. Crick (England), J Watson (USA) and M. Wilkins (England)
1955 Cockerel invented hovercraft (England)
1957 First artificial Earth satellite went into orbit (USSR)
1959 Integrated circuit (silicon chip) developed (USA)
1960 T. Maiman developed laser (USA)
1961 First manned space flight (Russia)
1964 Computer mouse invented by Engelhart (USA)
1967 First heart transplant by C. Barnard (South Africa)
1969 First manned moon landing (USA)
1970 Floppy disk developed by IBM (USA)
1971 Microprocessor patented by Intel (USA)
1978 Successful PC developed by Jobs and Wozniak (USA)
1979 Compact disk developed by Sony and Philips
1981 Space shuttle developed (USA)
1983 Satellite TV developed (USA)
1984 Genetic fingerprinting developed (Britain)
1989 Game Boy™ launched by Nintendo (Japan)
c1992 Virtual reality helmets devised (USA)
1992 First map of human chromosome (France, Britain, USA)
1994 Longest undersea tunnel, 50km-long Channel Tunnel opens (Britain, France)
1995 First DNA database set up (Britain)
1997 First successful clone of a mammal (Britain)
c.1997 Sikorsky developed robotic helicopter (USA)
1997 Biorobotics pioneered by Shimoyama's team (Japan)

Web Addresses

www.s9.com/biography

A biographical dictionary site with basic information on over 28,000 men and women who have shaped our world from ancient times to the present day. It also has book links to Barnes & Noble.

www.enchantedlearning.com/inventors

Visit Zoom Inventors and Inventions for a lively presentation of historical and technological facts.

www.howstuffworks.com

This is a site aimed at children and young adults explaining how things work. It covers a vast number of topics from cellphones, air conditioners and inkjet printers to animals, insects, credit cards, videos and guitars – an endless list.

www.bbc.co.uk/history/multimedia_zone

This is an enjoyable site with educational games and animations, including topics such as Stephenson's Rocket, blast furnaces, paddle steamships, spring mills and winding gear.

www.uspto.gov/go/kids

This is the kids' site for the United States Patent and Trademark Office. Highly interactive, it offers games, information and links, as well as resources for parents and teachers, including information on how to help a child to make a patent application.

www.cbc.ca/kids/general/the-lab/history-of-invention/default.html

An invention timeline that is constantly being updated. Did you know that the first fax machine was invented in 1843? Email with suggestions for inventions that you think are interesting.

www.brainpop.com

This is a science, technology and health site for kids, with lively graphics, quizzes and movies on anything from assembly lines to lasers, photography, refrigerators and televisions. Do experiments in the company of Bob the Rat and ask Tim and Moby, Tim's friendly robot, any science and technology questions that you have. There are lots of activities on this site, and for each one you can earn points and win prizes.

inventors.about.com/cs/younginventors

This kid's site is related to inventors.about.com with areas aimed at a variety of ages and levels. There is lots of information on the history and stories behind different inventions as well as explanations of how each thing works. Search by name, letter or by subject, such as famous inventors, famous inventions, women inventors or wacky patents. There are also lots of useful invention and inventing links, including a section of sites about children who have made and patented successful inventions.

www.build-it-yourself.com

This site is an inventor's club for kids between 8–16, aimed at inspiring young people to build whimsical toys. Discover how to 'build-it-yourself' and turn unwanted junk into trucks, boats, robots and much more.

edtech.kennesaw.edu/web/inventor.html

This site offers a variety of invention and inventor-related links, from the history of invention to invention games.

kids.patentcafe.com

This is a great site with lively graphics and plenty of activities. Learn about famous inventors and then try your hand at developing and creating your own inventions.

Quick-fire Quiz ANSWERS

Page 207 Writing and Printing
1.a   2.c   3.c   4.b

Page 209 Medicine
1.c   2.b   3.a   4.c

Page 211 Buildings
1.c   2.b   3.b   4.c

Page 213 Food and Agriculture
1.b   2.c   3.a   4.b

Page 215 At Home
1.c   2.b   3.a   4.b

Page 217 Clothes and Fabric
1.c   2.c   3.c   4.a

Page 219 Useful Materials
1.b   2.c   3.b   4.a

Page 221 Energy
1.b   2.c   3.a   4.c

Page 223 Calculations
1.b   2.c   3.b   4.b

Page 225 Computers
1.b   2.c   3.a   4.c

Page 227 Communications
1.b   2.c   3.b   4.b

Page 229 On Film
1.b   2.c   3.a   4.c

Page 231 Travel on Land
1.b   2.b   3.c   4.b

Page 233 On the Sea
1.b   2.b   3.c   4.c

Page 235 By Air
1.b   2.c   3.c   4.c

Page 237 Into Space
1.c   2.b   3.c   4.b

1000
QUESTIONS
& ANSWERS
FACTFILE

TRANSPORT

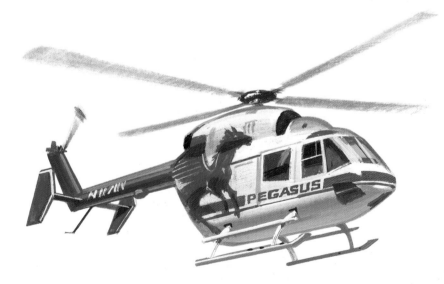

Contents

Early Transport

Before the invention of wheeled vehicles about five thousand years ago, few people travelled far from home, and when they did, they went by foot. Gradually, people learned to tame and ride animals such as horses and camels, but it was the wheel that enabled people to transport large loads with ease, especially when good roads were built.

How did early people transport heavy weights?

Many structures of the ancient world, such as the pyramids in Egypt, were built with huge stones that could weigh several tonnes each. We do not know for certain how people moved these stones to the building sites. They may have dragged the stones over wooden poles laid on the ground (above) or made sledges, mounted on wooden runners. It is possible that they laid wooden paths to help the sledges move more smoothly.

What was the 'ship of the desert'?

The camel was called the 'ship of the desert' when it was used in the deserts of Asia and northern Africa to transport both people and goods. Camels were prized for their stamina – they could survive long periods with little food or water. One-humped dromedaries and two-humped Bactrian camels were both in use by 1500BCE. Camels are still used today for transport.

Ceramic rider from China around 80BCE

What is a 'travois'?

The native people of North America were often on the move, hunting and gathering food. Many used a 'travois' – a simple sledge – to transport their goods. They tied two teepee poles to the harness of a trained dog and strung their baggage between the poles.

How did people manage before the invention of the wheel?

Some rich people were carried on 'litters' – platforms held up by parallel poles (left). Heavy loads were carried by pack animals – mules or donkeys in Europe and llamas in South America.

How did horse collars help transport heavy loads?

In the past, when horses dragged loads, they wore throat harnesses, which put great pressure on their windpipes, making breathing difficult. The Chinese solved this problem when they invented a padded collar that fitted around the horse's shoulders and neck, away from the windpipe. This collar enables horses to pull loads up to four times as heavy.

Can you ride without stirrups?

Yes! Early riders were very skilled at controlling horses with their legs and knees. Stirrups were probably invented in India around 200BCE, and they made horses even easier to control. Stirrups are loops for riders' feet and they are suspended from horses' saddles. Horses began to be used more in warfare because riders could perform the twists and turns needed in battle. Also, soldiers needed their hands less for controlling the horses and so could use weapons more easily.

How were the first wheels made?

The first wheels were made by nailing together planks of wood to form solid discs (above). They were strong but also very heavy and were used for carts and war chariots.

What were wheelbarrows first used for?

The Chinese invented the first wheelbarrows, which were simple wooden vehicles that were pushed along and used to transport people. Modern wheelbarrows are similar in design – they have one wheel at the front and two support legs at the back, but they are used to transport small loads – not people!

Cars

In just 100 years, cars have changed the world, bringing easy, convenient transport within the reach of ordinary people for the first time. There are now motor vehicles for every imaginable purpose, from ambulances and racing cars to buses and jeeps. However, all these vehicles cause problems, polluting the air and draining valuable oil reserves. Now the search is on for cars that use less energy and keep our air cleaner.

How long are limousines?

People who want to make a big impression often choose big cars – and cars do not get much bigger than a 30-metre-long stretch limousine (above). Stretch limos are usually about eight metres long and they often have problems turning street corners. Limos can often be seen ferrying the rich and famous around the world's big cities.

What was the first car?

The first true motor car was a three-wheeler built by the German engineer Carl Benz in 1885. It had a small petrol engine fitted underneath the passenger seat and this drove the back wheels to a top speed of about 15km/h. Benz went on to build many more cars, becoming the world's first motor-car manufacturer.

Can there be a low-energy car?

Manufacturers are trying to design cars that use less energy. They have designed lightweight cars that use less petrol, as well as electric cars. However, the generation of electricity for electric cars does use coal and oil, so these vehicles are not as low-energy as they seem. One day, we may ride around in solar-powered cars that are covered with light-sensitive panels (left).

What are 'crumple zones'?

Modern cars are designed to protect passengers in a crash. The passenger compartments are surrounded by metal bars to shield those inside. But the front and rear of cars are designed to crumple in a crash, absorbing some of the impact shock. These parts of cars are called 'crumple zones'.

Quick-fire Quiz

1. How many wheels did the first car have?
a) Two
b) Three
c) Four

2. What type of engine powered *Thrust SSC*?
a) Petrol engine
b) Diesel engine
c) Jet engine

3. What sort of tyres grip the road better?
a) Wide tyres
b) Narrow tyres
c) Thicker rubber tyres

4. What provides low-energy power?
a) Hydrogen
b) Oil
c) Solar energy

How fast can cars go?

By fitting jet engines to specially designed, streamlined cars, Englishman Richard Noble has built faster cars than anyone else. His most recent car, *Thrust SSC* (right), set a new record in 1997, powering to an amazing 1220.86km/h – faster than the speed of sound.

Thrust SSC

How does the engine drive the wheels?

In most cars, the engine is at the front, but drives only the rear wheels. A long rod called a propeller shaft connects the engine to the axle of the rear wheels. Between the engine and the propeller shaft is a gearbox, which allows the driver to select a low, powerful gear for accelerating, or a higher gear for fast speeds.

What prevents cars from skidding?

In wet conditions, cars are more likely to skid. This is why car tyres have a pattern of grooves called a 'tread'. Water from the road gathers in the tread and is pushed back on to the road, away from the path of the tyre. Modern tyres are quite wide to reduce further the risk of skidding.

247

Racing Cars

At the beginning of the 20th century, cars began to be designed for speed and special tracks were built for racing. Today, motor racing is huge – Formula One and Indianapolis 500 racing are multi-million dollar sports with amazing, hi-tech cars, skilled drivers and huge support teams.

What is pole position?

Pole position is the first place on the grid from which a race starts. The position of the cars on the grid is determined during the previous qualifying circuits, when the cars are timed as they drive the course. The driver with the fastest lap wins pole position, and the others line up behind him in the order of their qualifying times.

How do racing cars 'stick' to the track?

Formula One cars are lower and more streamlined than any other type of vehicle. The shape of the body is important in two ways. First, the streamlining enables air to flow easily over the vehicle, cutting down 'drag' (air resistance) and allowing the car to go faster. Second, the air flow, aided by specially shaped wings on the front and rear, pushes the car down on to the track, holding it close to the road.

Air flow

How do racing drivers choose their tyres?

If the weather is dry, racing drivers will choose tyres called 'slicks'. Slicks are wide tyres with no tread. They grip well on dry tracks and get sticky as they warm up, helping the cars to grip roads. In wet weather, slicks do not grip well and drivers usually switch to tyres with treads.

How powerful are car engines?

Most family cars have small four-cylinder engines, designed to travel comfortably at or near the maximum road speed limit, which is 113km/h (70mph) in the UK. Racing cars are designed for much higher speeds. Formula One cars can reach speeds of 322km/h and have very powerful, 12-cylinder engines.

Why can you remove the steering wheels?

To keep a racing car light, streamlined and efficient, nothing is bigger than is necessary. The cockpit, where the driver sits, is very cramped, and the driver's legs nestle under the steering wheel in the front, or 'nose', of the car. To squeeze legs into the narrow nose, the driver must first remove the steering wheel.

What happens in the 'pits'?

Formula One cars enter the 'pits' – service areas by the side of the tracks – at least once during races to refuel. Using special equipment, the highly skilled pit mechanics fill petrol tanks and change tyres in a matter of seconds. Also, the mechanics can usually sort out any mechanical problems very quickly.

Quick-fire Quiz

1. Which best holds a car on to the road?
a) The car's shape
b) The car's material
c) The car's size

2. Which tyres are used in dry conditions?
a) Tyres with treads
b) Slicks
c) Narrow tyres

3. Why are qualifying sessions important?
a) Points are scored
b) Grid position is determined
c) Drivers are eliminated

4. What is the front of a racing car called?
a) The bumper
b) The beak
c) The nose

How can we make cars even faster?

Fitting bigger engines makes cars faster, but also heavier, which slows them down. Because of this, racing-car designers concentrate on making the vehicles more streamlined, and they aim to use new materials that are very strong, but also very light in weight, such as carbon fibre. Designers use computers to try out new ideas in theory before testing them in practice on working cars.

Trucks

Early trucks were small, but as engines got larger, designers made larger trucks that could transport almost anything. Long-distance trucks have big engines, but there is still room in the 'cabs' for the drivers – sometimes there are even beds!

How many cars can you drive at once?

You can only really drive one car at once – but a modern car transporter can carry as many as nine. The upper deck of the transporter lowers at the rear so that cars can drive on to it. Then the deck is raised so that more cars can be driven on to the lower deck.

Wedges and straps stop the cars moving while the transporter is in motion.

Why do so many lorries carry containers?

Containers are large metal boxes that come in two standard sizes. Lorries can be standardized to carry both sizes, and cranes are also standardized to load the containers on to ships (below).

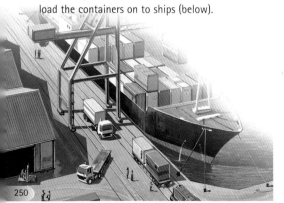

How does a 'tipper' tip?

To lift and tip a heavy load, a 'tipper' truck uses a powerful hydraulic system. Pressure is applied to a liquid, which pushes up a piston connected to the underside of the tipping container. When the pressure is released the tipping container lowers.

What is a 'juggernaut'?

A 'juggernaut' is any large cargo-carrying truck. The word comes from the name of a Hindu god, whose statue was carried on large wagons in religious processions in India. It is thought that worshippers threw themselves under the wheels of these wagons. Because of this, people began to call any large truck that could crush with its wheels a 'juggernaut'.

How do you drive a 'road train'?

A 'road train' looks like a normal truck from the front, and it is only when the long train of trailers winds into view that it is clear where this impressive vehicle gets its name. It is driven like a normal truck, but when the driver needs to turn corners, he or she has to swing out in the opposite direction to the bend so that the trailers follow in the right line. Road trains are often seen in countries that have long stretches of straight roads, such as Australia.

What can trucks carry?

Trucks can be adapted to carry virtually any type of load. Tankers carry liquids, special transporters carry animals and rubbish trucks have garbage-crushing machinery. Low-loaders (above) have long, low platforms to transport other vehicles or awkward cargoes, such as logs.

How many tonnes can a truck carry?

The trucks used on building sites are some of the world's biggest vehicles. Many trucks can carry more than 100 tonnes, but the latest 'monster' truck will take up to 330 tonnes – the weight of a jumbo jet!

How do articulated trucks work?

An articulated truck has two sections. The front section is the tractor, which contains the engine and the driver, and the rear section is the trailer, which carries the load. A joint links the two sections, allowing the truck to turn with more flexibility than a one-section vehicle of the same length. Cables connect the trailer's brakes and lights to the tractor, giving the driver full control.

Special Vehicles

Motor vehicles are the most adaptable form of transport. They can be used to rescue people in an emergency, harvest crops on the farm or build towering structures. Manufacturers start with the same basic machinery found on cars – wheels, gears, brakes and engines – and add any specialized equipment needed to create the best machine for the job.

What vehicles do police use?

Police forces use motorbikes to pass through busy traffic quickly, and heavily armoured vans to control riots. Police cars are fitted with flashing lights and sirens as warning signals, and they carry all kinds of equipment in their boots. Police drivers are specially trained to drive safely at high speeds.

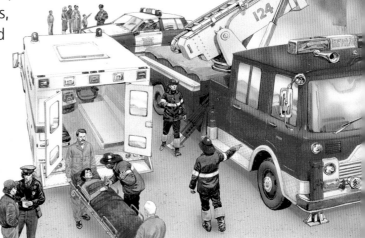

Why do tractors have such big wheels?

The rear wheels of a tractor are big in order to spread out the vehicle's heavy weight so that it does not sink into soft or muddy ground. The large wheels have thick tyres with chunky treads to provide plenty of grip on the ground. Many tractors provide power for other farm machinery directly from a connection on the rear of the tractors.

What are the special features of ambulances?

Ambulances are ordinary vans or cars fitted out with medical equipment to give emergency treatment to sick or injured people as they are driven to hospital. Ambulances must be seen and heard easily – they have sirens and flashing lights, and the word 'ambulance' is often written in reverse on the front so that other drivers can read it properly in their rear-view mirrors.

How do machines tunnel underground?

Special tunnel-boring machines dig tunnels, removing rubble with conveyor belts. If the rock is very hard, machines drill small holes and fill them with explosives to blast away the rock. Tunnels are usually lined with both steel and concrete in order to reinforce them.

How does a fire engine save lives?

There are several types of fire engine. Some have platforms or ladders that extend to just over 30 metres so that fire officers can rescue people trapped in burning buildings. Some fire engines are fitted with pumps powerful enough to deliver up to 2,840 litres of water in one minute.

When were tanks first used?

Tanks made their first major appearance in 1916, during World War I. They were heavily armoured to withstand machine-gun fire and explosions, and their 'caterpillar' tracks could easily plough through barbed wire and trenches. Tanks have many different features – gun turrets, ammunition stores, periscopes and armoured plating.

How does a trolley bus work?

A trolley bus looks like an ordinary bus but, instead of using a diesel engine, it runs on electricity. At the top of the bus are two 'arms' with 'trolley wheels' at the end. These wheels connect to two overhead wires that supply the power. A trolley bus can only travel along the routes laid out by the power wires.

Which digger is the best?

The JCB is the most versatile machine for digging. It has both a big scoop for picking up material from the surface and a shovel for digging holes, grabbing and other uses. The JCB has sturdy wheels as well as a series of strong steel props to prevent it toppling over when performing complicated manoeuvres involving heavy loads. Both the shovel and props are powered by hydraulics, which means that the driver can move them easily in any direction just by flicking a series of levers in the cab.

Trains

The first railway networks appeared during the 19th century in England, and soon railways were being built all over the world. They changed people's lives, allowing them to travel further and faster than ever before. The railways made it possible to transport heavy goods in bulk over land for the first time.

Were there trains before steam power?

Yes – as early as 1550, mine owners in Germany were hauling stone, coal and iron ore out of mines using trucks on tracks. The trucks were pulled by horses (above) or pushed along by the miners themselves. Most of these early railways were very short.

What were 'Big Boys'?

'Big Boys' were the largest steam locomotive trains ever built. They ran on the United States Union Pacific Railroad in the 1940s, and hauled heavy goods up the Rocky Mountains. The engines were 40 metres long, and could reach speeds of up to 130km/h.

How can trains run on electricity?

Many trains are attached to overhead electric cables that supply electricity to motors that turn the wheels. The trains are linked to the cables by special connectors that use adjustable springs that take up any slack when the trains are travelling uphill.

How fast are bullet trains?

The Japanese bullet train is built for speed, and the most recent model has reached speeds of up to 360km/h in test runs. It runs on special tracks without sharp bends, which would slow the train. The French TGV (Train à Grande Vitesse) can travel at a similar speed.

How do trains hover in the air?

'Maglev' (magnetic levitation) trains are held just above the track by magnetic force. This means that when they move, the trains do not touch the track, so there is no friction to slow them. Scientists believe that one day it will be possible to travel at speeds of up to 700km/h in maglev trains.

What was special about the *Rocket*?

The *Rocket* was a famous railway locomotive designed by British engineer George Stephenson. It was built in 1829, when a competition was held to find the best engine for the new Liverpool to Manchester railway. The *Rocket* was the winner, reaching a top speed of 47km/h.

What were the 'Flying Hamburgers'?

In 1933, new diesel express trains (left) were built to run between Berlin and Hamburg in Germany. They were sleek, streamlined and very fast for the time, reaching a speed of 175km/h. They became known as the 'Flying Hamburgers'. The trains were so successful that they were used on other German lines until the 1960s.

What are 'cowcatchers'?

The first American railroads were not protected by fences and cattle often wandered on to the lines. Special guards called 'cowcatchers' were fixed to the front of steam locomotives (right) to nudge the cows to safety away from the wheels. The first locomotive to have a cowcatcher was the *John Bull*, which was built in 1831.

Quick-fire Quiz

1. How fast could the *Rocket* travel?
a) 100km/h
b) 56km/h
c) 47km/h

2. What don't maglev trains experience?
a) Delay
b) Friction
c) Engine

3. Where were the earliest trains used?
a) In mines
b) In cities
c) On the coast

4. Why can a bullet train travel so fast?
a) Its tracks have no sharp curves
b) It does not stop at stations
c) It carries few passengers

Bicycles

Cycling is a cheap, healthy and fun way to travel. The modern bicycle, with its diamond-shaped frame and equal-sized wheels, appeared just over 100 years ago. Since then, manufacturers have made bikes for every sort of activity – from lightweight cycles for racing to BMX bikes for tricks. There are even folding bicycles that fit into car boots!

How did bicycles begin?

A machine called the 'hobby horse' (right) appeared in the early 19th century. It had a saddle, two wheels and handlebars, just like a modern bike, but no pedals – you had to stride along the ground while the saddle took most of your weight. Hobby horses were uncomfortable and hard to ride, so they did not catch on.

Were penny farthings safe?

With its giant front wheel and tiny rear wheel, the 1870 penny farthing was not easy to ride. Many people needed steps to climb on to it, and once in the saddle, it was very easy to fall off. Even so, many people bought penny farthings. They liked the idea that, unlike a horse, the bicycle did not need feeding or looking after!

Why are racing bikes so light?

The lighter its frame, the less effort it takes to pedal a racing bike, so the faster you go. Because of this, designers make the frames with very light metals such as aluminium alloys. Narrow, treadless tyres reduce friction between the wheels and the road and also make bikes faster.

How do you ride a unicycle?

A unicycle has a saddle and two pedals, but only one wheel. Unicyclists let the saddle take their weight and then rock the pedals back and forth to balance. Beginners usually ask two friends to support them as they pedal, but after a couple of hours, riders can usually balance on their own. Skilled riders can learn to play basketball, hockey and tag on unicyles.

What makes mountain bikes special?

Mountain bikes need to be extra strong for cross-country riding. They have tough metal frames, tyres with deep treads to provide lots of grip and plenty of gears to make cycling up and down hills easy.

Quick-fire Quiz

1. What was unusual about the hobby horse?
a) It had no saddle
b) It had no pedals
c) It had no handlebars

2. How did people get on to a penny farthing?
a) By jumping
b) With steps
c) With a mechanical lifting device

3. How many people could ride the *Décuplette*?
a) Two
b) Five
c) Ten

4. Which tyres do racing bikes have?
a) Narrow, treadless tyres
b) Thick, rugged tyres
c) Solid tyres

Which bikes are the fastest?

Professional racing bikes (left), which are the fastest bicycles, need to be very streamlined. The frame, wheels and handlebars are all designed to reduce drag (air resistance). Hi-tech materials that are strong and light, such as carbon fibre, are used. Even the cyclist is streamlined – he or she wears a special helmet to reduce drag.

What can bicycles transport?

In many parts of Asia, few people can afford a car, and tricycles are popular alternatives. These vehicles often have platforms for carrying goods (right) and many riders earn money by making deliveries. Trishaws – tricycles with small seats at the rear – also provide income for riders who ferry passengers around.

How many people can ride on one bike?

Some people like riding tandems – bicycles made for two (above), but at the end of the 19th century, some bikes were built for even more people. A number of four-seaters appeared, and there was even one French bicycle, the *Décuplette*, that carried ten people!

Motorbikes

The very first motorcyle, or 'motorbike', was built in 1868 and was powered by a small steam engine! But ever since Daimler made his first machine in 1885 (below), motorbikes have had petrol engines. There are all sorts of different machines from slow, economic scooters to powerful, expensive bikes that give exhilarating rides on open roads.

Why was Daimler's first motorbike made of wood?

When German engineer Gottlieb Daimler made his first petrol engine, he tested it by fitting it to a home-made wooden bicycle, creating the first-ever motorbike with a petrol engine (above). He probably used wood because many vehicles were wooden in those days, but he may have regretted his choice when the bike was destroyed by fire in 1903!

How are motorbikes built for speed?

Motorbikes, especially those designed for racing, have large, powerful engines and streamlined frames to reduce drag. The seats are set back and the handlebars are low so that the rider's head and shoulders are kept down. This helps cut drag even more, enabling the rider to gain valuable seconds.

What's special about scrambling bikes?

Scrambling bikes are designed to be raced over muddy, bumpy courses at high speed. They have sturdy frames, thick tyres with deep treads and big mudguards to protect the rider from the mud and stones that the wheels throw up. Good suspension does help to absorb some of the shock, but scramblers must still expect a rough ride!

How do you 'corner' at speed?

Motorcyclists turn bends, or 'corner', by leaning into the curve. On fast bends, racing riders lean so far that it looks as if they will topple over! Professional riders know just how far to lean to give them the best route around the curve at the fastest possible speed.

When is a bike not a bike?

When it's a trike! Three-wheeled bikes, or 'trikes', are more stable than ordinary bikes because of the support from the extra wheel. This means that trikes can be used off-road over bumpy ground. Trikes are also used for racing. Some trike owners fit large seats for extra comfort.

What is a 'chopper'?

A 'chopper' is a motorbike with a low seat, raised handlebars and a long fork that supports the front wheel. Most choppers do not start out like this – they are ordinary bikes that have been altered or 'customized' by their owners. The biker has to 'chop up' the original bike, alter it and then put it back together. In this way, a unique 'chopper' is made.

Which motorbikes are best in the city?

For many people, scooters or mopeds are ideal in the city. Scooters first appeared in the 1940s in Italy, but are still very popular today. They are not too expensive and are quite easy to ride. Scooters' engines are small, but suitable for busy city streets where you cannot go too fast. Often the engines are covered to keep noise to a minimum.

Why were sidecars invented?

Sidecars were originally made to enable motorcyclists to carry extra passengers in comfort. But it was not long before another separate class of motor sport developed – racing motorcycles with special flattened sidecars attached. During races, the sidecar passengers must move about, shifting their weight into the best positions to keep the machines stable at speed.

Quiz
he
first
ve?
he
he
ngine
d
gers
ight

Boats

From the canoe to the most modern speedboat, there are [boats] for every need and water conditions in every part[...]. In the past, people use[...] simply for getting ar[...] jobs such as fishing, s[...]p and down rivers and[...]ts. Many of today's b[...]t for pleasure – either for [...]r cruising.

What is an 'outrigger'?

An 'outrigger' is a boat with a long wooden 'float' attached to one side by poles called 'booms' (above). Outriggers were developed to make boats more stable when fitted with sails. Normal narrow dug-out canoes capsized easily when rigged with sails. The float of an outrigger does not add too much extra weight, and the boat remains stable and swift.

What we[...]oats like?

The first boats [...]m simple materials that [...] ind and work with. Re[...] tightly together to fo[...]ertight boats (above). [...]oes were another [...] watercraft, bu[...]ic people thousa[...]go and still used [...] parts of the world. [...]de from tree trunks, w[...]lowed out in the mid[...]h [...]ne tools or[...] that [...]d away [...]od.

Are two hulls better than one?

The hull is the main body of a boat or ship. Boats with twin hulls are called 'catamarans' (left). They are very wide and can accommodate large sails, which means that the craft can sail fast. Catamarans were developed thousands of years ago in islands of the Pacific Ocean. They are now popular for both racing and leisure.

Which boat can you carry on your back?

The coracle is a tiny, lightweight boat that has been around for thousands of years and is still used today in some parts of England and Wales. It is made from leather, which is stretched over the wooden framework, and is just big enough to carry one fisherman. When the fisherman returns to shore, he lifts out the boat, hoists it on to his shoulders and walks home.

Which boats are best for racing?

People race all sorts of boats, from tiny dinghies (small boats without decks) to large yachts. Races are organized in different classes so that boats of the same type race against each other. Most racing craft have sleek hulls made of strong, lightweight materials. Large sails are vital for speed.

Which are the fastest boats?

The fastest watercraft are speedboats, which combine powerful engines with sleek, pointed hulls. Swiftest of all is the hydroplane (above), which rises up out of the water as it speeds along. The world record for speed over water is 511.11km/h. This was achieved by Ken Warby of Australia in a hydroplane.

Can boats sail uphill?

Yes, with help from 'locks' – sections of a canal or river that can be closed off by gates. Lock-keepers open the lower gates, allowing the boat in, and the lock fills with water until it is the same level as the water upstream. Then the upper gates open and the boat sails out. To sail downstream, the process works in reverse.

Quick-fire Quiz

1. How many hulls has a catamaran?
a) One
b) Two
c) Three

2. What are dug-out canoes made from?
a) Tree branches
b) Tree trunks
c) Planks of wood

3. What is the main advantage of an outrigger?
a) It is stable when fitted with a sail
b) It can carry more passengers
c) It looks good

4. Which type of boats are the fastest?
a) Dinghies
b) Coracles
c) Hydroplanes

Boat sails through lower gates of lock

Gates close and water enters lock   Upper gates open

Ships

Ships have been used for thousands of years because it was often easier for people to sail along a river or coast than to build a road. Over time, bigger and better boats were built – from the small wooden sailing craft of early times to the vast liners and tankers of today that can sail right around the world. Since the 19th century, ships have also had engines and no longer had to depend on a good wind to get them moving.

What were the first sailing boats like?

The world's first sailing ships probably sailed about 5,000 years ago in the Mediterranean Sea and along the River Nile in Egypt. They had solitary square sails on tall, wooden masts (above). Their hulls were made of wood, and they were steered by a large wooden oar at the stern.

How did clippers race across the oceans?

Clippers were the fastest sailing ships of the 19th century. They often carried tea from China to Europe. Clippers had sleek, streamlined hulls, and many large sails, which enabled them to skim through the water at speed. One clipper sailed from Melbourne, Australia, to London, England, in just 85 days.

Which ships are the biggest?

The world's biggest ships are supertankers. These enormous vessels weigh up to 500,000 tonnes and are about 450 metres long. It would be possible to build tankers even bigger – up to one million tonnes – but no port in the world would be large enough to handle such vast ships.

Why did early steam ships have sails?

There were several reasons for keeping a set of sails on a steamer. By using sail power when the wind was favourable, ship-owners could travel further on a single load of coal. This meant that they saved money on coal. Also, by using sails occasionally, less coal needed to be carried, allowing more room for cargo.

Why are oil slicks dangerous?

When a tanker spills oil, the oil floats on the surface of the sea in a thin layer called a slick. The slick from a large tanker can spread out for many kilometres, and it causes damage wherever it goes. Oil sticks to the feathers of sea birds, often killing them. Oil-polluted beaches can take months to clear.

Which ship is the most luxurious?

Perhaps the most luxurious ship is the cruise liner *Grand Princess* (right). Her 12 decks offer her 2,600 passengers everything they could expect in the best hotel, and more – a casino, a theatre, a virtual-reality centre and many different restaurants. The swimming pool even has a movable roof to protect it in bad weather.

Grand Princess

Submarines

Submarines add a new dimension to warfare, enabling forces to creep up on enemy ships and launch surprise attacks. As a result, these powerful craft played an important role in both World Wars. But underwater vessels also have peaceful uses – they can be used to explore the deep, dark trenches of the oceans, discovering new species of marine life.

Turtle

What were early submarines like?

Early submarines were small wooden vessels that could hold only one person. They were operated by handles and foot pedals that moved two propellers – one to dive and ascend, and one to travel forwards. The *Turtle* (above), a famous early submarine, was built in 1776 during the American War of Independence to plant explosives beneath British ships.

Air out

Compressed-air tanks

Compressed air in

Water in

Ballast tanks

Submarine dives

Water out

Submarine rises

How do submarines dive?

The hull of a submarine has two walls and in between these walls are large containers called ballast tanks. When the tanks contain air, the submarine floats on the surface like a normal ship. When the captain wants to dive, the tanks are gradually filled with water. This makes the vessel heavier so that it dives towards the bottom of the ocean. When it is time to surface, compressed air is released into the ballast tanks to force the water out.

Why do submarines have 'wings'?

Submarines have small 'wings' called hydroplanes. These can be moved up and down in order to help submarines climb and dive. The hydroplanes can also tilt submarines sideways to change direction.

How useful are nuclear submarines?

The submarine below is powered by an onboard nuclear reactor. The advantage of this form of power is that the craft can sail an almost unlimited distance without the need to refuel. This is useful in wartime, when vessels may have to travel thousands of kilometres from port. The drawback is that nuclear submarines are difficult and costly to service, and produce hazardous waste that needs to be treated with great caution.

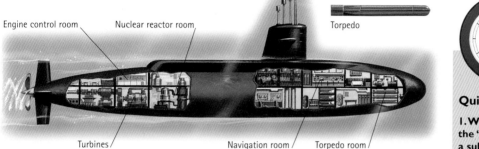

Engine control room | Nuclear reactor room

Turbines | Navigation room | Torpedo room

Do submarines have weapons?

Most submarines are military machines used for patrolling the oceans. Submarines may have to fire at enemy craft and for this reason they are equipped with special missiles called torpedoes. Torpedoes propel themselves through the water, often over very great distances.

Torpedo

Quick-fire Quiz

1. What are the 'wings' of a submarine called?
a) Hydroplanes
b) Hydrofoils
c) Hydroponics

2. What happens to a submarine when it dives?
a) Water empties out of the ballast tanks
b) Oil flows through the ballast tanks
c) Water flows into the ballast tanks

3. What weapons do submarines sometimes use?
a) Torpedoes
b) Heat seekers
c) Submersibles

4. What is the deepest known place on Earth
a) The Dead Sea
b) The Marianas Trench
c) The South Pacific

Why are submarine hulls so strong?

The deeper underwater a submarine dives, the greater the pressure applied to it from the water. In 1960, when two scientists dived 10,911 metres into the Marianas Trench, the deepest underwater gorge known on Earth, their vessel, the *Trieste* (right), had to be heavily reinforced in order not to be crushed.

Trieste

How can you see above the surface?

Submarines use a device called a 'periscope' to enable those on board to see what is happening on the surface. A periscope is a long tube with an angled mirror at either end. The submariner looks at the lower mirror and sees the reflected image of what is above. When the vessel dives deep, the periscope tube is lowered into the body of the submarine.

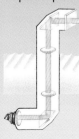

What is a 'submersible'?

A 'submersible' is a small submarine used for all sorts of underwater jobs – exploration, marine biology, repairs to oil rigs and laying pipelines. Some submersibles are remote-controlled. *Deepstar IV* (left) can operate at depths of more than 1,200 metres.

Deepstar IV

Hovercraft and Hydrofoils

There are several types of craft that work by skimming over the surface of the sea. The most common are hovercraft and hydrofoils, which use two very different designs to keep their hulls out of the water. Hovercraft and hydrofoils are some of the fastest and most efficient craft afloat, but they do tend to be uncomfortable, and even unstable. Because of this, they are not used as much now as they were in the past.

Is this ship taking off?

No, it's a hydrofoil! It has a set of foils that lift the hull out of the water as it moves. The less contact the hydrofoil has with the water, the less drag it experiences, and the faster it can go. The vessel is efficient and this reduces the amount of fuel it uses.

Water flows over foil

Upward thrust

How do foils work?

As the hydrofoil speeds along, water flows over the foils, which are specially curved to provide an upward thrust. The faster the vessel travels, the greater the lift produced from the foils.

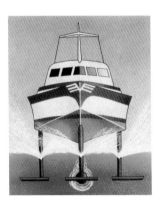

Fully submerged hydrofoil

Surface-piercing hydrofoil

Which type of 'foil' is best?

'Foils' are the underwater fins or wings beneath hydrofoils. There are two main types – those that stay submerged and those that pierce the surface of the water. Submerged foils are popular as they allow high speeds and operate well in rough seas when used with an automatic control system. Surface-piercing foils are useful when boats tip to one side as more of the foil on that side is pulled underwater and this creates forces that pull the boat upright again.

How does a hovercraft hover?

A huge fan pumps air into the area under a hovercraft (below). This creates a cushion of air on which the craft rides, or 'hovers'. Because air escapes from around the edge of the vehicle, the fan has to keep working whenever the craft is in motion to prevent it sinking into the sea.

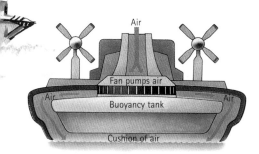

Air
Fan pumps air
Air
Buoyancy tank
Air
Cushion of air

Can hovercraft travel over both land and sea?

Hovercraft are 'amphibious' – in other words, they can ride over both land and sea. Because they have no wheels, they can even travel over bumpy terrain and marshland where it is difficult for wheeled vehicles to go. Surfaces such as ice, mud and even quicksand pose no problems for hovercraft.

What are hovercraft used for?

Hovercraft are normally used for ferrying cars and passengers. They are ideal for this type of job because they can cover short journeys at high speeds. Sometimes armed forces use hovercraft to travel over all sorts of different terrains.

Who invented the hovercraft?

Hovercraft, or 'Air-Cushion Vehicles' (ACVs), were invented by the British engineer Christopher Cockerell in the 1950s. Cockerell tested his designs with a hairdryer and two tin cans.

What is a hovercraft's 'skirt'?

Most hovercraft have a length of flexible rubber that goes all the way around the underside of the vehicles. This is called the 'skirt'. The skirt raises the hovercraft higher and is very flexible. This helps the craft to ride easily and smoothly over the waves. The skirt also helps to keep in the cushion of air underneath the hovercraft.

Quick-fire Quiz

1. What do the foils on hydrofoils do?
a) Protect the hull
b) Help you climb on board
c) Lift the hull out of the water

2. What do hovercraft ride on?
a) A pair of wheels
b) A cushion of air
c) A layer of rubber

3. Which word describes hovercraft?
a) Amphibious
b) Ambidextrous
c) Ambiguous

4. Why are hovercraft good ferries?
a) They are fast
b) They are comfortable
c) They are quiet

Aeroplanes

American brothers Wilbur and Orville Wright built the first aeroplane (below) in 1903, and flew it for only 12 seconds. Today, there are jet airliners that can fly for hours, carrying hundreds of people vast distances in comfort. It is now possible to fly faster than the speed of sound.

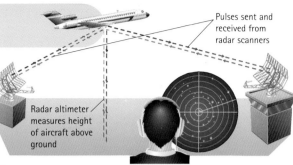

Pulses sent and received from radar scanners

Radar altimeter measures height of aircraft above ground

How are planes found in thick cloud?

Air-traffic controllers need to keep track of hundreds of aircraft in the sky in order to prevent collisions. They are not able to see most aircraft with the naked eye because of darkness, poor weather conditions and long distances. This is why air-traffic controllers use radar, which bounces radio waves off objects to work out their position. The aeroplanes appear as dots on the radar screens in the airport control tower.

The Wright brothers' *Flyer 1* – the first successful powered aeroplane

Why do aeroplanes need instruments?

A modern aeroplane is a complicated piece of machinery that uses all sorts of different systems such as engines, hydraulics and control surfaces. The pilot needs to know how all these are functioning, and the instruments in the cockpit give the answers. Also, navigational instruments indicate how high the plane is flying, how fast it is going and in what direction.

How do you steer a plane?

The wings and tail of an aeroplane have movable flaps, called control surfaces, that the pilot can adjust at any time during a flight. By moving controls in the cockpit, the pilot can change the control surfaces to make the plane climb or dive and turn left or right.

Quick-fire Quiz

1. Who flew the first aeroplane?
a) The Wright brothers
b) The Montgolfier brothers
c) The Marx brothers

2. What is the nickname for the Harrier aircraft?
a) Lightning jet
b) Jumbo jet
c) Jump jet

3. What is forced out of the back of a jet engine?
a) Exhaust gases
b) Hot water
c) Hot air

4. What do air-traffic controllers use?
a) Sonar
b) Radar
c) Metal detectors

How do planes fly so fast?

The fastest planes normally have jet engines, which create a force in a similar way as when air is let out of a balloon. The engine burns fuel, and forces the exhaust gases out of the back of the engine at high speed. This creates a huge backward force, and the reaction against this force pushes the aircraft forwards.

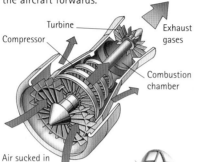

Turbine

Compressor

Exhaust gases

Combustion chamber

Air sucked in

Why did Concorde's nose 'droop'?

Concorde's long, pointed nose made it sleek and helped it to fly faster than any other airliner. But the nose obstructed the pilot's line of vision during take-off and landing, so a special mechanism was used to lower it into the 'drooping' position.

Flight position

Take-off and landing position

How can a jet jump?

Vertical Take-Off and Landing (VTOL) aircraft are useful in places where there are no runways. The first aeroplane able to take off vertically was the British Hawker Siddeley Harrier, known as the 'jump jet'. The nozzles of its jet engines, which point backwards in normal flight, swivel towards the ground to give the vertical force needed for take-off.

A Harrier 'jump jet'

Which are the largest airliners?

The biggest passenger-carriers are the wide-bodied super jets. The first and best-known is the Boeing 747, often called the 'jumbo jet'. About 70 metres long, it can carry almost 500 passengers and cruises at around 1,000km/h.

Lufthansa

Gliders

Gliders are simple, lightweight aircraft with no engines. They are cheaper to run than powered aeroplanes and have been popular with flying enthusiasts for years. Hang-gliders give an even greater feeling of freedom in the skies. Both types of aircraft are simple, but require special skills and training to fly.

What were the first hang-gliders like?

The first hang-gliders aimed to copy the flight of birds (above), but failed because they focused more on flapping than gliding. German inventor Otto Lilienthal experimented with fixed-wing gliders and made important notes about control surfaces. He crashed to his death in 1896 flying one of his inventions.

How do you control a hang-glider?

The first hang-gliders were steered by the pilot shifting his or her weight towards the desired direction. More modern hang-gliders have tails with movable surfaces, similar to those on full-size aeroplanes, that can be adjusted by using hand controls.

How do you launch gliders?

A glider has no engine so it is pulled along to gain the speed needed for lift. Usually, a powerful car or an ordinary aeroplane tows the glider, and when there is enough lift, the glider pilot releases the tow rope and is able to glide smoothly away.

What is an 'aerofoil'?

An 'aerofoil' is the cross-section of a wing that is shaped to produce an upward motion, or 'lift', with little drag. Aerofoils are curved on the top to force air to flow over them quickly, creating lift. The faster the air flows over the wings, the more lift is created, so gliders must fly at a certain speed to stay airborne.

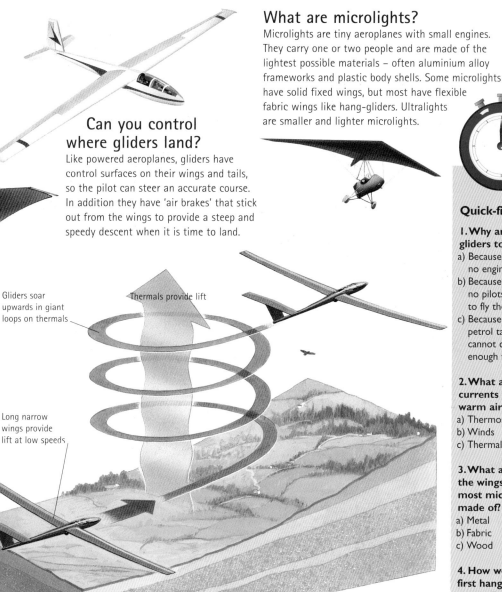

What are microlights?

Microlights are tiny aeroplanes with small engines. They carry one or two people and are made of the lightest possible materials – often aluminium alloy frameworks and plastic body shells. Some microlights have solid fixed wings, but most have flexible fabric wings like hang-gliders. Ultralights are smaller and lighter microlights.

Can you control where gliders land?

Like powered aeroplanes, gliders have control surfaces on their wings and tails, so the pilot can steer an accurate course. In addition they have 'air brakes' that stick out from the wings to provide a steep and speedy descent when it is time to land.

Gliders soar upwards in giant loops on thermals

Thermals provide lift

Long narrow wings provide lift at low speeds

How do gliders keep going without engines?

It is not only aerofoils that provide lift, gliders also rely on 'thermals' (currents of warm air) to keep going without engines. Like birds, pilots search for the thermals, which swirl up into the atmosphere and provide lift. Experienced pilots can stay aloft for hours soaring on thermals.

Quick-fire Quiz

1. Why are gliders towed?
a) Because they have no engines
b) Because they have no pilots to fly them
c) Because their petrol tanks cannot carry enough fuel

2. What are currents of warm air called?
a) Thermos
b) Winds
c) Thermals

3. What are the wings of most microlights made of?
a) Metal
b) Fabric
c) Wood

4. How were the first hang-gliders steered?
a) By the pilot shifting weight
b) By using control surfaces
c) By using steering wheels

Helicopters

Helicopters are the most versatile of all aircraft. They can take off and land vertically and can hover in the air like a bird of prey. Helicopters are built in all sizes, from small craft used for business travel to huge craft used for transportation. Helicopters are also used by the emergency services to get to danger scenes quickly and easily.

What keeps helicopters in the sky?

Instead of wings, helicopters have at least one set of whirring blades, called rotor blades, or 'rotors'. The rotors spin around at high speed, acting like huge propellers to pull helicopters up into the air. This lift effect is reduced by speed so helicopters usually cruise at only 130 to 240km/h, much slower than most aeroplanes.

Why are helicopters ideal for rescue work?

Helicopters are the most manoeuvrable of all aircraft. In the hands of skilled pilots, helicopters can fly very slowly, change direction easily and even hover directly over one spot, allowing people to be winched on board from below. Helicopters can also land in very confined spaces and so can access awkward rescue sites.

Why do helicopters have extra rotors on their tails?

Without tail rotors, helicopters would spin around in circles. The turning of the tail rotors creates forces that are opposite to the ones created by the main rotor blades, preventing the spinning. The tail rotors are also used for steering – changing the angle, or 'pitch', of the blades alters the direction a helicopter flies in.

What is an 'autogiro'?

An 'autogiro' (right) is an aircraft that has a normal propeller at the front to drive it forwards as well as a set of horizontal rotors. The rotors are not powered like a helicopter's, but spin freely as the aircraft moves to provide lift for take-off. Autogiros, invented by the engineer Juan de la Cierva, were popular in the 1930s.

How are helicopters used in warfare?

In warfare, helicopters are used to transport troops and equipment. This is because they can land and take off quickly in very confined or awkward spaces near battlefields. In fact, helicopters can remain almost motionless when they hover in the air and so sometimes they don't need to land at all. Some military helicopters are large enough to carry vehicles such as armoured cars or troop carriers.

Forward flight – rotor blades tilted forwards

Backward flight – rotor blades tilted backwards

Hovering – rotor blades at same pitch

Who invented the helicopter?

It is thought that many centuries ago, the Chinese made tiny helicopters as toys, but the first serious design for a helicopter as a means of transport was made by Leonardo da Vinci, the artist. His design relied on a screw-shaped wing (right) that aimed to provide lift by winding itself up into the air.

How do you control helicopters?

The pilot of a helicopter controls the aircraft by altering the pitch (angle) of the rotor blades. In the cockpit, there are two controls – the 'collective pitch' and the 'cyclic pitch'. These allow the pilot to adjust the blades to the appropriate position for climbing, descending, hovering or even for flying backwards.

Spacecraft

In 1957, the Russians sent the first satellite, *Sputnik I*, into orbit around Earth – the space age had begun. Since then, astronauts have visited the Moon, and scientists regularly work on board space stations. At first, astronauts travelled in tiny capsules, sent into space by throw-away rockets. Now they use space shuttles – spacecraft that can be used again and again, just like aeroplanes.

What is 'escape velocity'?

The Earth has a strong gravitational pull and so lots of power is needed to get away from the planet and into space. Spacecraft use rockets – the only devices with the power to fly at the speed required to 'escape' Earth's gravity. This speed is known as 'escape velocity' (velocity means speed) and is about 40,000km/h. Because of the pull of gravity, shuttles do not need the rockets when they return to Earth.

How are space shuttles launched?

Space shuttles are launched by being blasted into the sky by a pair of rockets, which are fuelled from a huge tank that sits between them. When the shuttle has left Earth's atmosphere, the rockets parachute back to Earth, where they are collected and recycled. The fuel tank has to be discarded.

What can space shuttles carry?

Space shuttles are large craft that carry astronauts as well as lots of scientific equipment, which is used to conduct experiments once the shuttle is in orbit. Shuttles also carry satellites, which are released in order to circle Earth. The satellites are used for communications or for sending back information about the weather.

What was the first creature in space?

The first creature in space was a dog named Laika (right), who spent a week in orbit on board the Russian *Sputnik 2* in 1957. The first human in space was the Russian astronaut Yuri Gagarin, who left Earth in *Vostok I* on April 12, 1961.

Where do space stations get power?

Space stations run mainly on solar power. They have huge panels of solar cells, called solar 'arrays'. The arrays gather sunlight, which is converted into electricity. This means that space stations do not need to store fossil fuels, such as coal or oil.

Solar panels

Mir space station

Can astronauts travel outside their spacecrafts?

Astronauts may need to go outside their spacecraft in order to perform external repairs. Astronauts wear Extravehicular Mobility Units (EMUs) and must either remain attached to the spacecraft or operate Manned Manoeuvring Units (MMUs). MMUs are special backpacks with rocket thrusters that control direction and movement (left).

Quick-fire Quiz

I. Which part of a space shuttle is thrown away?
a) The fuselage
b) The rockets
c) The fuel tank

2. What is a space station's main source of power?
a) Coal
b) Oil
c) The Sun's rays

3. Which type of probe visits more than one planet?
a) Fly-by
b) Orbiter
c) Landing probe

4. How fast is escape velocity?
a) 4,000km/h
b) 40,000km/h
c) 400,000km/h

What are 'probes'?

Space probes are unmanned spacecraft that collect data. They are able to send back to Earth beautiful images from outer space. 'Fly-by' probes gather information as they pass different planets. 'Orbiters' fly towards a target planet, go into orbit around it and observe it over a long period. Landing probes send down craft on to a planet's surface. Probes use the gravitational pull from planets to travel about.

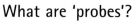
A Viking probe orbits Mars

Can you drive a car in space?

Yes! Special cars called 'Moon Buggies' or 'Lunar Rovers' (right) have been driven on the surface of the Moon. In 1997, a small rover travelled over the rocky surface of Mars as part of the Mars Pathfinder Project. This rover, the *Sojourner*, unlike the Moon Buggies, was remote-controlled and could journey only a short distance.

Unusual Transport

Some forms of transport cannot be categorized as cars, trains, boats or aeroplanes. New vehicles have come about because of the need to travel in difficult conditions, such as snowy, icy or steep ground. Other machines have developed because people keep on inventing new forms of transport to carry us in ways that are faster, easier or just more fun!

How do you speed through the snow?

In the frozen regions of Canada, getting around quickly can be a problem. Canadian inventor Joseph Armand-Bombardier came up with the answer in the 1930s – a vehicle that had tracks driven by a petrol engine at the back and steerable ski-like runners at the front. These first 'snowmobiles' were used by the army as troop carriers, but today's vehicles are smaller, designed for one person to ride like a motorbike (below).

How do you build a railway where there is not enough room?

Build a monorail! A monorail is a railway that runs on a single rail. There are two main types – ones that run along rails on the ground and ones that hang from overhead rails (above). In some cities, the overhead rail system has been used to save space on the ground.

Which type of transport is the most fun?

Simple, cheap devices, such as skateboards, rollerblades and ice skates, allow us to speed about and have lots of fun. It is even possible to play sports and perform tricks while using them – but this may take a little practice!

When is drag useful?

Drag is resistance from the air and is a problem for many forms of transport as it slows them down. Parachutists, however, rely on drag for a safe landing. The large 'canopy' of a parachute is the opposite of streamlined – it is large and rounded in order to trap as much air as possible to slow descent.

Canopy

Steering lines

What is a 'personal watercraft'?

A 'personal watercraft' is a small vessel like a water-going motorbike, and is known as a 'jetski'. Jetskis carry one or two people quickly through the waves. They are powered by water-jet engines, which force water out of the crafts' sterns, creating forces like the ones from jet engines on aircraft.

K-153

How can you travel up steep mountains?

In mountainous areas, a third rail, called a 'rack rail', is laid in between the two normal train tracks. The rack rail is toothed and connects to cog wheels, or 'pinion wheels', under the carriages of the train. This locks the train tight to the track. Cable cars, which travel along cables strung between high towers, are also used as they avoid contact with the ground altogether.

Web Addresses

www.brainpop.com

This kids' science, technology and health site offers lively graphics, quizzes and movies. Do experiments in the company of Bob the Rat, and ask Tim and Moby, Tim's friendly robot, any science and technology questions that you have. There are lots of activities on this site, and for each one you can earn points and win prizes.

www.enchantedlearning.com

Visit Zoom Inventor and Inventions on this site to find out about all sorts of types of transport and navigation, from the aeroplane, aqualung and astrolabe to traffic signals and windscreen wipers.

travel.howstuffworks.com

This is a very useful site for children and young adults that covers topics such as cars, engines, aviation, space travel, jets, GPS, Concorde, rollercoasters, hot-air balloons, air-traffic control and, even, how time travel *could* work!

www.bbc.co.uk/education/dynamo/history/show.htm

This site offers fun animations and games for younger children, showing how types of transport such as trains and planes have changed over the years.

www.ltmuseum.co.uk

This London Transport Museum site is a resource for teachers, parents and other adults, and offers information on the museum and events, as well as access to other resources. A kids' site called The Wheelies offers facts, figures and quizzes, and Busabout gives a history of London buses.

www.nasm.si.edu/wrightbrothers/

The Smithsonian National Air and Space Museum online, with an introduction by Wilbur and Orville Wright. Includes a history of flight and flying machines, the restoration of the Wright Flyer, plus interactive experiments and classroom activities.

www.faa.gov/education/kidcornr.cfm

A fun site from the Federal Aviation Authority, separated into age groupings, aimed at kids from five years to teens. It offers plenty of activities, from colouring books to crosswords and easy experiments to do at home, including how to make styrofoam gliders and paper helicopters.

www.kidgrid.com/kgmachines.htm

This site lists many useful links to transport, inventions and technology websites.

www.transport-pf.or.jp/english

This is a superb website for kids, covering all aspects of transport, from its history to the future. Follow the Tran family on travel adventures and play transport games.

inventors.about.com/library/inventors/blrailroad.htm

The history of the railroad. Includes links to information about other forms of transport.

inventors.about.com/library/inventors/blcar.htm

The history of the development of the motor car.

Quick-fire Quiz
ANSWERS

Page 245 Early Transport
1. b   2. a   3. a   4. c

Page 247 Cars
1. b   2. c   3. a   4. c

Page 249 Racing Cars
1. a   2. b   3. b   4. c

Page 251 Trucks
1. c   2. b   3. a   4. b

Page 253 Special Vehicles
1. b   2. b   3. b   4. c

Page 255 Trains
1. c   2. b   3. a   4. a

Page 257 Bicycles
1. b   2. b   3. c   4. a

Page 259 Motorbikes
1. b   2. a   3. b   4. b

Page 261 Boats
1. b   2. b   3. a   4. c

Page 263 Ships
1. b   2. c   3. a   4. b

Page 265 Submarines
1. a   2. c   3. a   4. b

Page 267 Hovercraft and Hydrofoils
1. c   2. b   3. a   4. a

Page 269 Aeroplanes
1. a   2. c   3. a   4. b

Page 271 Gliders
1. a   2. c   3. b   4. a

Page 273 Helicopters
1. a   2. b   3. a   4. b

Page 275 Spacecraft
1. c   2. c   3. a   4. b

Page 277 Unusual Transport
1. b   2. a   3. c   4. a

INDEX

A

abacus 222
acid rain 81
acropolis 144
advertisements 207
aerofoils 270, 271
Africa 126, 142, 143, 146, 154, 157
agriculture 69, 70, 71, 76, 77, 76, 77
aircraft 233, 234, 235, 268–269
air-cushion vehicles (ACVs) 267
air-traffic control 268
Albertosaurus 102, 103, 104
Alexander the Great 142, 146, 148, 149
Allosaurus 100, 102, 106, 108
ambulances 252
Andrews, Roy Chapman 94, 95
animal life 52, 56, 67, 69, 70, 71, 72, 73 74, 75, 80, 81
Ankylosaurus 104, 105
Anning, Mary 112
Antarctica 66, 67, 75, 80
antiseptics 209
Apatosaurus 90, 99, 111
Apollo 11 spacecraft 30
aqualungs 232
aqueducts 156, 210
Archaeopteryx (bird) 120, 121
Archelon 113
archers 183, 186, 188, 196
Arctic 66, 67, 75
armour 167, 181, 183, 184, 185, 196, 198
armourers 184
articulated trucks 251

artificial limbs 209
arts 126, 130, 137, 140, 142, 145, 152
Ashurbanipal, King 140
Assyrians 140–141
asteroids 19
asteroid belt 19
astrolabes 222
astrology 12
astronauts 30, 236, 237, 274
astronomers 10, 11, 14, 15, 16, 17, 18, 23, 30, 31, 32, 35, 36, 37, 38, 39
Babylonians 10
Chinese 10
Copernicus, Nicolaus 18
Egyptians 10
Galileo 10, 35
Herschel, William 38
Lowell, Percival 41
Mayans 10
Tombaugh, Clyde 41
astronomy 10, 11
Atlantic Ocean 50, 53, 65
atmosphere 46, 49, 50, 63, 64, 72, 80
atomic energy 221
Augustus, Emperor 153
autogiros 273
Avimimus 100

B

Babylon 138–139, 140, 141
bacteria 208
baileys 167, 170, 171, 200
bailiffs 192, 193
Bakelite 219
ballast tanks 264
ballpoint pens (biros) 207
barbarians 156, 157
Baryonyx 101

baths 147, 155
battle-axes 182
battlements 173, 189
battles 179, 180, 181, 182, 183, 201
beds 174, 199
Benz, Carl 246
Big Boys 254
bicycles 230, 256–257
black holes 15
blood flow 208
boats 22, 260–261, 262–263
boiling oil 188, 189
bows and arrows 182, 183, 186
Brachiosaurus 90, 91, 97, 98
bridges 210, 211
Britain 142, 153
building castles 168–169
buildings 210–211, 214, 215
bullet trains 254

C

cable cars 277
Caesar, Julius 156
calculators 222, 223, 225
caltrops 181
camcorders 229
camels 244
cameras 228, 229
Camptosaurus 107
canal boats 261
cannons 198, 201
cars 230, 231, 246–247, 248–249
car transporters 250
carpenters 168, 169
castles 167, 168–175, 186–189, 191, 198, 199, 200, 201

catamarans 261
catapults 186, 187
cavalry 166, 198, 200
celestial sphere 12, 13
Celts 152–153
central heating 215
Centrosaurus 105
Cetiosaurus 119
CFC (chlorofluorocarbon) 63, 80
chariots 128, 140, 141
Charlemagne 166, 200
Chasmosaurus 105
Château Gaillard 177, 201
Children's Crusade 190, 201
china (porcelain) 219
Chinese 10, 150–151
chivalry 194, 200
choppers 259
chronometers 249
cinema (movies) 228, 229
cities 76, 126, 128, 143, 144, 157, 158
Athens 144
Babylon 138
Carthage 143, 157
Çatal Hüyük 126
Chichen Itza 159
Constantinople 156
Harappa 128
Knossus 136
Mohenjo-daro 128
Nineveh 140
Persepolis 149
Pylos 137
Sparta 144
Ur 129
clippers 262
clocks 223
clones (animal) 213
clothes 126, 129, 130, 143, 146, 152, 154, 158, 175, 184, 198, 216–217